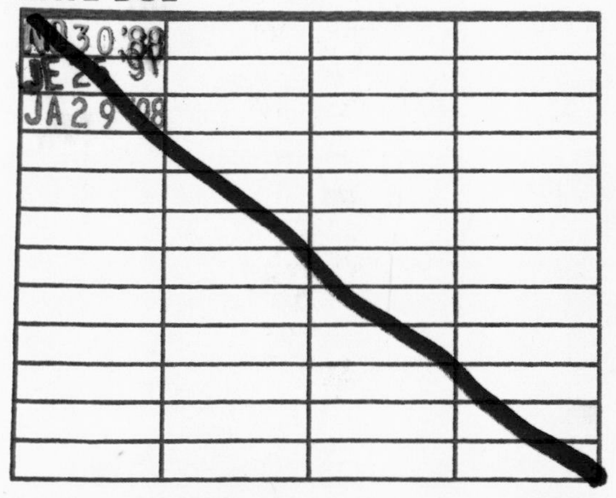
9213
GV
885
.H64
Holzman
Holzman's
basketball
DATE DUE

HOLZMAN'S

BASKETBALL

HOLZMAN'S

BASKETBALL:

Winning Strategy and Tactics

RED HOLZMAN

AND

LEONARD LEWIN

THE MACMILLAN COMPANY

NEW YORK, NEW YORK

COLLIER-MACMILLAN LIMITED

LONDON

To our patient wives
Selma and Phoebe

All photographs, unless otherwise indicated, are by George Kalinsky.

The Macmillan Company
866 Third Avenue, New York, N.Y. 10022
Collier-Macmillan Canada Ltd., Toronto, Ontario

Library of Congress Catalog Card Number: 72-90551

FIRST PRINTING

Printed in the United States of America

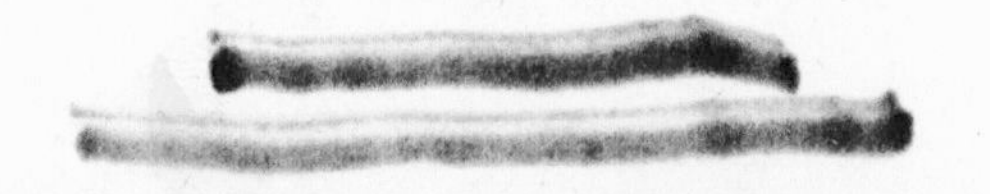

CONTENTS

FOREWORD

I first met Red Holzman during my tenure as head basketball coach at St. Bonaventure University. At that time he was scouting for the New York Knickerbockers under head coach Fuzzy Levane. I spent many evenings with Red, and from the very beginning was impressed with his knowledge, not only of pro basketball, but also of college basketball.

Red, who played his college basketball under Nat Holman at City College in New York, has been associated with the National Basketball Association ever since its inception in 1946. After eight playing seasons with the Rochester Royals, he went to the Milwaukee Hawks where he was named player-coach of the team during the 1953–54 season, one year before the Hawks moved to St. Louis. Red remained as the Hawks' coach until 1958 when he came to the Knicks as Chief Scout.

When I accepted the job as Head Coach with the Knicks in 1961, my first order of business was to meet with Red and request that he continue as Chief Scout. I sincerely believe that this was one of the wisest decisions I ever made.

There are two ways of putting a championship team together: 1) through the college draft, and 2) by trades within the league. In order to be able to make a trade, you have to have talent to trade, and it was through Red's knowledge of college players that we acquired this talent in the drafts.

With Red as Chief Scout the Knicks' draft choices read like a Who's Who of pro basketball. Through Red's recommendations the Knicks drafted Willis Reed, Howard Komives, and Emmette Bryant in 1964, Bill Bradley,

Dave Stallworth, and Dick Van Arsdale in 1965, Cazzie Russell and Freddie Crawford in 1966, and Walt Frazier, Phil Jackson, and Mike Riordan in 1967.

Reed, Bradley, Stallworth, Russell, Frazier, Jackson, and Riordan all played vital roles on the 1970 World Championship Knick team and Reed, Bradley, and Frazier have been accorded All-NBA status for several years.

Red not only has been an excellent judge of talent but one of the game's best teachers. He has proven not only to pro coaches but also to college and high school coaches as well the importance of teaching fundamentals both defensively and offensively. He also has shown that individual goals come second to team play.

Nobody is better qualified to write a book on how to play basketball. Red has an awareness and sharp insight into the game. He knows how to cut through all the words and get to the heart of things. He knows how to explain basketball in a way that is easily understood by anyone—players, coaches, and even fans.

This book is a fine example of his unique way of clarifying things. I have always found it somewhat confusing reading some of the books on basketball. They are inclined to become too technical. It is not easy at times to decipher the Xs and Os in the suggested plays. Red has considered this and employs a different technique. In place of the Xs and Os, he has devised a simple modification by using the names of players. Therefore, instead of X_1, X_2, X_3, etc., you will find DeBusschere, Bradley, Frazier. A little thing but important to those trying to grasp the information as part of the learning process.

Red Holzman exemplifies the contributions basketball has made to the American sports world and to the world of human understanding in the past twenty-five years through his genuine concern for others.

Eddie Donovan
Vice-President, General Manager
Buffalo Braves Basketball Club

HOLZMAN'S

BASKETBALL

CHAPTER

1

BASKETBALL: GROWTH AND CHANGES

It is presumptuous for any coach to assume he knows everything about basketball. It is ridiculous for any coach to suggest he is the author of new techniques. The fundamentals of the sport are the same for everyone. They never change. It comes down to how the fundamentals are applied.

Each coach has his own philosophy, but the fundamentals are the same. You learn basketball the same way you learn mathematics or how to play the piano or drive a car. You absorb the fundamentals and practice. The peak of efficiency depends on individual awareness and the ability to get maximum mileage out of inherent talent.

In effect, a coach, like a student, is only a by-product of his education. My education began in the streets and schoolyards of Brooklyn. If you grew up in Brooklyn when I did, there were only two sports—baseball and basketball.

You either rooted for the Brooklyn Dodgers and went to Ebbets Field to see them play or you headed for the schoolyard to play basketball. I played basketball. You had to arrive at the schoolyard early and you had to be good if you desired any reasonable amount of playing time. Winners stayed on. Losers watched.

You would start your basketball experiences by dropping around and watching the older boys. At first, they would be just a swarm of moving, leaping bodies. They would run, shoot, and argue but you would not understand. You would sit on the cold stone and watch with curiosity. Once in a while, the basketball would roll or bounce your way.

This was your moment. You would grab it with your small hands and heave it back and wait for some sign of recognition. Nothing. The bigger boys would go back to playing 2-on-2 or 3-on-3 and you would kill more time. Once in a while, someone in the game would ask you to run to the corner and get him a soda. You would run. It was your involvement. Your first involvement. You were thrilled by the recognition.

On occasion, when the bigger boys went home, which was close to dark, you had your chance to shoot a few baskets. Maybe you had a friend who managed to save enough money to buy a basketball. Maybe you were lucky enough to have an uncle who gave you one for a birthday present. Or maybe the other kids in the neighborhood would let you slip in and join them.

When you are around seven, and your hands are small, and the strength is not there, you find it difficult making that big ball reach the hoop. You fling with all your strength and it falls short. But you don't give up. You keep trying.

Soon the ball is moving closer and closer. Then, one day, the ball goes through the basket and you get a nice feeling. It is the same feeling Willis Reed or Jerry West or Oscar Robertson got when they made their first basket. That never changes. No matter how profound a coach may be, no matter what techniques he employs, the object still is to put the ball in the basket.

James A. Naismith, a Canadian, conceived the idea in 1891. He was a physical education teacher who had been searching for a new indoor activity for the students at the International YMCA Training School in Springfield, Massachusetts.

Dr. Naismith had a soccer ball and that's all. He knew he wanted to do something involving the ball—but what? He decided on shooting the ball into boxes. He had the ball. Now he had to get the boxes. "As I walked down the hall," Dr. Naismith wrote, "I met Mr. Stebbins, the superintendent of buildings. I asked him if he had two boxes about eighteen inches square. Stebbins thought a minute and then said:

" 'No, I haven't any boxes, but I'll tell you what I do have. I have two old peach baskets in the storeroom.' I told him to bring them up, and a

NBA CHAMPS. This is the team that brought the Knicks their first league title in the 1969–70 season. Front row: John Warren, Don May, Walt Frazier, President Ned Irish, Chairman of the Board Irving Mitchell Felt, General Manager Ed Donovan, Dick Barnett, Mike Riordan, and Cazzie Russell. Back row: Coach "Red" Holzman, Phil Jackson, Dave Stallworth, Dave DeBusschere, Willis Reed, Bill Hosket, Nate Bowman, Bill Bradley, Scout Dick McGuire, and Trainer Danny Whelan.

few minutes later he appeared with two baskets under his arm. They were round and somewhat larger at the top than at the bottom. I found a hammer and some nails and tacked the baskets to the lower rail of the balcony, one at either end of the gym."

That is a procedure that prevails to this day throughout the United States and other parts of the world. It is not unusual to drive through sections of the country, as I have in my thirty-four years as a player, scout, coach, and general manager, and see youngsters shooting a basketball at a peach basket nailed to the side of a barn.

In the more affluent areas of our society, you will find backboards attached to garages. The driveway becomes the family basketball court where Dad, and sometimes Mom, indulges in the joy of shooting baskets. Many basketball stars cut their teeth competing family style in the backyard.

There was no such thing when I grew up in Brooklyn. You played in the schoolyard or not at all. You played when the court was open—when the bigger boys were not there to chase you off. Otherwise, you had to wait until you grew a little taller and stronger. Then you played and you chased the younger boys off.

By then, you had learned a few things. You began to understand the movement of the game. If it was 2-on-2, you worked with your partner to free one another. You would pass the ball to him when he was open and you would step in front of his man to free him. You learned how to set a "pick" without anyone telling you how.

These were the things you had picked up watching the bigger boys play. Things such as playing your man in a manner that would prevent him from getting open for a pass and a shot. Or switching to pick up your partner's man to keep him from getting an easy shot. You learned the terminology for those fundamental moves much later. You did it before you really understood why. It was the foundation of your basketball education.

From there, you graduated to the older boys and high school basketball. By then you were obsessed with the sport. Your mother was not happy. She wanted her son to go to school and study and someday go to college so he could earn a good living. How could a young man earn a good living from basketball?

Not in those days. Pro basketball was a honky-tonk sport. Joe Lapchick, an old friend and a former coach of the New York Knickerbockers, lived the game in the early days of professional basketball as a member of the Original Celtics. His teammate, Nat Holman, was my coach at CCNY and, therefore, responsible for a large part of my basketball education.

You learn from the experiences of men such as Lapchick and Holman. They represented an integral contribution to the development of basketball as a major sport and institution in this country. They were bred in the schoolyards. They played the game and taught it. They were the pioneers of the tremendous interest the sport has generated.

Playing conditions were not very good in those days. They played in antiquated arenas. They played in dance halls. They played in cages or nets. There was only one referee and he had to be as much concerned for his own safety as for officiating the game.

I was part of that era where the semi-pros and organized pros played in dance halls, high schools, or broken down gyms for a few dollars. My knowledge of what happened in pro basketball before my time is confined to some of the stories I heard from Holman and Lapchick about their experiences with the Original Celtics.

There was one story Lapchick told about the time he was first breaking into pro ball with the New England Carpet League back around 1919.

He was reminded of it by the way the game has progressed in every respect—from playing arenas to the officiating. Only one thing seemed to have avoided the ravages of time and the inroads of change and that's the hometown fans' desire to see their team win.

"Those hometown boys made ugly noises in the stands to sway officials and usually helped gain that hometown victory," recalled Lapchick. "Once in a great while, though, the visiting team won—and that's when the victors had to worry about getting out of town.

"There was the night in Albany that Amsterdam had the temerity to win, a triumph attributable in no small part to the rough and rugged play of Marty Friedman. After pushing their way through the irate crowd, with the help of the police, the Amsterdam team dressed hurriedly and left the building in one big rush.

"Crossing the bridge on the way to the station, however, the team was ambushed by the hot-headed crowd. Somebody spotted Friedman, and, in no time at all, Marty was lifted high over the heads of the crowd and was apparently headed for the frozen river below. Luckily, the Albany players arrived just in time to intercede and save Friedman the dunking that might have been as tragic as it seems amusing after all these years."

Pro basketball was a rough game in the days of the Original Celtics. It still was a rough game when I graduated from City College and was invited to join the pros. The nets and cages were gone but a player still took his life in his hands every time he tried to drive to the basket. Sometimes you would wind up with a better seat than many of the spectators with the help of an opponent's hip or shoulder.

There wasn't much money in it, a few dollars here and there, and the traveling conditions were far from first class. We moved around by automobile for the simple reason no one could afford the train or even a team bus. Sometimes it was by subway if we had a game scheduled for the Broadway Arena in Brooklyn or the St. Nicholas Arena in Manhattan.

Those areas primarily were used for boxing, which gives you an idea as to the stature of pro basketball in those days. The seating capacities were three to four thousand and the average crowd was around five hundred on those nights when we were fortunate to draw well. Few of these arenas that permitted pro basketball to use the building strictly as an accommodation, and for the rental, had the basic facilities.

Promoters had to bring in their own backboards. They had to lay out the court by placing tape on the floor to indicate the required lines. You had to provide your own towels and soap, and there was a great chance that the water would be cold when the players took their showers after the games.

That was pro basketball until the major building operators throughout the country moved it into the big arenas in 1946. It is a fairly accurate description of what pro basketball used to be. What mother, I repeat, would want her son to be involved with anything like that, assuming she knew anything about pro basketball.

Today, of course, pro basketball, as is the case with professional sports in general, has become big business. It offers the youth of America a career with tremendous financial inducements. Played in glamorous indoor complexes, such as Madison Square Garden and the Los Angeles Forum, it has out-distanced the era when games were held in smoke-filled bandboxes in conjunction with dances.

Today, any mother would be proud if her son came home and informed her he had just signed a lucrative deal to play pro basketball. While she might have preferred he had become a lawyer or doctor, the money and pro basketball would provide her son with a good start in life. And if a mother really wanted to rationalize a little harder, she might recognize that her son was involved in a huge industry that has attracted some heavyweights from the world of big business.

When I played ball for the Rochester Royals, a salary of $25,000 was practically unheard of. Wilt Chamberlain broke the log jam and triggered the move that sent pro basketball salaries skyrocketing. He came into the NBA with the Philadelphia Warriors as a $75,000 player. He was the first to reach the $100,000 level. "If he gets a hundred thousand dollars," said Bill Russell, the architect of eleven championships in thirteen years for the Boston Celtics, "then I want one dollar more."

There are now more players earning $100,000 in the NBA than in any other sport. Of course, when I was sneaking out of the house to play basketball in Brooklyn, my mother never dreamed of anything like that. She wasn't even sure a basketball was round. She did not want me wasting my time playing basketball. I read it, ate it, slept it. I watched it grow and became a part of that growth.

First there was the explosion of college basketball set off by Ned Irish when he introduced intersectional doubleheaders to the old Garden. That created an infusion of ideas and techniques that had a major influence on the way the game developed. Many things changed because certain players, coaches, and teams were given the opportunity to communicate and exchange ideas.

LOOK WHO'S HERE! Recognize him? It's a young, or younger, Red Holzman when he played with the Rochester Royals before they joined the NBA in 1948. Notice the kneeguards on everyone. (*Photo courtesy of Selma Holzman*)

Hank Luisetti of Stanford came to the Garden and introduced the one-hand shot to New York fans. He was considered unorthodox by many advocates of the two-hand set, the Eastern vogue in those days. Now if you shoot with two hands, the stylists think there is something strange about *you*.

The center jump after every score (basket or foul shot) disappeared to help speed up the game. Rhode Island State, under coach Frank Keaney, excited the New York basketball public and media with "racehorse basketball"—the forerunner of the fast break in the East. It was only an extension of the fast-breaking style employed in the Mid-west, fundamentally, and what the Boston Celtics were to use so successfully in their glory years.

Keaney's idea was to have his son, Frank, Jr., clear the board and fire a release pass to a teammate around midcourt. Young Frank was built like a bull. He would take the ball and fling it like a baseball to Ernie Calverley or to Stan Modzelewski, later an NBA player and referee after changing his name to Stan Stutz. It was a technique employed effectively later by Bob Pettit with the St. Louis Hawks, Wes Unseld with the Baltimore Bullets, Wilt Chamberlain with the Los Angeles Lakers and, of course, Bill Russell with the Celtics.

The game changed in another respect. Basketball generally was a sport of little men—especially in the East. There were no seven-footers. At CCNY, where I played, for example, our centers were Julie Gersoon and Dave Laub, both six-foot-one. These days they would have trouble making the backcourt in pro basketball with that size.

Clair Bee of Long Island University was the first of the New York college coaches to recognize the value of big men in basketball. He introduced six-foot-eight Art Hillhouse to Eastern fans. Art was considered unusually tall by the standards that existed in New York basketball.

New York had seen a big man on occasion but never on any of its teams until Bee unveiled Hillhouse. There once was an Olympic elimination tournament in the Garden, back in the 1930s, and the Phillips Oilers brought in two towering players: Willard Schmidt, six-foot-ten, and Joe Fortenberry, six-foot-nine. Otherwise, the only tall people New Yorkers ever got to see appeared in the circus freak show.

Then Loyola of Chicago came to New York with a six-foot-nine center named Mike Novak. His specialty was planting himself near the basket and swatting away shots. He was the first of the goaltenders. In fact, he was responsible for the goaltending rule that helped basketball to partially neutralize the advent of the *really* big men.

Novak provided an awesome problem to a team and a coach in those days. The responsibility of solving it fell to the fertile mind of Clair Bee, whose LIU team was scheduled to play Loyola in the Garden as part of a doubleheader. Bee, Holman, Lapchick (St. John's), and Howard Cann (NYU) constituted the coaching force behind the Golden Era of college basketball in New York.

They each had a distinctive approach to the game. Bee was considered an outstanding strategist. He analyzed things quickly. He not only recognized the problem but had the capacity to find the solution. Thus, when Novak, the terror of the Mid-west, came into the Garden, the Loyola team was not really prepared for Bee's response to the goaltending threat.

It was simple after it worked but it took a sharp, analytical mind to complete the diagnosis. Bee had his players work the ball to the sides and bank their shots high off the boards. They were out of Novak's reach and LIU won. Then came the era of Bob Kurland and George Mikan, two giants. Basketball was growing up in many ways.

College basketball interest was incredible in those days. You couldn't buy a ticket to any of the Garden doubleheaders. Pro basketball had died out for all practical purposes. There were a few leagues here and there and the Harlem Globetrotters generated some interest, but there was no national impact until 1946. Then a group of hockey arena operators got together and decided pro basketball could be an economically feasible addition to their operations.

On June 6, 1946, the Basketball Association of America was born. It consisted of franchises in New York, Boston, Chicago, Cleveland, Detroit, Philadelphia, Pittsburgh, Providence, St. Louis, Toronto, and Washington, D.C. The owners named as their commissioner Maurice Podoloff, then president of the American Hockey League.

The National League was operating at the time in Chicago, Detroit, Rochester, Ft. Wayne, Syracuse, Sheboygan, Oshkosh, Indianapolis, Anderson, Moline, Youngstown, and Toledo. In effect, the National League had the name players because it had been in business since 1937 and offered the only haven for college stars if they wanted to play pro ball. The East had its American League, a weekend operation only that eventually became the Eastern League.

Two years later, or in 1948, the BAA and the NBL merged and became the National Basketball Association. Merge is not really the proper word. Rochester, Ft. Wayne, and Minneapolis (originally Chicago) quit the NBL to join the BAA. With the move came such great players as George Mikan and Jim Pollard of the Lakers and Bob Davies, Fuzzy Levane, Bob Wanzer, Al Cervi, and Arnie Risen of the Royals, in addition to a young man named William (Red) Holzman.

Rochester, my team, was made up of Eastern style players. Players from other sections were more physical—bigger, stronger, and more suited for the contact game they played in Mid-west colleges. It was significant that Les Harrison, the owner-coach of the Royals, had to reach out to Indianapolis to get Risen of Ohio State, a big man, for us little Eastern guys.

It took time but the NBA began catching on. People had to be reoriented. They fundamentally were college basketball fans, especially in New York. Pro basketball had to find a way to stimulate interest in its product. It had the natural resources in the college stars and the attendant national publicity they attracted. All that was needed was some means of funneling the tremendous public appeal of college basketball into the pros.

A few changes in the pro rules provided the momentum—helping to speed up the game and eliminating some of the deterrents. The six-foot lane was widened to twelve feet and then eighteen feet to neutralize the advantage of size and open the middle for driving plays. Max Winter, owner of the Minneapolis Lakers, the same Max Winter who now owns the Minneapolis Vikings, objected because he said the pros were legislating against Mikan, alone. "Baseball wouldn't change the rules to hurt Babe Ruth," was the argument he offered.

Winter lost. While the owners recognized the excitement and public appeal of Mikan, they were more concerned about the progress of the sport. The change served the purpose of moving the big men away from the basket on offense and putting a greater premium on their ability to shoot and maneuver for their shots.

There were other changes—most notably the twenty-four-second clock, which prevented a team from stalling and turning a game into a bore for the spectators. It revolutionized the game at a time when the teams were killing the clock and threatening to kill the game. By then, the pros were determined to streamline everything. They wanted a game that would be entertaining and skillful and played at top speed.

There were too many low scoring games. There was too much stalling in the backcourt. There was too much fouling in the backcourt. So they adopted the college ten-second rule, which prevented the team that was leading from using the backcourt to freeze the ball. A two-shot foul in the backcourt went along with it. Penalty shots for too many team fouls in a quarter were introduced to minimize excessive fouling.

These changes did not come overnight. They were the by-products of the growing pains pro basketball endured over many years. Eventually, the owners came up with the streamlined, fast game we know today, expanded immensely to all corners of the United States and televised nationally for the entertainment of millions every week.

The metamorphosis of basketball had taken place and the pros firmly were established as a national product. There were changes that astound me when I look back. I can recall playing with a big, fat basketball into which you would pump air through a rubber valve with a bicycle pump or at the gas station. That ball just about fit through the hoop. Now you can almost fit two of the slick, molded basketballs into the 18-inch hoop at the same time.

Smaller basketballs is one reason why shooters are better today. Another reason is that there are better shooters. The jump shot is a lot tougher to defend against than the two-hand shot of my day.

Basketballs were precious items when I was growing up. Today, most youngsters can afford to buy their own. Today, a pro team gives away more autographed basketballs in a week than we used at CCNY in a season. Today, endorsing a basketball can bring a pro player anywhere from five to ten thousand dollars, depending on sales. That's more money than most players earned when the league was formed.

Progress. Pro basketball grew up and many things changed. The players got bigger and bigger and bigger. There was a time when six-foot-five forwards were considered in-between players: too small for up front, too big for the backcourt. Even that changed. It no longer is unusual to see six-foot-five guards or even one who is six-foot-seven, if his name is Dave Stallworth.

Stallworth played the backcourt many times for the Knicks in an emergency. He had the quickness and ballhandling. Dave DeBusschere, when he was a six-foot-six rookie with the Detroit Pistons, was used in the backcourt by coach Dick McGuire at times. The Knicks even proved that a six-foot-eight center could operate efficiently against seven-footers such as Wilt Chamberlain, Kareem Abdul-Jabbar, and Elmore Smith if he has the finesse, intelligence, and execution of a Jerry Lucas.

Only one thing seems to have resisted the ravages of time. Fundamental basketball has remained fundamental basketball. The basketball I learned as a youngster is basically the same basketball that is played today, with some refinements. A pick is still a pick, a screen is still a screen, a switch is still a switch, a give-and-go is still a give-and-go, post plays are still post plays, ad infinitum.

Each coach has his own way of applying the fundamentals and maybe teaching them but they are still the same for everyone. Each coach has his philosophy, depending on his education, experience, and awareness.

John Wooden of UCLA, for example, is a man who teaches all aspects of the game but emphasizes defense. His teams are well-coached in the press because he believes in the value of putting pressure on the offense. Al McGuire of Marquette is the same way as was Jack Ramsey when he was at St. Joseph's of Philadelphia. Eddie Donovan, when he coached at St. Bonaventure, was considered the master of pressure defense.

It was different in the pros. For a long time, most teams stressed offense because there were so many good shooters. The jump shot gave the offense a tremendous advantage over the defense. Towering centers created another problem for the defense. It was easier for a coach to allow his players to do what came naturally rather than invest valuable time thinking about and working on defense.

There were times when a team did not have the attacking power, so it was forced to think more of defense. That was the situation when I was with the Rochester Royals. We had smart ballplayers and good shooters —fellows such as Bob Davies, Arnie Risen, Jack Coleman, Arnie Johnson, and Pep Saul. We were forced to work a little harder on defense because there were teams much tougher on offense. We managed to put it all together sufficiently to beat the New York Knickerbockers, 4–3, for the championship in the 1950–51 season.

That was the era of George Mikan and the Minneapolis Lakers. They won five NBA titles in six seasons primarily because of the brute strength and skills of Mikan, the finesse of Jim Pollard, the power of Vern Mikkelson, and the craftsmanship of little Slater Martin. The league was not to see domination by another team until the Boston Celtics obtained Bill Russell in a trade with the St. Louis Hawks.

Ben Kerner, owner of the Hawks, negotiated the deal ostensibly to acquire Easy Ed Macauley, who had played his college ball at St. Louis University. With the transaction just about completed, Kerner informed Red Auerbach, his former coach at Tri-Cities, that he would like Cliff Hagan thrown into the deal. Ben pointed out that Hagan was in service at the time and the Celtics, in effect, would not be losing anyone immediately.

Russell was late reporting to Boston because he was representing the United States in basketball at the Olympic Games in Australia. The appearance of the six-foot-nine, former San Francisco University center in pro basketball had a major impact on the game. The Celtics went on to establish the longest reigning dynasty before Russell retired and gave someone else a chance.

There was one other significant spinoff of the Bill Russell era. The game philosophy changed. Most teams thought offense first. Russell and the Celtics made everyone more conscious of defense. They established, quite effectively, that an offense can work off the defense.

It was the beginning of a radical change in fundamental thinking that was to set off a chain reaction. No longer was the NBA to remain an offense-minded league. Russell, under the guidance of coach Red Auerbach, turned the Celtics and the NBA in a new direction.

Boston always had outstanding offensive players through the years. Bob

Cousy, Bill Sharman, Frank Ramsey, Jack Nichols, and Macauley had the shooting power but they did not win a championship until Russell arrived. That was when Auerbach shrewdly built his game around Bill's defensive genius—his ability to block shots and intimidate an offense.

With Russell behind them to operate as a traffic cop, Cousy, Sharman, K. C. Jones, Sam Jones, Tommy Heinsohn, John Havlicek, and others were able to gamble. They played the ball. Russell—quick, smart, and coordinated—protected the inside. He was a one-man team defense. He was a one-man zone.

Zones are barred in the NBA to prevent big men such as Russell from standing under the basket. That did not bother Bill at all. He had such tremendous range and quickness for recovery, his man could take him outside and he still managed to drop in time to prevent layups. He not only was the greatest shot-blocker to ever play the game, but he had the uncanny knack of recovering the ball before it got out of bounds.

Finding another Bill Russell was not easy. But the league began to think more about team defense. NBA owners no longer looked entirely to former players as the source of supply for coaches. Ned Irish turned to St. Bonaventure and Eddie Donovan. The Philadelphia 76ers plucked Jack Ramsay out of college in their backyard.

That was the start of an influx of college coaches into the pro game. It provided the impetus for the team defense concept that has altered the philosophy of pro basketball and, also, helped the New York Knickerbockers win their first world championship.

As I have said, every coach approaches a situation in his own way. My way is defense. Team defense. Helping out defense. Not exactly the way the Boston Celtics played it because the Knicks had no Bill Russell. Defense is the backbone of the game. It is the same in all sports.

Baseball long ago recognized that a team must be defensively strong down the middle. Pro football did more to glamorize and emphasize defense than any other sport. Hockey championships are won and lost by the ability of goalies and defensemen to hold the other team's scoring down.

Basketball is no different. In my opinion, the offense in basketball works best off the defense. That is why I approach the game through defense. That is why we spend 80 percent of our time on the Knicks working on defense. That is why when fever runs high in Madison Square Garden, the fans begin to chant: "DEE-fense! DEE-fense!" They recognize the name of the game just as I got to know it through thirty-four years of association.

CHAPTER

2

INDIVIDUAL OFFENSE

A strong defense can create an offense, but it is important to know what to do with the ball when you have it. A team is only as effective as its parts and certain individual skills are required to create and exploit scoring opportunities.

Possession may change in many ways. Sometimes quickly enough to allow little time to think. A player has to react instinctively under certain conditions. When that happens, there are three things available to the man with the ball: dribble, pass, or shoot. These fundamentals are not learned overnight.

Everyone approaches them from different directions but arrives at the same spot, eventually. I remember Carl Braun, for example. Carl was one of the best shooters among all the Knicks. He had a fine touch from outside. Way back in 1947, when points did not come that easily, he once scored 47 in a game at Providence. A great shooter who obviously had spent a lot of time acquiring that touch. As a youngster, Carl would pop ping-pong balls at the head of a milk bottle for hours. It sounds silly on the surface but he sensitized the fingertips long before he realized that's where the touch is.

Walt Frazier did it another way. When he was fourteen, he and a friend had jobs in a drive-in down in Atlanta. They would do their chores, such as policing the area and little odds-and-ends. Between assignments and hamburgers, they would hang a paper cup on a tree, crumple another cup into a ball and shoot baskets.

Terry Dischinger of the Detroit Pistons would work out in a nearby schoolyard with his wife—proving you are never too old to learn. Mrs. Dischinger would take a broom and try to block her husband's shots. Terry was practicing against a moving target. It is always a better idea to work with someone, not alone. The objective is to work against the distractions an opponent will provide.

Easy Ed Macauley of the Boston Celtics and St. Louis had a favorite routine to improve concentration. It was a little game of 1-on-1 foul shooting. The non-shooter was allowed to do anything to distract the shooter but obstruct his vision or hit him.

One trick was to stand along the foul lane near the shooter and, as he straightened his knees while in the act of shooting, the non-shooter would bend at the knees sharply. Another time the non-shooter would walk behind the shooter and breathe heavily as he was about to shoot. If that did not work, the non-shooter would whistle as the shot was about to be taken.

Bill Bradley was full of little tricks. For shooting, he would go into the gym and pile chairs until they reached about eight feet high. He would make believe he was playing against Wilt Chamberlain. He would drive at "Chamberlain," fake, and go over with his hook shot.

Bradley kept moving the chairs to different spots on the floor to sharpen his range and variety of shots. He had a unique drill for dribbling. He would take eyeglass frames without lenses and insert pieces of cardboard so he could not see the ball. He had to dribble with his head up—eyes in a position to see what was going on ahead of him at all times. The idea was to perfect finger control and dribble without looking at the ball. He went even further. He took five chairs and spaced them evenly from foul line to foul line. Then he would dribble in-and-out while wearing his special glasses.

He worked on improving his jumping by wearing weighted shoes. He worked on his timing by shooting on the move from the foul line, deliberately bouncing the ball off the rim, faking, and then trying to nail the rebound while it still was in the air. He sharpened his passing and receiving by throwing a basketball against the wall.

Bradley discovered early in life that it was wise to be familiar with all the shooting areas. He had a six-foot-wide court laid out in his driveway and would practice shooting blindly from all spots. He got to know every inch of the court that was within his shooting range. Then he would invite some neighborhood friend over for a game of "Horse" (matching shots) and give him a lesson.

Hard work and practice constitute the best ways to acquire all skills. Everything starts with shooting. In any game of basketball, the team that scores the most points wins; so shooting is the heart of the game. No matter what else takes place, the object is to put the ball through the basket.

Shooting can be taught. Shooting can be improved by practicing. All this can happen if the shooter understands the fundamentals. Once the knowledge is acquired, a player must know when to shoot and from where.

Shooting comes down to what we in basketball call "the percentage shot." The closer to the basket, the better the percentage. Of course, once in a while a Jerry Lucas comes along and defies percentages. He is quite accurate from twenty-five to thirty feet, which ordinarily would be considered a bad percentage shot—especially for a big man. Yet, that shot is within his range, so, for him, it is not considered a bad shot.

A good or percentage shot also depends on body control. A shooter may be in a good percentage range, yet not have a good shot. He may be off balance or his man may be playing him too tightly. Every bad shot hurts a team. Shooters must have patience. They must concentrate on taking good shots from within their range.

It is a good idea to practice all kinds of shots from different ranges. As shots are perfected, spend time working on weaknesses. Adolph Schayes, a member of the NBA's all-time All-Star team, was a great example. He was a natural right-hander but learned how to shoot with his left hand. He also learned how to dribble with his left hand. He broke his right hand one year while playing for the Syracuse Nationals, yet he was able to play with a heavy cast only because he could dribble and shoot with his other hand.

I realize that Schayes was a rarity, but he represents what it can mean if a player has the desire to work on his weaknesses and improve. Of course, first perfect certain shots before you move on. Find your shooting range and the type of shots that come naturally and work on them. If you cannot get enough players together for a game, try to play 1-on-1 with someone.

Individual skills are enunciated in 1-on-1 situations. They develop during a game when the offense moves across midcourt and a player finds only one opponent between him and the basket. A 1-on-1 player must be a good shooter. He may drive, fake, or pull up, but the shot is the objective.

In the days when I learned how to play, all players used the two-hand set for long shots or drove for layups. There was no in-between, no intermediate shot. It was either inside or outside. The one-hand shot and jump shot took care of that.

Hank Luisetti set off the revolution with the one-hand shot. Joe Fulks of the Philadelphia Warriors perfected the jumper from long range. Paul Arizin of Philadelphia and Bill Sharman of Boston perfected it from the baseline. Basketball had entered another era. Now surveys indicate that over 80 percent of the shots are taken within eighteen feet of the basket —an area in which the defense concentrates. All because of the one-hand shot and the jump shot.

ONE-HAND SHOT

The body is positioned with hips and shoulders squared. Eyes on the target. Think of an imaginary line from the nose to the middle of the front rim. Aim for that. Knees are relaxed and feet are spread about the width of the shoulders. Right foot a few inches ahead of the left for right-hand shooters; left foot ahead for left-hand shooters.

THE GRIP. Shooting accuracy depends on sensitive touch in the fingers. Dave DeBusschere shows how the fingers balance and direct the ball.

The fingers are spread. The thumb and the little finger are the pressure fingers. They grip the ball tightly. The middle three fingers rest along the lateral seam or groove of the ball. They balance the ball and provide the natural backspin that controls the flight of the shot.

The index, or trigger finger, should be lined up with the nose and the front rim of the basket. The ball is going wherever the index finger directs it. Be sure the elbow is pointed toward the basket—not down or sideways. The wrist is cocked. Ball over head. Eyes focused on the front of the rim. Feel comfortable, with the ball resting in the fingers, not in the palm of the hand.

Now release the ball. Flip the fingers and follow through making sure the trigger (index) finger goes directly at the hoop. If you shoot properly, the fingers on the shooting hand should be bent toward the head prior to release and there should be backspin on the ball.

Once you get the ball going in the right direction, concentrate on getting the shot high enough. The basket is ten feet high, and the ball must come in from an arc above it. Some shooters, such as Jerry West, are so accurate they can shoot line drives and make them. An arc is recommended because the shot comes in softer and has a chance of bouncing in off the rim. How much height on the shot depends on the individual.

Bill Bradley uses a medium-sized arc when he shoots his favorite shot from the corner. Jerry Lucas prefers the rainbow—thirty feet away, thirty feet up, and thirty feet down. The secret to consistency is to keep aiming at the front rim and not let anything distract you.

Remember, keep your eye on the target at all times. It is no different than the expert golfer, who keeps his eye on the ground through the swing and does not look for the ball until the hit is accomplished.

JUMP SHOT

This is the one-hand or two-hand shot off the jump. How high should one jump? That depends on the defensive player: How tall he is. How high he jumps. How he reacts to your moves. How far he has you from the basket. The idea is to get the ball over his hand and through the hoop.

Sometimes, if he is guarding closely, it is best to fake and make him commit himself before shooting. Dick Barnett is a master at the technique. He pumps once, twice, or even three times. He gets his man off his feet, then goes up with the jumper. It accomplishes two things: (1) Barnett gets free for the shot, and (2) he invariably draws a foul as the defender falls into him.

It is a good idea to start practicing one-hand shots and jumpers near the basket. Begin about six feet from the hoop and work out to the foul line, which is fifteen feet away. If you are a guard, develop a range from

UP HE GOES. Jerry Lucas has just removed his left hand from the ball and is inches above Wes Unseld with his shooting hand. Luke is a study in concentration as he keeps his eyes glued on the basket despite the defensive distraction.

eighteen feet out to twenty-eight. If you are a forward, concentrate on up to twenty feet. If you are a big man, stay within a range of fifteen feet.

There are exceptions. Willis Reed has excellent range for a big man—from twenty to twenty-five feet. He developed his touch as a lanky youngster in Bernice, Louisiana, where he would go into the playground at night and shoot baskets with his friends.

Not only can the fifteen- to twenty-foot jump shot be accurate, but it is almost impossible to stop. Footwork and balance are the most important elements. A shooter must be prepared to maneuver into shooting position off a dribble, after taking a pass on the move, or while stationary.

Jerry West is the ideal model for shooting the jumper off the dribble. He will maneuver with the ball until he reaches his percentage area. He will move the defender back or to the side and then suddenly pull up for the shot. He will come to a quick stop with his lead foot and square off to the basket as on any other shot. He will be completely balanced and in control of his body and the ball as he springs off the floor. He goes straight up, with his eyes picking up the front rim of the hoop as soon as they can and fixing on it.

The position and force of the ball depends on the distance from the basket. The shorter the shot, the higher the ball can be held—sometimes higher than the head, if that comes naturally. The higher the ball, the quicker the release and the less chance of getting it blocked.

Do not release the ball too soon. Get it off at the top of your jump. Watch the top shooters and you will notice a slight hesitation on the shot at the peak of the jump. The split second before the shot enables the shooter to zoom in a little longer on the hoop.

There aren't many players who can shoot the jumper, after cutting to take a pass, better than Bill Bradley. He received enough practice on the Knicks. For one thing, he is constantly on the move. For another, we run a lot of plays for him because he is so proficient shooting off a pass.

The secret here is the ability to take a pass on the move and then quickly get set for the shot. You cannot slide into position. You have little time to think. You must jam on the brakes and effect shooting balance before the defense can recover.

Bending the knees the proper way is necessary. Try to stop short without bending your knees and you will better understand why. One pet play in the pros is to run a forward along the baseline and circle around a teammate. The forward will take a pass while heading for the corner. He now has to stop, turn, and shoot. All in a split second. He pivots on his lead foot and squares away in one motion. He goes up for his jumper with the ball firmly in control, body balanced, and eyes picking up the hoop as soon as they can.

DeBusschere and Jerry Lucas are the stationary jump shooters on the Knicks. Most times, DeBusschere gets the opportunity from along the sidelines or the corner. He will fake at the defender as though he intends to drive but then pulls back for the shot. The important thing to remember is to face the basket as soon as you get the ball. This puts pressure on the defensive man because he does not know where you intend to go or what you are going to do with the ball.

MR. CLUTCH. Jerry West goes up and over Walt Frazier with perfect rhythm. West has found his spot on the floor and is in full control of his body and the shot.

Lucas gets his stationary shots deep along the sidelines or straightaway. Many times he is the safety valve and receives the ball with time running out on the twenty-four-second clock. He has a different kind of jump shot. Most players start the ball close to the chest and move it toward the head before releasing. Lucas starts the ball near his right shoulder and pushes it past his ear, like a shotput. In every case, the shooter springs off the floor and releases the ball at the most comfortable stage of his jump.

Hal Greer, one of the more prolific NBA scorers and an excellent jump shooter, uses the shot at the foul line. A player should employ whatever foul shooting technique that results in maximum efficiency. Rick Barry, a top jump-shooter, prefers the two-hand underhand free throw that coaches such as Nat Holman recommended in the old days.

ON THE LINE. Bend the knees, concentrate, and use the shot that is most natural.

Bob Boozer, once with the Knicks, decided the best way for him was to shoot one-handers from a sharp angle. Wilt Chamberlain, who made twenty-eight of thirty-two attempts the night he scored a hundred points against the Knicks in 1962, has employed many varieties. He started with the one-hand shot. Then he went to two-hand underhand like Barry. He finally settled on a one-hander from three feet beyond the foul line. And then there is Don Nelson of the Boston Celtics. He goes into a severe crouch and shoves the ball toward the hoop with a complete follow through that sometimes sends him off balance.

FADE-AWAY JUMP

This is the same as the regular jumper except that the shooter "fades away" from the defender instead of going straight up. Walt Frazier has this shot in his arsenal. It helps a player who likes to drive. He can go right at his man and then pull up for the jump shot on which he leans away from the defender. The thing to remember is balance—go back, not to either side.

TWISTING JUMP

Another maneuver off the regular jump shot. The difference is that the shooter starts this shot with his back to the basket. Mostly used around the pivot or inside. It is a good substitute for the hook shot by big men. For example, Elvin Hayes of the Baltimore Bullets. He likes to station himself on a high post with his back to the basket. He will leap high, twist in the air, and release the ball while facing the basket. Tough to stop because the "Big E" gets up high on the shot. Also, he is on the way up before his man realizes it, unless the defender is smart enough to anticipate the shot. Elvin still hits a good percentage of them.

HOOK SHOT

This is primarily for big men from the pivot. There are times when the hook shot has value in a moving game. Dave DeBusschere employs it on some of his drives. Bill Bridges of the Atlanta Hawks and Philadelphia

76ers likes to use it while sweeping across the foul lane. I remember a night in St. Louis, when the Hawks were based there; Bridges hit a sweeping hook from the side to beat the Knicks by a point on the final shot of a game.

No one is more destructive with the hook shot than Kareem Abdul-Jabbar. He sweeps the ball way out from his body and sails it high over the heads of everyone; since he is well over seven feet tall, and has a fantastic reach, it is almost impossible to block. That is the real value of the hook shot—it is not easy to block.

The shot is not that popular in professional basketball anymore. Almost every center used the hook out of the pivot in the old days. Johnny Kerr of Syracuse and Neil Johnston of Philadelphia were its leading exponents. So was George Mikan, who used a full turn sweeping hook—or the buttonhook, a fake and a turn the opposite way for a quick rolling hook.

Nowadays there is too much congestion around the middle for the big pros to rely on hook shots. The foul lane also has widened. The pros prefer twisting or fading jumpers. High school and college players are different. There is a distinct advantage in the hook shot for those big men.

THE HOOK. Willis Reed reaches way out in order to discourage Walt Bellamy from getting any ideas about blocking his shot.

The shot is taken by stepping away from a defender and hooking over his head. If the shooter is right-handed, the left foot is the pivot and the step is taken with the right foot. The ball is in the fingers, with the normal grip for any shot. It is released as the head and shoulders turn to the basket and the eyes pick up the hoop.

Protect the shot by stepping far enough away from the defender to get out of range. Also make sure you are not turning into another defender who might be dropping off on the blind side. Be sure to follow through so you can be in a position to rebound. If you are shooting properly, you should wind up facing the basket on the follow through.

UP-AND-UNDER

A fine weapon out of the pivot. Willis Reed scored many baskets and got fouled using this one. It starts with the back to the basket. Reed would fake a hook or indicate he might roll in. The defender reacts instinctively and throws up an arm to block the intended shot. Willis then would lower the ball and sweep it up underhand. In effect, Reed would draw the foul as the defender's arm automatically lowered across his as Willis came up with the shot.

This is a tricky maneuver the old-time pros used more than this generation. Harry Gallatin of the old Knicks was superb at it. You will be surprised how many three-point plays the up-and-under can get a pivot man.

TAP-IN

This shot is not as lucky as it may appear at times, but there are players who practice it. There are drills where two players work against each other and perfect the timing the shot needs. Tall players have an advantage but I have seen smaller players, such as Dean Meminger, six-foot-one, tap in a rebound amid a crowd of giants.

In addition to good timing, tap-ins require the ability to get into rebounding position. Tommy Heinsohn of the Boston Celtics was as efficient as anyone. So was Bailey Howell, who started out with the Detroit Pistons and played a few seasons with championship teams in Boston. Not being boxed out helps. The offensive rebounder must determine quickly whether to try and tap the ball in or get it back to a teammate for a better shot.

There are times when the percentage play calls for grabbing the rebound and not trying to out-scramble the other team. If you are going for the tap-in, get up as high as you can and either steer the ball back to the hoop with your fingers or, if you cannot effect some control, slap it.

Tap the ball higher than the rim. If you cannot tap it directly into the hoop, then aim for the white tape that forms the square on the backboard. Use it as a guide. Unless you are all alone under the board, it is extremely difficult to get finger control of the ball. When you are competing with other players for the rebound, the tap-in must be with the fingers and strong enough to lift the ball against the board—hopefully at the right angle so it will bank in.

LAYUP

The most aggravating shot in the book. There seems to be no logical reason why anyone should ever miss a layup, but it happens. Why? Mostly because the player takes his eye off the backboard or basket or has not gauged his speed or the takeoff properly.

A player should come into the hoop at an angle—45 degrees, if that is possible. In other words, bisect the angle that is formed by the baseline to the hoop and the hoop out to the foul line. Why an angle? Because the best way to make a layup is off the backboard and that requires a player to drive in at an almost perfect angle, unless he is tall enough to dunk the ball.

Big men have that advantage in the pros; in the colleges stuffing the ball is not permitted. A Kareem Abdul-Jabbar or Wilt Chamberlain does not have to worry about the backboard. They can jam a ball through the hoop straightaway or from the side. Picture little Cal Murphy of the Houston Rockets or Nate Archibald of the Kansas City Royals trying that. Or even a big forward if Abdul-Jabbar or Chamberlain is lurking near the basket.

The proper way to make a layup is off the backboard. Pick a spot above the part of the rim nearest you and lay the ball softly against the board so it can carom into the hoop. If you come in off the right side, the takeoff is from the left foot—and vice versa.

Control the ball with both hands on the takeoff. The left is the guide hand at the start and then is released and is used to protect the ball and distract the defender. The right hand carries the ball up and delivers it against the spot on the backboard you have picked out.

HOW HIGH IS UP. Dean Meminger drives the hoop and is about to lay the ball up off his fingers. He is stretched out as far as he can go and has his eyes on the basket—not the traffic around him.

NEW YORK
7
DAVIS
23
ATLANTA
3

There should be no spin or English on the ball. This is a true shot all the way and it requires the utmost concentration. Do not worry about the defender. Many layups are missed because the shooter is looking to be fouled and winds up getting nothing. Go to the board as hard as you can and make sure you do not takeoff too soon. The timing is no different than those layups you work on in practice.

There is no excuse for missing one. I would say 99 percent should be made. Actually, the success is somewhere down around 88 percent, which tells you something. It is mostly a lack of concentration. I even have seen a few professional basketball players go in for an uncontested dunk shot and miss, primarily because they were uncertain.

Why? Maybe the crowd noise. Maybe they were undecided as to whether to lay it up or jam it through. Maybe they were thinking how easy it was and relaxed enough to lose concentration. Treat every play as though a championship depended on it and no one will accuse you of not concentrating.

Practice making layups on both sides of the hoop. Try and learn to lay up the ball with either hand—the right hand coming off the right side, and vice versa. That will establish a maneuverability that will enable the shooter to protect the ball better when a defender comes at him.

Take time to work on all shots and techniques. Work on coordinating the eyes and muscles. If shots fall short, focus on the back rim. If they are long, focus on the front rim. All shots are made with the fingertips, not with the palm of the hand.

The arms have nothing to do with a shot. It is a flick of the wrist and fingers. If you are short from the eighteen to twenty-five foot range, use more wrist and finger action, not the arms. Make sure you do not use the other hand on a one-hand shot as you release the ball. Otherwise you will affect the backspin and the direction of the ball.

It is the same principle as the barrel of a rifle. The bullet is given a spin by the grooves and rotates directly at the target. Any outside influence, such as windage, alters the direction. The middle three fingers of the shooting hand represent the rifle barrel and they are responsible for the proper spin that will keep the ball on a true course.

The knees should give a little on all shots. They should be relaxed. The longer the shot, the more the knees are flexed in order to provide greater leverage and, therefore, distance.

Use the backboard on layups and certain shots from angles. Sam Jones of the Boston Celtics was the most accurate bank-shot artist in pro basketball. Dave DeBusschere is good at it, so are Oscar Robertson, Walt Frazier, Jerry West, and all good shooters. They find it is more accurate for them to bank the ball off the backboard on angled shots from fifteen feet in than to shoot straightaway at the basket.

The further from the basket, the higher the spot on the backboard where the ball should be placed. Most pivot men use the board for their hook shots. They are stepping away from the basket on a shot out of the pivot, and the backboard offers them a better target.

DRIBBLING

This is one phase of the game that remains constant. The only radical change in the art of dribbling came when Bob Davies, then playing for Seton Hall, introduced the behind-the-back move. Davies brought it into the professional game as a teammate with the Rochester Royals and Bob Cousy glamorized it during the years he played for the Boston Celtics. Now most backcourt players in pro basketball use the behind-the-back dribble to help them change direction against a defender applying pressure.

Cousy, Frazier, and Lennie Wilkens of the Seattle SuperSonics represent the finest type of dribblers. Not only have they mastered the technique, but they dribble with a purpose. They use the dribble as an attacking weapon. They dribble to set up plays and control the movement of the game.

The dribble is all fingertips. The ball is pushed at the floor with the fingertips, not the palm. Pete Maravich of the Atlanta Hawks has a drill that helps acquire the touch. Everything he does is aimed at producing fingertip control without looking at the ball.

He bounces the ball rapidly a few inches off the floor. He will bounce it behind him and to the side and to the front. He will get on his knees and bounce it in a circle around his body and through his legs. Never looking at the ball.

Dr. Naismith recognized the necessity of not running with the ball when he invented the game of basketball. This is the way he covered it in his original set of rules: "When a player, having gained control of the ball, gives impetus to it by throwing, batting, bouncing, or rolling it and touches it again before it touches another player . . ."

There was a time when a movement started in basketball to eliminate the dribble. Some people saw the Original Celtics move the ball down-

AVOIDING TRAFFIC. Pistol Pete Maravich sees an opening and heads for it. Notice how he has full control of the dribble, which is high because no one is near him. He will drop the ball closer to the floor when the defense closes in.

court without putting the ball on the floor and considered it a thing of beauty. Nat Holman, my coach at CCNY and a member of the Original Celtics, helped discourage the change.

He reasoned that while professional players might be advanced enough to be able to play without the dribble, high school and college players would find it too difficult. Holman was right, as usual. Yes, there are times when a coach, even a coach of a professional basketball team, thinks there is too much dribbling. But the dribble is an integral part of the game and can be responsible for the flow of an offense if employed judiciously.

There are many types of dribbles. There is the quick dribble, or the escape dribble, that is used after recovering the ball off the defensive backboard. There is the controlled dribble that is used to bring the ball down-

TRICKY DICK. Dick Barnett is on his way with the ball. He doesn't waste any time looking at the ball as he pushes downcourt at top speed.

court. There is the change of pace and change of direction dribble to beat the defense in the attacking zone or in a press.

Dribbling is a fine offensive weapon if you know how and when to use it. Learn to dribble without looking at the ball so you can see what is developing ahead of you. These are some of the more important things to keep in mind:

1. The ball is pushed ahead with the fingers, not the palm.
2. Keep your head up and see what is going on in front of you.
3. Dribble at a height that is comfortable—but not too high—and close to your body to protect the ball from being slapped away or stolen.
4. Set the speed of the dribble to coincide with what you are trying to accomplish. If you want to slow the pace of the game, then slow the dribble. If you are being pressed or time is important, then quicken the dribble.
5. The direction or purpose of the dribble depends on what your opponent, and the defense in general, is doing.
6. Learn the habits of an opponent and use fakes to exploit them.
7. After a fake, push the first bounce of the ball as far as possible to get a step on your opponent.
8. Perfect the dribble with either hand so you can give body fakes without changing stride or fool an opponent with a change of pace.
9. Learn to switch hands on the dribble in order to change direction easily. The lower the dribble, the easier to change.
10. Stop and start occasionally on the dribble to throw an opponent off balance.
11. Dribble with the hand farthest from the defender to protect the ball. If you are dribbling with the right hand, do not drive left unless you can switch the ball away from the defender into your other hand. Always keep your body between the defender and the ball.
12. Be prepared to pass quickly off the dribble. Generally speaking, the dribble is used to move the defense and set up a pass to a teammate.

Keep in mind that under all circumstances the dribble should never get higher than the waistline. In situations where a player wants to escape pressure from the defense, the dribble should be below the knees. The shorter the distance from the floor, the quicker the ball can be moved in a different direction.

When going around an opponent, keep the ball away from him. So

EITHER HAND. Earl Monroe is ready at all times to dribble in any direction. A natural righthander, "The Pearl" moves the ball smoothly to his left hand to get around a defender.

many times I have seen Walt Frazier steal the ball from a careless player who exposed the dribble.

A dribbler always should look around to make sure he is not moving into a trap. He should be aware at all times that a defender is not sneaking off his blind side while he is concentrating only on his own man. Dribble with a purpose and not for show.

Dribbling requires alertness. It is a thinking man's weapon if the mind is trained to think. Here are a few situations that require a player to dribble with a purpose:

1. Freezing the ball to kill the clock.
2. Shaking a closely-guarding opponent.
3. Setting up a play.
4. Clearing out on a fast break.
5. Driving to the basket for a layup or to draw the defense over so the ball can be laid off to a teammate.
6. Spreading the defense to give the offense more room to maneuver.
7. Moving across the midcourt line to get into the attacking zone within the ten-second limit.
8. Setting up for a shot behind a screen or a block.
9. Drawing fouls.
10. Avoiding traps.

It is wise to remember that the less you put the ball on the floor, the fewer steals or turnovers. Do not dribble too much against a pressing defense or zone. Check the floor before every game away from home to familiarize yourself with the bounces. Each floor is different and your dribble might be affected. It is better to discover a loose board or a bad bounce before the game than during it.

Do not get fancy. Forget about the behind-the-back or between-the-legs dribbles. Leave that to the professionals. The secret of a good dribbler is to have complete control of the ball so he can use it as an attacking weapon. Walt Frazier has mastered that control so he can do things with a basketball that can be quite amazing. In one game against Baltimore, he dribbled into the attacking zone rather leisurely. His man reacted accordingly by staying in front of him. Clyde's opponent made one mistake: he relaxed for a split second. Frazier was past him with one big step off a change of pace.

That was only the beginning. Clyde saw an opening down the middle and drove for the basket. The Bullets switched to help out. They tried to close the gap. Clyde took one more dribble and took off for the hoop. Wes Unseld went at him. There seemed no way that Walt could avoid getting the shot blocked. But Clyde had one more weapon left. As he got to the hoop and Unseld's menacing hand threatened to jam the shot, Clyde switched the ball from his right hand to his left in mid-air and laid it in off the backboard. This tremendous control is one reason why the dribble is a dangerous weapon in the hands of a Frazier.

A smart dribbler tries to penetrate the defense to set up better scoring opportunities. Lennie Wilkens is an outstanding example. He would drive the middle and go all the way if the lane remained open, as it did for

PENETRATION. Walt Frazier puts pressure on the defense down the middle. He will drive the hoop and if Bob Lanier (16) switches, Clyde can pass off to Jerry Lucas.

Frazier. If there was a switch, Lennie would lay off the ball to Don Smith, his center, or Spencer Haywood, his forward, or even Dick Snyder, his backcourt partner, for an open shot.

The Knicks had an awful time with Archie Clark of the Baltimore Bullets in the 1971–72 playoffs. Archie is one of the finest dribblers in the league. He has quick hands. He can change direction faster than anyone I have ever seen for the simple reason that he keeps the ball low and then moves it the opposite way faster than his opponent can react.

He kept cracking the middle of our defense with his dribbling. Once he penetrated, he either pulled up for a short jumper or passed off to Unseld, Jack Marin, or Mike Riordan for an open shot. He scored over thirty points in three of the six games. The best we could do was find a way to keep him from penetrating the middle.

The ball can move quicker by passing but there are times when no one is open for a pass. That is when the ballhandler should dribble away from congestion and open the defense. A dribbler or playmaker must create the rhythm for the offense. He is responsible for moving the ball in a direction that will establish the best scoring opportunities.

Frazier does that for the Knicks. He does the orchestrating. He sets the tempo. He cannot monopolize the ball. He must be conscious at all times that he has teammates and he has the ball most of the time purely because he is the quarterback. He should dribble only enough to keep the defense moving and the offense flowing.

Players fall into the bad habit of bouncing the ball as they get it. They forget that even one bounce constitutes a dribble. How many times have you seen a pivotman get the ball and immediately bounce it? Now he has nowhere to go. He must stand there or force a shot. He has given the defense an edge. Some players bounce the ball from habit to get into a certain scoring position. It is a sort of reflex action that they have acquired because they did not discipline themselves not to waste a dribble.

Young players are the worst violators. They put the ball down as soon as they get it and leave themselves no place to go when an opponent closes in. When a player gets the ball, he should regard the dribble as a precious commodity. Do not put the ball down unless it is the start of a dribble. If you get the ball in a standing position, look around and determine what is going on before putting it on the floor.

PASSING

Passing enables the offense to carry out its patterns and methods. As in everything that takes place on a basketball court, there always should be a purpose to passing. Do not get rid of the ball just to get rid of it. Remember, it takes two to pass. Make sure there is a clear passing lane to your teammate, who, in turn, should move toward the ball to avoid interceptions.

The shorter the pass, the less risk. Make all passes crisp. Lazy passes are easier to steal or deflect. That does not mean the passer should fire the ball so hard it cannot be handled. The passer should move toward the ball for a return pass if necessary because he is more aware of where it is and, therefore, in a better position to help if the receiver gets trapped.

TEAMWORK. Dennis Layton of Phoenix has released a two-hand chest pass. Clem Haskins moves toward the ball to cut down the risk of interception.

Since passing is the fastest way to move the ball, it becomes more important to the offense than dribbling. In the development of the Knicks, I put the entire emphasis on the involvement of five men. We wanted everyone on the floor participating in our attack. We did not want to build a team around any one player and, therefore, enable the defense to close in at any critical point.

Our whole concept on offense is to move the ball until the man with the open, or best percentage, shot gets it. We could easily have allowed Willis Reed, Bill Bradley, Dick Barnett, Jerry Lucas, Earl Monroe, Dave DeBusschere, or Walt Frazier to take most of the shots. They are all good shooters. We preferred moving the ball and the defense until the player with the best shot took it. That has been the strength of the Knicks since they were built into a winning team.

"I like our chances in a close game," DeBusschere has always said, "because we have five players on the floor who are capable of taking and making the last shot." It is nice to know the players feel that way. It is gratifying to a coach to know that the hard work for everyone reached that stage of accomplishment.

In the game of professional basketball, the ultimate is a team that executes under pressure. There are teams that have one, two, or three favorite players they go to when the game is on the line. On the Knicks, we have been fortunate not to live by any distinctions. Anybody who gets the ball in the best position to shoot, shoots.

Getting the ball in the best position to shoot requires good passing. When I was at CCNY, we ran some passing drills. Nat Holman estimated that on the fast break it took four or five passes, including the pitchout, to complete the layup at the other end. In ordinary maneuvers, with no time limit, it generally took more than five passes before a shot was taken. Sometimes as many as ten.

It is obvious that there is more passing in high school and college games than in professional basketball, where the twenty-four-second clock has cut down on stalling. "Whenever we called a timeout," recalled Bill Russell, speaking of the days when he was player-coach with the Celtics, "any suggested play that required more than two passes I would throw out."

We have no passing quota on the Knicks. We move the ball as long as it takes to get an open shot—as long as it does not take more than the maximum twenty-four seconds. We concentrate on the fundamentals of passing. That means short passes. We are talking about when the ball is in the attacking zone. It is totally different on the fast break, where the long pass is required to get the ball out deep.

The long pass is dangerous in the attacking zone because it has to travel past so many players. Sometimes it is necessary to get the ball to a teammate all alone on the side or in the corner. I grew up having it drilled into my head to never throw crosscourt. Nothing that has happened in basketball has changed my mind about that. If you must get the ball to a teammate crosscourt, play safe—do not throw it.

Helping the passer

A teammate may be an outstanding passer, such as Frazier or Oscar Robertson, but that does not mean he should make the play all by himself. It is important for the man getting the ball to help out. DeBusschere, for example, might be playing inside and want the ball to his right. He will fake going to his left to get his opponent moving that way, then cut back to his right for the pass.

It is up to the receiver to move out of the traffic and create an open passing lane. Unless he is coming out deep to take the ball from a guard in a weave, he should not run in a straight line. He should use deception so the defense cannot anticipate the pass and steal it: a head feint, a change of direction—anything that will shake his man and permit the passer to get him the ball unmolested.

The passer must be careful that he does not misread his teammates' moves. Many times the passer will interpret a fake toward the basket as a cut and throw the ball away as his teammate doubles back. There are times when these split-second mistakes are unavoidable and excusable. But in general, it is the man with the ball who has the responsibility of making the pass good. There are times when a passer can gamble, but the basis for judging any situation is execution, and even in a gambling situation, the passer has to be careful throwing the ball.

There are many varieties of passes. By the time a player enters professional basketball, he has mastered the techniques he will have to employ. It is rather late for a coach to start teaching a pro player the kind of passes he should use in certain situations. He should know the following techniques or there would be no reason to draft him in the first place.

Hook pass

This pass is employed when a defensive man is in your way. It is especially effective against a taller opponent who is blocking your vision and path. Step away from him, go up in the air, and hook the ball with one hand to a teammate. It is similar to the hook shot. Never take your eye off your teammate. You should wind up facing him if you have made the pass properly.

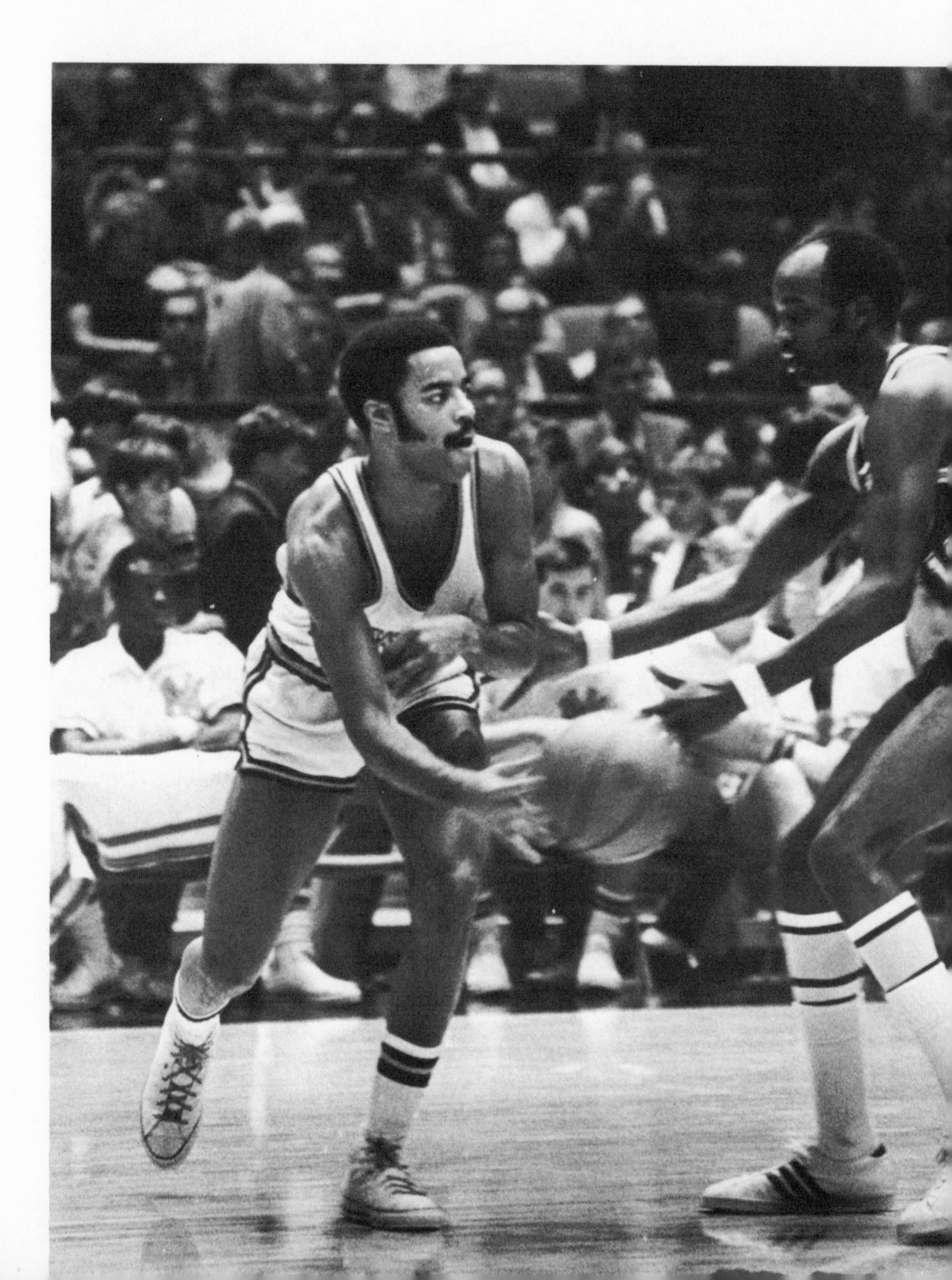

Baseball pass

This is for speed and distance—from thirty feet or more. Keep both hands on the ball until ready for release. Spread the fingers of the throwing hand along the seams or the groove for grip control. Heave it past your ear like a baseball or football and follow through. Wes Unseld, Bill Russell, and Wilt Chamberlain used the baseball pass to trigger the fast breaks that meant so much to their teams. It gets the ball out in a hurry after a defensive rebound.

Bounce pass

This is used to avoid interceptions—especially when the pass is more than twenty feet. It helps get the ball through traffic and beneath the hands of the defense before it can react. The surprise is what makes the bounce pass effective. The defense always anticipates a pass in the air. Try and hit a spot about two-thirds of the way toward your teammate. The one thing to remember is that the ball should be past the defender before it bounces. The trick is to complete the pass on one bounce. It is thrown most of the time with one hand (like a baseball pass) but there are occasions when a two-hand bounce is useful. It depends on your position and balance. Do not use the bounce pass too often.

Chest pass

This is a two-hand pass for less than twenty feet. It is ideal for fast breaks and set patterns in the attacking zone. The ball is in both hands with the middle finger of each hand on the grooves for balance. Elbows are close but not touching. The fingers cover the sides of the ball, with the thumbs and palms behind it. Push the ball straight from the chest to a teammate and follow through. Always step in the direction of the pass.

Two-hand overhead

This is the best pass into the pivot. It is a snap pass made with the wrists. Get the ball high over your head, gripping it, like the chest pass,

GET THE BALL THERE. Walt Frazier flips the ball underhand as the quickest way to get it to an open teammate.

with both hands. Flip it sharply to your teammate. Tall men should use the overhead pass more often because of their physical advantage. I have seen it used on the fast break but it is not advisable unless you have the strength of a Wes Unseld. He amazes me everytime I see him clear a rebound, turn, and fire a two-hand overhead pass to Archie Clark or Phil Chenier covering almost the length of the court.

Two-hand underhand

This type of pass is used to hit a teammate cutting past the pivot or a block. It really is a shovel pass with little spin and not too much speed. The idea is to place the ball where your teammate can dribble or shoot with one motion. Keep the elbows out to protect the ball and pass from a crouched position to effect control.

One-hand underhand

This is used to get more speed on a short flip. The ball should be controlled by both hands until the release. Follow through. This will get you

moving as soon as the pass is made. It is a dangerous pass for distance because the longer the throw, the more difficult it is to control.

There are other types of passes that are suited for various stages of a game. Some players, especially rebounders, have perfected the tap pass. At best, the tap pass is something to be used in an emergency—clearing a rebound or getting the ball out of a scramble. The best pass is the controlled pass if you can get a hand or two on it for possession.

The bounce pass off a dribble is not recommended. It works in isolated cases but it is too erratic. Dribblers or ballhandlers should concentrate on passing the ball in a manner that does not interrupt the flow of motion. Try not to surprise your teammate. I have seen too many players hit in the foot or in the head by passes they never expected.

If a teammate is coming toward you, aim at his chest with a simple pass. If he is cutting left, lead him to his left. If he is coming around a screen or block for a shot, get the pass to him around the shoulders. If he is breaking behind the defense, lead him with a lob pass. If he is cutting behind you, drop it over your shoulder or shove it back.

There is one other pass the professionals have perfected and turned into a useful weapon—the "between-the-legs bounce." The dribbler uses it to set himself up as a one-man screen for his teammate. He will dribble toward the corner or side, then turn into his man. Meanwhile, a forward will drive the baseline and curl behind the dribbler, who will bounce the ball to the forward between his legs. The dribbler just stands there and protects the shooter. It takes perfect timing but is effective to shake a player loose for a shot.

While players know just about all they are going to know about the different types of passes, they still get to sharpen things in fast-breaking drills. The three-man fast break is the best way I know to work on some of the passes that are required under accelerated conditions. One man goes down the middle and the other two flank him. The ball moves without touching the floor. No dribbling. It is fundamentally two-hand chest passing, with an occasional hook at the end or a bounce feed.

The drill helps sharpen the reflexes and the timing that is necessary for accurate passing. Carry the break all the way to the basket with the ball revolving around the middle man. The wingmen can crisscross for variation. When the play is completed, the same three men go the other way after the middle man clears the rebound and triggers the break with a release pass.

BEAT THE DEFENSE. Bill Bradley is improvising to get the ball under the arm of a defensive player. He is hooking it with one hand.

MOVING

There are certain refinements that enable players to get maximum mileage from fundamentals. These refinements come in two forms: (1) moves with the ball and (2) moves without the ball. They are the dimensions of individual performance that establish all-around efficiency.

Moves with the ball fall into one-man, two-man, and three-man categories. That is the way I approach it, anyway. In one-man moves, we talk about picks and screens and feints and assume everyone understands. Not necessarily so. Feinting, changing pace, changing direction—these are the moves that put pressure on the defense. They are important moves that come into play every game and determine the result.

Feint

The idea is to make the defender commit himself so you can shake loose. Test him by faking in one direction with your head, trunk, arms, and the ball—always protecting the ball. If he goes for the fake, or feint, you are free to move in the other direction. Take a small step in the direction of the feint, making sure the pivot foot is firmly on the floor. Now a long step in the opposite direction with the front foot, while twisting the trunk away from the defender.

This is a fine maneuver against a bigger man with slower reflexes. Feint one way and go the other. Sometimes you can do it with one fake of the head. Archie Clark has his own technique. He drives at his man, shaking from side to side like a TV antenna caught in a high wind. His purpose is to keep his man off balance and guessing which direction Archie will go. Generally, the opponent finds out when Clark is past him.

Change of pace

This is fundamentally for the dribbler though quite useful when moving without the ball. Dribble slowly downcourt as though you are going nowhere and just surveying the situation. Keep the brakes on your speed under control. Establish that you are waiting for something to develop behind the defender that he cannot see. As soon as you have him relaxed,

OOPS. This is what can happen when Walt Frazier changes speed and direction on an opponent. Clyde indicated he was going left and, without breaking stride, went the other way with this result.

open up. Take a quick or long step—anything that will give you the jump on him before he has time to recover.

You will be surprised what you can do if you mix things up on an opponent and lure him into thinking you are doing something you have no intention of doing. Meminger is adept because he has different speeds and can shift gears quickly. He will come down the sidelines with the ball not too fast, not at top speed. The defender will move over, thinking he has Dean trapped. Then Dean will put on a burst of speed that gets him through the small opening along the sideline and he has an alley to the basket and a layup.

Wally Jones of the Milwaukee Bucks is a series of constant movements when he brings the ball up court. He has a herky-jerky motion that can be confusing to an opponent. He stops and starts. He slows down and picks it up—all with the intention of probing the man playing him and setting him up. You never really know when Wally is going to turn it on and drive past.

Change of direction

Maybe the most important maneuver on offense without the ball. Indicate you are going in one direction, then go the other way. You can change direction while dribbling right at a defender or coming out of the corner or driving to the baseline. A man in deep may indicate he is coming out to the ball and then cut for the basket and the pass. Pro teams frequently use "backdoor" plays to go behind the defense along the baseline. A player will take a step or two toward the ball and then pivot off the front foot away from the defensive man—catching him going in the wrong direction. The offensive players will swing back toward the baseline for a bounce pass. Sometimes a forward can come out toward the the ball, take the pass, and then reverse direction with a three-quarter turn while the momentum of his defensive man carries him the other way.

Using screens and picks

The man with the ball should learn how to use his teammates to shake himself loose for a shot. Frazier will maneuver his man and run him into Lucas (pick), enabling Clyde to keep driving for the basket or pull up for a shot. On the screen, Frazier will dribble behind Lucas, who sets himself between Clyde and, let's say, Wes Unseld. All teams have plays where they run players behind screens with or without the ball. The purpose is to give a player room to shoot.

Pivot

Either foot is used for pivoting, depending on which direction a player intends to go. Generally speaking, the left foot is used if a player wants to pivot right, and the right foot if he desires to pivot left. The idea, of course, is to pivot away from the man, not into him. Also, by using the opposite foot, it eliminates the possibility of tripping yourself by crossing your legs.

There are exceptions. A pivotman looking to roll right would pivot off his right foot. But if the pivotman wanted to hook with his right hand, he would have to pivot off his left foot.

Two-man moves

One of the most effective two-man maneuvers is the give-and-go. We learned it when we were playing in the schoolyard. Outstanding coaches such as Nat Holman emphasized it because it required little ballhandling and could beat a defense quickly.

It takes only two players. A guard bringing the ball across midcourt sees the defense spread out. He spots a forward along the sideline. The guard passes to the forward, fakes going toward him, and then breaks for the basket. The forward hits the guard with a bounce pass for a layup.

There is nothing spectacular about the play but it is very effective against a switching defense or one that has a tendency to relax. It is best executed by two teammates who know every move of the other. They must be able to recognize the opportunity for the give-and-go and use it without hesitating or a signal. Not even a nod should be necessary. It is a bang-bang play.

Another two-man play for guards depends on the ability to set up the defense with a fake. The man without the ball fakes toward the ball and then takes his opponent away from the ball. The dribbler brings the ball toward the other guard and they create a tight screen. If there is no switch, the guard without the ball is open to drive for the basket and take a pass.

Sometimes the play is worked with the forward and guard. The forward will work from deep in a corner. He will take his man toward the basket or foul line, then double back to the ball indicating with his hand where he wants the pass. The guard gives the forward the ball and swings around him to the baseline for a return pass and shot.

There is an option on the play. The forward may set up a screen. He will come at the guard as though he is going to take a pass and then stop. If the guard's man switches, the forward will take a long step toward the foul area for a pass and a jump shot over a smaller defender.

Sometimes the forward will hand off to the guard and go to the corner. The forward tries to create a switch so he can take the guard's man to the baseline in a mismatch. If there is no switch, the forward buttonhooks back and takes a return pass from the guard for a jump shot.

Another time, a team may run the change of direction with a guard and forward. The forward sets up in deep and takes a pass as the guard runs at him. The guard's man anticipates a baseline play, naturally, and moves toward the forward, while protecting the back door. The guard pulls up, changes direction, and doubles back behind the forward for a pass and shot.

If the guard's man runs into the forward and gets picked off, the guard has an alley along the baseline. If the forward's man switches to block off the baseline, the guard pulls up sharply and takes a pass for a shot. There are many variations on every play. Everything depends on how the defense reacts. A good team must be prepared to surprise the other team at any time.

Pick and roll

A favorite maneuver in the pros. Every team is equipped to use it. Every team has some big men and some small ones. The object is to create a mismatch, which happens often in a fast-moving game where the defense is required to switch often and quickly.

The pick and roll requires a good shooter and a big man. Oscar Robertson and Kareem Abdul-Jabbar are an outstanding example. Frazier and Reed might even be a better example because Willis is a good outside shooter in addition to being strong and big enough to set the effective pick that is necessary.

Frazier will dribble laterally and Reed will move out to set a pick on Oscar. Now everything depends on what Abdul-Jabbar does. If Kareem lays back, Clyde has an open jump shot over everyone. Should Kareem decide to switch and go for Frazier, then the "Big O" is left with Reed, the mismatch.

Now Reed is in position to take advantage of the situation by rolling to the basket and taking a pass from Frazier for a layup. This play requires perfect timing. Willis must release quickly and Clyde must lob the pass so that Reed does not have to reach or break stride. Frazier must be aware that the other Milwaukee players are in no position to steal the ball.

Three-man moves

The Chicago Bulls probably use the set offense more than anyone in professional basketball. Dick Motta has installed a number of three-man plays that put great pressure on any defense. The Bulls concentrate on slicing the guards or forwards off a high post set by Tom Boerwinkle or Cliff Ray, the other center.

Bob Weiss, one of the guards, will give the ball to Boerwinkle, fake right, and drive left around the big center. Jerry Sloan, the other guard, has faked left and now swings around the slicing Weiss to take a pass for a jump shot.

Nobody worked the three-man play off the high post better than the Boston Celtics and Bill Russell. They had many variations. Tom Sanders would feed Russell from the side, take two steps toward Bill, and then cut left to set up a deep screen near the baseline. John Havlicek would run his man into Sanders and swing around Satch for a pass from Russell and an open jump shot.

The Philadelphia 76ers had a play where they ran a forward off the high post. Billy Cunningham would slice around Luke Jackson, and Hal Greer would move toward the high post from the other direction. The defense would expect Greer to complete the double slice and take a pass from Jackson while cutting to the basket. Instead, Hal would change direction and drive straight past Luke on his right rather than swing around him. That catches the defense going in the wrong direction and leaves Greer to take a back bounce pass from Jackson for a layup or short jumper.

There were variations. Greer would pass to Cunningham and then go at him for a return pass. Jackson could come to set a screen and Cunningham would run his man into it. Billy then would move to the foul line for a pass from Greer and a jump shot.

At times, the 76ers would run it the same way except Cunningham would not get the pass from Greer right away. Billy headed for Jackson as he set a screen at the foul line but doubled back behind Greer. A back pass from Hal and Cunningham had a jump shot or was in position to drive off Greer for the basket.

The Atlanta Hawks have a variation they used against us in the 1970–71 playoffs. Pete Maravich flipped the ball into Walt Bellamy, then sliced around him. Walt Hazzard sliced the other way. The guards moved

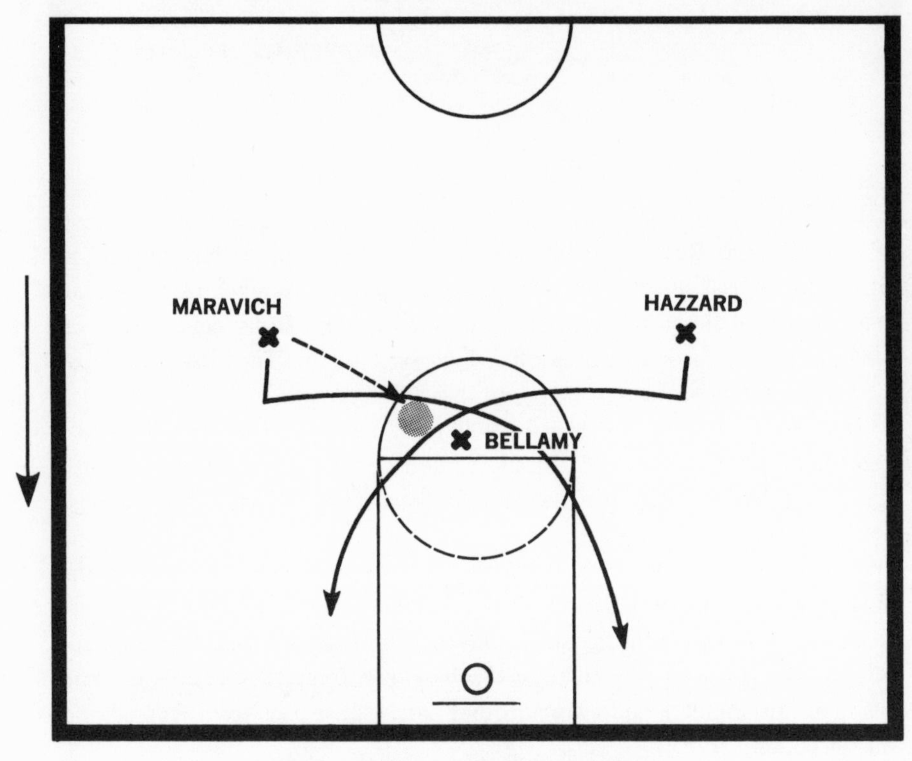

Diagram 2-1 Slice Around Post

their men toward the corners, leaving Bellamy to go 1-on-1 against Reed for a drive to the basket or a jump shot (see diagram 2-1).

In another option, Maravich might pass into Bellamy in the high post. Having seen the guards slice around Walt a few times, the defense might be influenced by a decoying maneuver. So Lou Hudson will cut directly for the basket as soon as Maravich gives the ball to Bellamy and be in position for a pass and shot (see diagram 2-2).

Another play off the high post might have Maravich passing to Hudson, the other guard. Pete will move left as though he is cutting behind Bellamy but then swing around Walt for a return pass. Or Maravich will move right as though he is going to swing around Bellamy but cuts behind Walt and heads for the basket and a return pass from Hudson (see diagram 2-3).

The Boston Celtics use a guard and forward option on slice or scissor plays. Jo-Jo White will hit Dave Cowens on a high post, go right, and then

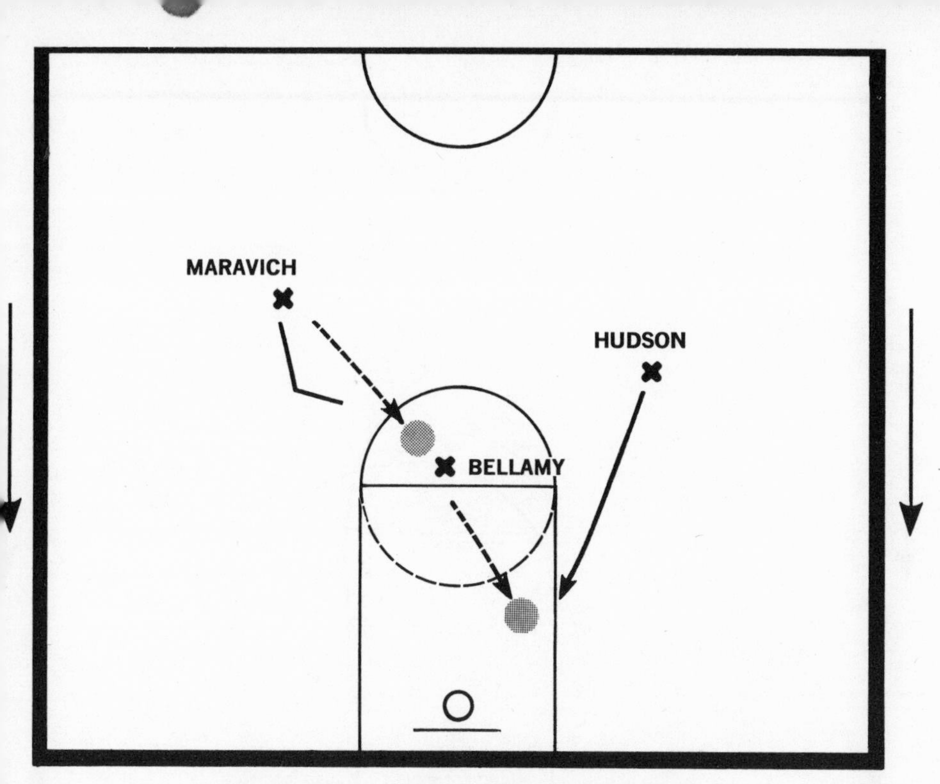

Diagram 2-2 Option: Slice Around Post

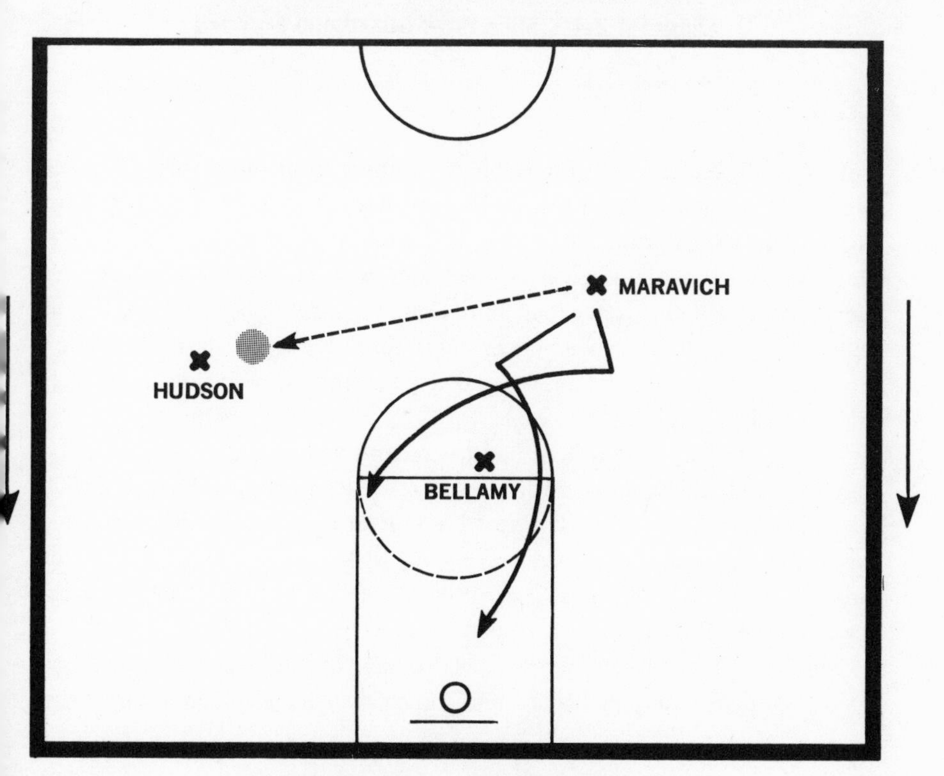

Diagram 2-3 "Shuffle" Cut

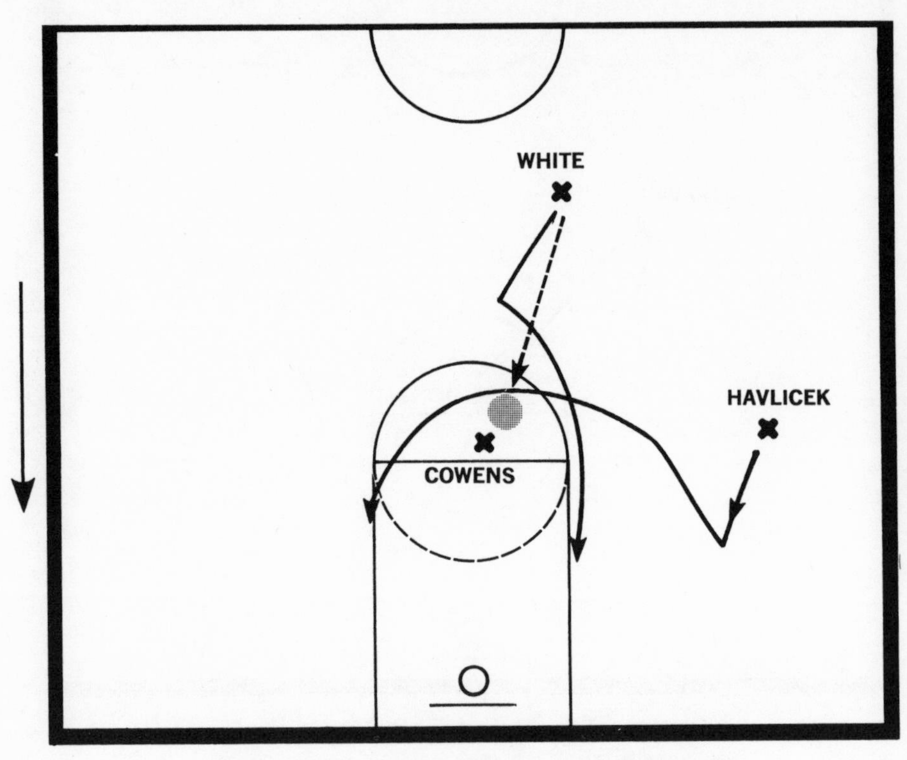

Diagram 2-4 Slice Play: Guard and Forward

cut left to set up a screen for Havlicek, coming from the corner. Havlicek will swing around White to the high post and take a pass behind Cowens for a shot (see diagram 2-4).

Sometimes, the Celtics will go backdoor with Havlicek off this formation. White will throw the ball into Cowens, fake right, and cut left as though moving to set up a screen. This time, Havlicek starts in White's direction but goes backdoor to take a pass from Cowens on either side of the basket (see diagram 2-5).

One of the plays the Knicks had to contend with in the 1971–72 championship with the Lakers involved Jerry West, Jim McMillian, and Wilt Chamberlain. On the dribble, West hit Wilt in the pivot. McMillian faked toward the baseline, and then moved out to set up a screen. West came around McMillian for a pass from Wilt and a shot from the side or corner (see diagram 2-6).

The 76ers work it another way. Hal Greer, on the move, gives the ball to Bill Bridges and goes behind him for an over-the-shoulder return pass.

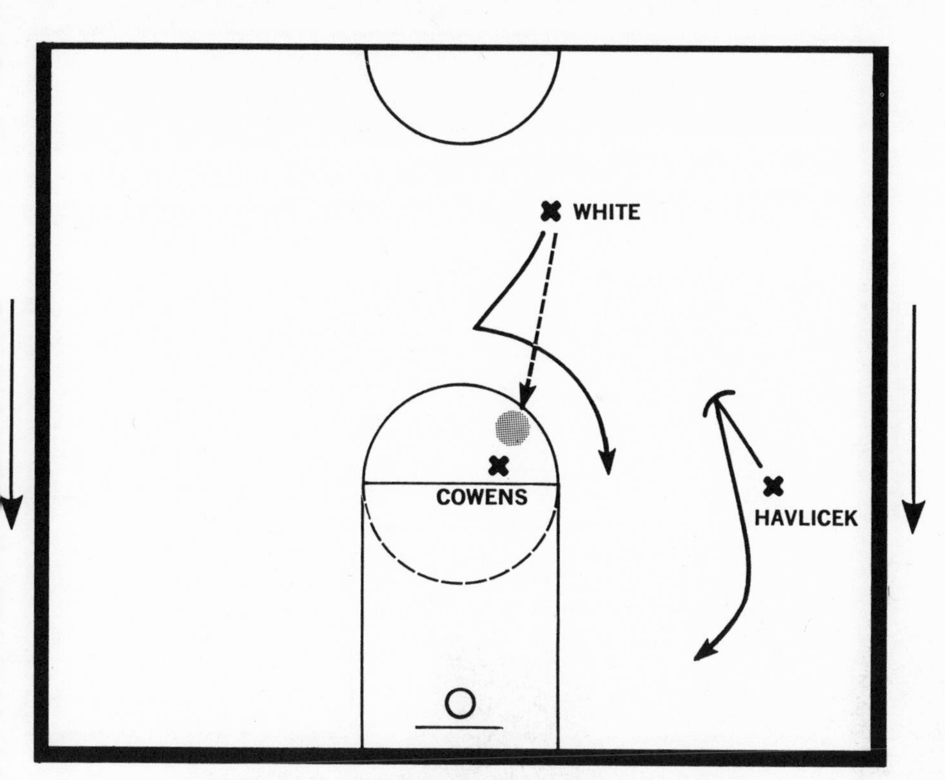

Diagram 2-5 Slice: "Back Door" Play by Forward

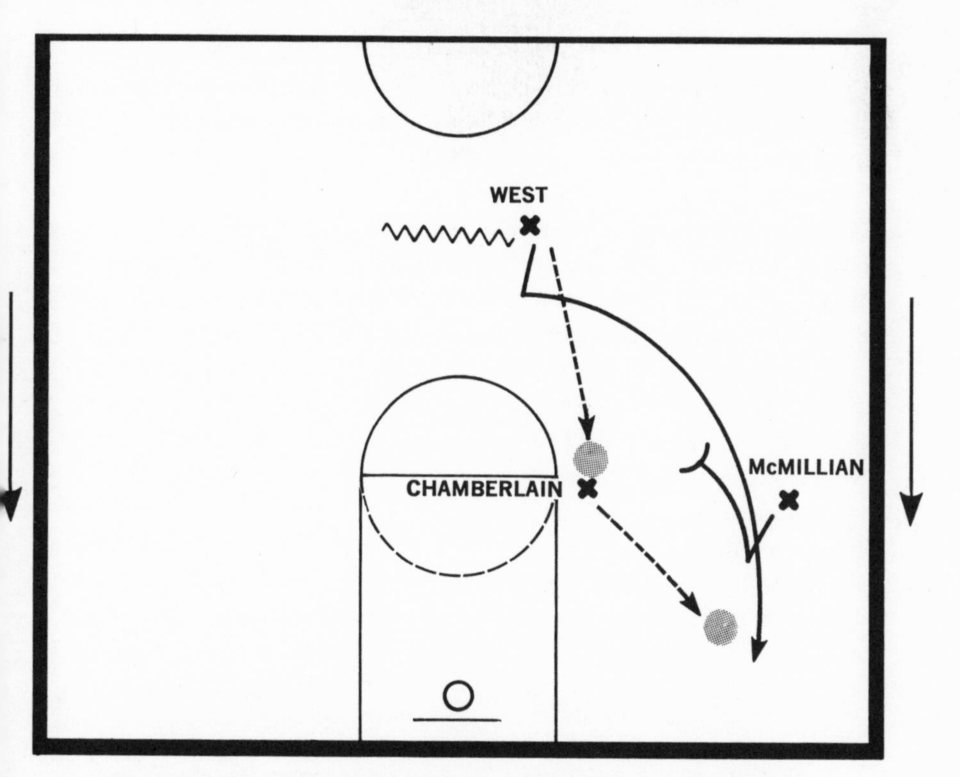

Diagram 2-6 Slice Play: Guard and Forward on Strong Side

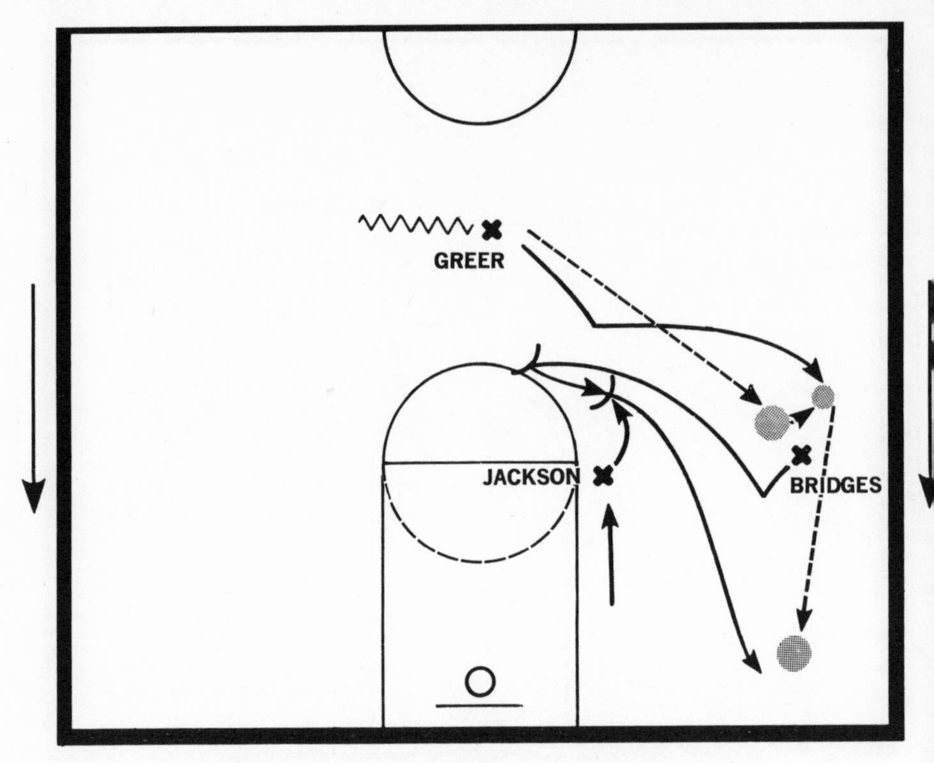

Diagram 2-7 Clear Out: Screen for Forward

Bridges clears out to the top of the key. Luke Jackson has moved out to set a screen on Bill's man. Bridges then cuts back toward Greer and heads for the corner and a return pass (see diagram 2-7).

The Bulls have a play that is good for a big pivotman who is not too fast. Jerry Sloan gives the ball to Chet Walker off a dribble. Sloan moves behind Walker for a return pass. Chet clears out and moves behind Tom Boerwinkle's man to set a screen. Boerwinkle steps out and takes a pass from Sloan for a short jump shot (see diagram 2-8).

On this play, Walker has to be careful about not violating the three-second rule by hanging around in the foul lane too long. He should move right out and into an effective rebounding position as soon as Boerwinkle is released for the pass and shot.

It is imperative for all players to work on the timing and execution of individual offensive moves. Learn to do things instinctively. Basketball is a game of speed and reaction, there is little time to think. If a player stops to wonder what he should do under certain conditions, the play will be lost.

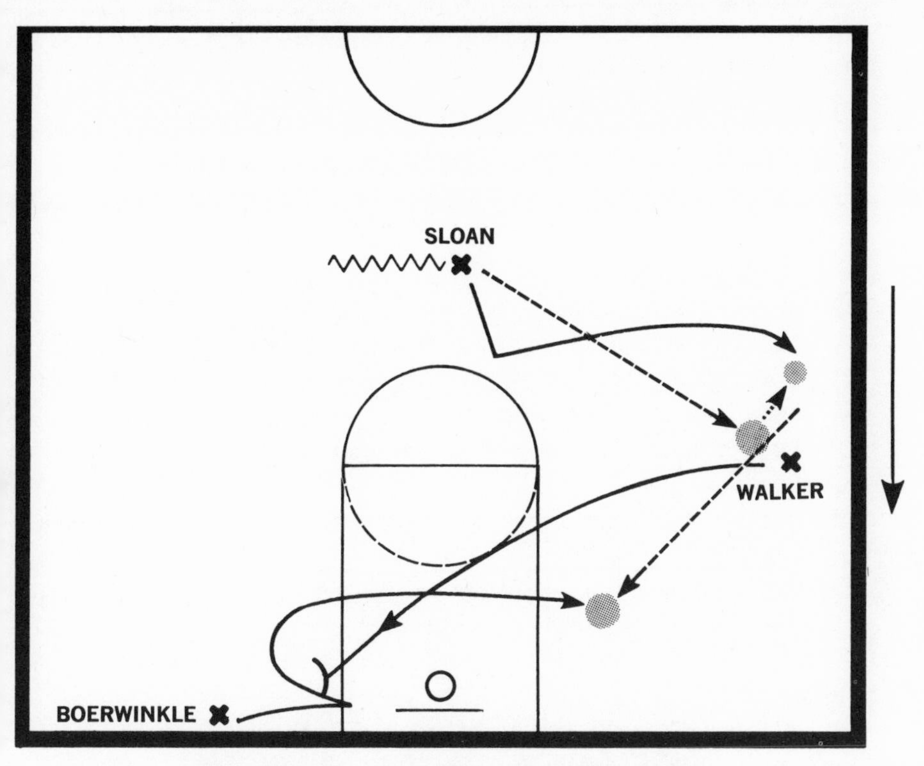

Diagram 2-8 Clear Out for Big Pivot Man

Practice, practice, practice. Get to know the little and big things as well as you know your name. Here are a few important reminders about your offense:

Handling the Ball

1. Protect the ball with your body. Keep your body between the defender and the ball to reduce the risk of the ball being stolen.
2. Do not bounce the ball needlessly and waste a dribble.
3. Pass to a teammate who is aware the ball is coming. A messed up pass generally is the fault of the man passing the ball.
4. Advance the ball with as little dribbling as possible. Everytime you put the ball on the floor, the risk of it being stolen or lost is greater.
5. Avoid crosscourt or lob passes. These are bad percentage passes and are the easiest to intercept.
6. Avoid crossing with a teammate to minimize steals or double-teaming. If you have the ball, avoid dribbling into traffic. Stay out of trouble.

7. Do not tip off passes. Always remember that the defense can be smart, so do not let it anticipate where your pass is heading.
8. Fake a pass against an opponent who plays the ball. Make him commit himself with a little fake and then get rid of the ball. Great for the give-and-go.
9. Do not get fancy. Make the simple, short, safe pass.
10. Pass quickly and not too hard to handle.
11. Avoid getting trapped in the corners or along the lines. Always give yourself room to maneuver.
12. Dribble no higher than the waist and as low as possible for protection.
13. Use the right hand dribble for driving right, the left hand dribble for driving left.
14. Do not dribble too far in front of you once you near a defender.
15. Make passes letter-high or to the chest.

Shooting

1. Always look at the basket and follow through with hands and head for accuracy. Pick up the rim before you shoot.
2. Do not force shots.
3. Learn your range and take only percentage shots. If you haven't got one, give the ball to someone who has.
4. The softer the shot, the better chance of the ball bouncing in off the rim. Try to get some arc on the ball. Line drives must be more accurate.
5. Practice shooting when you are tired to simulate game conditions. The same for foul shooting. Learn how to shoot under stress.
6. Try to practice with someone rather than alone. That way you will be able to work against a moving, defensive target—similar to what you will face in a game. You do not get many uncontested shooting opportunities in a game.
7. Learn to use the backboard for difficult shots taken from an angle.
8. Keep the ball high and the elbows in and low. Release the ball with a snap of the wrist, not the arms.
9. Concentrate. Study the backboard before a game and get a good mental picture of the shooting area.
10. Adjust if you are missing. Do not keep making the same mistakes. If you are too long, shorten the shot; if you are too short, lengthen it.

11. Concentrate on making your first few shots. This builds confidence. Some players, such as Dave DeBusschere, can shoot themselves out of a bad stretch. Others miss at the start and do not hit the rest of the way. If you find yourself pressing, that means you have lost concentration. Go to something else for a while and then come back to shooting.

CHAPTER

3

MOVING WITHOUT THE BALL

Someone once conducted a study for college basketball. The object was to determine just how long a player handled the ball in a forty-minute game. It was discovered that the average player handled the ball about four minutes.

That should tell you something. It kind of explains why moving without the ball is so important. As long as they play the game with one basketball, the players without the ball must learn what to do with themselves. Where to go. How to keep the defense moving and guessing so the offense remains fluid and effective.

In reality, moving without the ball is the heart of the Knicks' game on offense. Everything we do is based on Bill Bradley, Dave DeBusschere, and Jerry Lucas making moves before the ball comes in their direction.

Bradley is the finest example. John Havlicek is another. I find it rather difficult not to be distracted when these two play each other. The moves they use are classic examples of what players should do when a teammate has the ball.

They use changes of direction, changes of pace, screening, colliding, and perpetual motion. They look like something out of the Penn Relays as they chase each other in an attempt to establish some daylight between their bodies. I have to laugh, sometimes, when Havlicek will try and sneak behind a big body, such as that belonging to Dave Cowens, only to have Bradley discover his hiding place.

Moving without the ball is an important part of a basketball player's understanding and application of the fundamentals. Over a season of eighty-two league games in the NBA, you might discover that the Knicks have the ball twenty-four mintues, give or take a few minutes depending on turnovers. Assuming we used only five men in the forty-eight-minute game, each player would have about five minutes with the ball if possession was divided equally. Simple arithmetic then establishes each player should be without the ball for about nineteen minutes.

What do they do with that time? Do they stand around and watch? Do they hang around the middle and clog up their own offense? That is what goes through the mind of a scout when he goes out to look at a college player perform. Everything else considered, the scout will be influenced by a player's moves without the ball; it reflects an intelligence as well as an awareness of the team concept.

"Young players," says Bradley, "have a tendency to neglect moving without the ball. It's one of the most important phases of the game. When you pass the ball, you have to make sure you move immediately after the ball is passed and always move away, not toward, the player to whom you've passed.

"Don't run away. Screen a man and run your opponent off the screen. There are many reasons for moving without the ball and many directions you can take. It can be to clear an area and avoid the possibility of double-teaming, to set a screen, or to increase the possibility of offensive rebounding. When you move, you may not always be moving directly toward the basket, but ultimately your movement should carry you to the basket."

Bill never stops running but his movement *always has a purpose.* He will move in relation to our offense. He may be moving to set up a screen for Dave DeBusschere or Walt Frazier or to clear out an area for Earl Monroe to move into for a shot. He may just be creating motion so the defense cannot set up and pressure our offense.

In a spontaneous, or freelance offense, which seems to have unrelated movement, there are basic rules that guide the flow. For example, if a player is stuck and doesn't know what to do, he moves away from the ball. This prevents double-teaming. It also enables the player to set up a screen on the weak side or away from the ball.

A player must always be conscious of his area of responsibility and concentrate his movement within it. Guards, for example, are responsible for the "horseshoe" area that extends from the backcourt into the corners —fifteen to thirty feet from the basket (see diagram 3-1).

Forwards have the responsibility from the baseline and eighteen feet out. The basic movements generally take the shape of a "figure eight." On a clear-out, cut screen for a guard, or two-man play, the forward moves through the center of the scoring area into the corner. Then he weaves out and back to where he started in the "figure eight" maneuver.

The pivotman or center is responsible for the inside. He moves low post, key, high post, opposite key, and opposite low post. The basic pattern of the pivotman can be equated with the shape of a diamond.

Those are the basic areas of circulation. There are times when players change patterns to confuse the defense but it is important to understand the fundamental areas of responsibility. That way they will not wander aimlessly and get in the way of their teammates. The one thing to keep

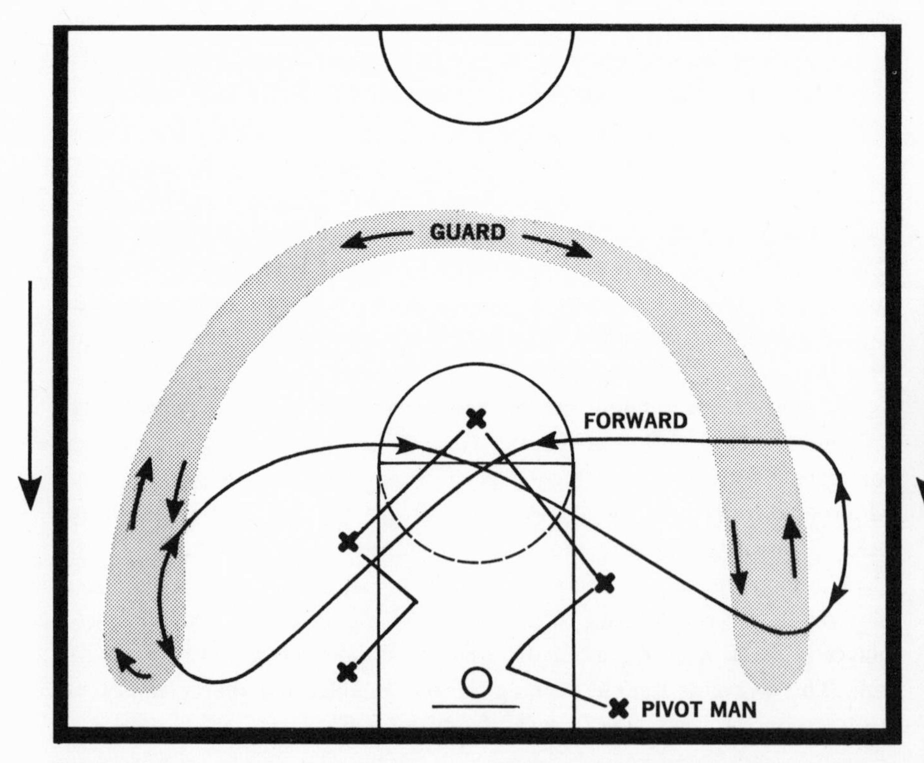

Diagram 3-1 Concepts of Movement: Position and Areas of Responsibility

in mind is not to allow the defense to bunch up at the spot where the shot will be taken.

The modern game has accelerated. It is much faster than when I played. Speed is essential. Players must be prepared to make their moves quickly and decisively. The trend in professional basketball has been toward tougher team defense, which means the offense is being placed under greater stress.

The team with the ball has to keep moving. The players without the ball have to keep moving. The idea is to keep the defense busy. Don't let the other team or players drop off and close the middle to cutters or passes. By keeping in motion, the man without the ball also enables the offense to maintain proper balance and spacing.

For example, how many times have you seen a backcourt man cut through the middle and then stand underneath the basket? This can be disastrous. He is clogging the scoring lane. He is risking a three-second violation. He has taken himself out of the play unless the pass gets to him quickly. His team is vulnerable to a fast break because he is out of position to protect in the backcourt.

If a guard cuts for the basket but does not get the pass, he should clear out immediately and head for the backcourt. That goes for all players. They have established areas of responsibility and should keep that in mind when they are out of a play.

Players without the ball who move continually with a purpose will assure good rebounding position and constant readiness for a quick change in tactics. They place maximum pressure on the defense. A player always should be thinking of what he can do to make himself useful to the team.

You do not need the ball to be effective. It is easy for a defense to key on the ball. The good player has available many moves that will enable him to contribute more and make his team more flexible and resourceful.

FEINTING

Dave DeBusschere and Bill Bradley find this an effective weapon against an opponent playing closely. It takes a man with extremely fast reflexes, such as John Havlicek, to recover when Bradley pulls the feint. Bill will make believe he is going in one direction by taking a half step to his right, keeping his knees relaxed so he can shift gears and go in the opposite direction. Now Havlicek has to change direction. If he is fast enough, Bradley is gone.

Sometimes Bradley will feint directly at his man, indicating he is going around him. The natural reaction of the defensive player is to take a step back. That enables Bradley to stop and drop back for a pass and quick shot. Sometimes it takes only a head fake to deceive an opponent.

The idea is to keep the defender guessing. Never let him read your moves. Most times, he is concerned with the man with the ball, so the man without the ball has a slight advantage. The defender has a tendency to react to the first move under those conditions and that is why a quick feint may get him.

SCREENING

People talk about the Knicks hitting the open man without realizing what it takes to create an open man against intelligent defenses. It wouldn't be possible if Bradley, DeBusschere, or Lucas did not move without the ball and set up screens.

The 1971–72 Knicks were not a big team as big teams go in the NBA. We had no Wilt Chamberlain, Nate Thurmond, Bob Lanier, or Kareem Abdul-Jabbar at center. We were actually a three forwards, two guards team with Lucas in the pivot. That created greater stress on moving without the ball and setting up screens because the defense was able to switch more on us. The defense did not have to fear mismatches that much.

Pro basketball players learn screening real fast. They see so much of it in every game that it is humanly impossible for them not to improve their knowledge and execution. Teammates learn to help each other get open for shots against a top brand of defense.

If Portland wants to work a screen for the guards, Rick Adelman, without the ball, would head toward Geoff Petrie and let his teammate slip behind him for a shot.

If the Blazers want to set up a screen for Sidney Wicks with a guard, Petrie might break around a screen by Adelman and move in deep. Wicks can then step behind Petrie for the pass and shot.

A forward on the weak side can provide a screen for a guard. Adelman can give the ball to Wicks. On the opposite, or weak side, Petrie moves around a screen set by Gary Gregor, the other forward, and can break underneath for a pass from Wicks. This may work well against defensive players who drop off the man without the ball.

Sometimes Petrie can join in double screens with Dale Schleuter, the

SCREENED OUT. John Havlicek of Boston gets help in his frequent confrontations with Bill Bradley. Bradley finds himself screened out by Dave Cowens as Havlicek goes over both of them with a jump shot.

HAVLICEK
17
24

center, or Wicks. On this maneuver, Geoff becomes the man without the ball after he gives it to Adelman. Now Petrie heads to a spot alongside Schleuter, standing at the top of the key. Adelman, meanwhile, dribbles toward Wicks and gives him the ball. Gregor swings around Adelman and Schleuter to take a pass from Wicks for a jump shot or layup.

On another screen without the ball, Petrie can pass to Wicks, then move away from the ball to set a screen for Adelman. If the passing lane is clear, Wicks feeds Adelman. If not, Wicks can pass to Schleuter in deep and Petrie will cut through the middle to take a pass.

Once a man passes in from out-of-bounds, he becomes a man without the ball. Adelman can hit Petrie, who will give the ball to Gregor. In the meantime, Adelman has moved around Petrie and set screens for Wicks and Schleuter, who cut around Rick. Then Petrie buttonhooks to the backcourt to maintain offensive balance and be available for an escape pass should everything become clogged.

All these moves without the ball depend on teamwork. There is no sense creating screens if a team does not recognize them or does not see them developing. The screen is completely ineffective if the shooter does not anticipate and move to it for an open shot.

There are moves without the ball that help a cutting game. Any player with the gift of speed or quick reflexes may develop into a fine cutter with the proper training. It requires good timing, the ability to feint and go while in motion, and a change of pace that will confuse the defender and exploit him if he relaxes for a split second.

Most teams prefer to cut off the weak side because there is less traffic and the defensive man has a tendency to turn his head to look for the ball. There are times when a team can create this type of situation by clearing out the middle, which is the responsibility of the pivotman and forwards.

Golden State, for example, might move the ball around-the-horn, the ball going from Jeff Mullins to Cazzie Russell to Nate Thurmond. As the ball reaches Nate, near the sideline, Jim Barnett, the other guard, fakes his man to the left and cuts right. Barnett will drive the middle for a pass from Thurmond as Clyde Lee, deep in the corner, clears his man out.

There are times when a team desires to break a guard quickly to the basket. Barnett will pass to Thurmond on the high post. Lee will swing into the corner to draw his man away. Russell will move out on the opposite side to open the defense more. Mullins then will cut off Thurmond for a pass and a drive down the middle.

These are all basic maneuvers without the ball. They are not the sole possession of anyone. That is why I can discuss them with candor. There are no secrets in the coaching business. I believe if a team works on fundamentals and perfects execution of its plays, the defense can know what is coming but still be unable to prevent it.

COLLIDING

Moving without the ball might enable a player to run his man into a teammate. You would be surprised how many times that happens to the man who plays Bradley; or to us when we are chasing Havlicek or Jim McMillian or Jack Marin.

A player may maneuver a defensive man into picking off a teammate by cutting. Bradley will weave in and out of traffic, slicing around Lucas or DeBusschere, and hoping Havlicek will run into Dave Cowens or Satch Sanders along the way.

The idea is to get the defender moving in the direction you desire by first feinting him the opposite way. That makes him concentrate more on you. He loses sight of what is going on around him. Now you drive him toward the blind side of a teammate. Another time you may indicate you are going around a teammate but you then drop back and leave your opponent in the traffic jam you just created for him.

This is another example of moving without the ball but with a purpose. It is hard for a defender to know what is going on behind him or on the side without turning his head. He doesn't want to do that because he doesn't want to lose sight of his man. So if you can get him to concentrate on you, it is easier to run him into somebody.

REBOUND POSITIONING

Most defensive rebounders turn their heads as soon as a shot is taken. They want to see where the ball is heading. They want to get into rebounding position. When they do that, you have a split-second advantage. You can move away before the defender reacts and boxes you out.

Tommy Heinsohn, now the Boston coach, and Bailey Howell, now retired, used to drive the Knicks crazy with their offensive rebounding. They were tricky. They always seemed to be in the right spot at the right time. It was no accident; they were smart. As soon as the shot went up, they knew everyone would be looking at the shot. So they would sneak away and move inside their men. By the time their men realized what was happening, Heinsohn and Howell would have the offensive rebound or a tip-in basket.

They traveled the path of least resistance. Most players stand and watch. They let their men box them out. Then they try and fight over the ball, which in most instances accounts for rebounding fouls. If there is a brick wall in front of you, it is better to go around than through.

Some players have an offensive rebounding move on foul shots, but I haven't seen it often enough. Willis Reed has used it many times to get a basket he never should have had. When the shot goes up, the man inside Reed will move into the middle with the idea of boxing Willis out. Most players walk right into that rebounding trap automatically; but not Reed. Sometimes he will fake heading into the lane on the shot. Then he will reverse pivot as the inside man protects the front of the basket, which is the percentage area if a shot is missed. Foul shots do not bounce too far from the hoop because they lack speed.

There is no percentage in trying to beat Wilt Chamberlain, Nate Thurmond, or Kareem Abdul-Jabbar to a missed foul in front of the basket. So once in a while, Reed decides he will gamble that a shot might bounce to the unprotected side. As soon as the shot is taken, the inside man heads into the lane. Willis will move in the same direction with a half step of his inside foot, then spin away from the hoop and completely around.

Reed actually has to use only one step to reach the unprotected area of the basket after he pivots. It is a wise maneuver even if it doesn't work. It gives an opponent something else to think about when he lines up along the foul lane.

DUMMYING

This is a play for a big man. We have worked it at times for Reed, and Chamberlain and Abdul-Jabbar are ideal for it. Sometimes the defense will overplay and provide the opportunity for the big man; other times, the big man can make his own opportunity.

Chamberlain, with the help of Jerry West, pulled it on the Knicks in the 1971–72 championship. He worked his way behind Lucas while Jerry was fronting him and cutting off a pass that might come into him. We were overplaying because West had the ball along the sideline.

Wilt, behind Lucas, dropped back toward the hoop. Lucas turned to find him. Wilt just stood there innocently as though the play was still progressing on the side. West flipped a lob pass and Chamberlain was up in the air and the ball was in the basket before another tick on the twenty-four-second clock.

Anyone can pull the "dummy" on an opponent who does not know where the ball is. The idea is not to tip off the pass. Do not react until the ball gets to you. The longer you wait, the less time your man has to react.

PLAYING THE CORNERS

This is generally for forwards. They create most of the movement on offense without the ball. The guards and centers handle the ball most of the time in most attacks. They are required to stay away from the corners whenever possible.

I always think of Bradley doing this. How he works the corners so he can be closer to the scoring area. How he drives for rebounds. How he sets up screens. How he sets up moving pivot plays by taking a pass and feeding a cutting teammate.

If you set up a moving pivot play, clear out of the area once the pass is made. That way you will not jam the middle and you will be able to get a return pass if necessary. Once you move from the area, go to the opposite corner and draw your man away from the ball.

Bradley gets a great deal of work done from the corner. It is tough for a man to play you and still see the ball if it is on the opposite side. He has to turn his head. Or he has to assume a position between you and the ball.

That gives a player like Bradley an edge because he has worked on moving without the ball. If a man overplays and gives Bradley the baseline, he will fake out and then drive to the basket for a pass. If a man plays deep to protect the baseline, Bill will move at the man and then swerve out to set a screen for Frazier or Monroe.

FOULING

We were playing the Milwaukee Bucks on our way to the 1969–70 championship. The game was close. There was a lot of activity on the floor. We had the ball. Milwaukee had just scored and we brought the ball downcourt. Frazier and Dick Barnett were maneuvering in backcourt. Bradley was conducting his own little marathon in close.

Suddenly the whistle blew. I couldn't figure it out. I had been watching the ball along with everyone else. I hadn't seen a foul. But the officials did. They called one on the man playing Bradley. He had been grabbed at some stage of his feinting and direction changing.

Little things like that win ball games. "I made a survey once," said Bill Sharman, whose coaching credentials were established when his professional teams won titles in the American Basketball League, the American Basketball Association, and the National Basketball Association, "and I discovered that up to forty percent of pro basketball games were decided by one point, one basket, or in overtime. Thus, small details make the difference."

Small details such as Bradley drawing a foul when he doesn't even have the ball and is far off the play. Small details such as not wasting time when you do not have the ball. Find something to do that will help the team. If you have any doubt, remember it is always better to get in the other team's way than your own.

Here are a few things to remember about moving without the ball:

1. Do not clog the middle. Clear out and keep it open for scoring opportunities unless you are setting a screen for a teammate.
2. Keep moving. Do not stand around and allow the defense to capitalize and jam up on your teammates. If you have nothing to do, at least move and take your man with you.
3. Never run in a straight line. Make it tough for an opponent to "read" you. Use changes, fakes, or feints.
4. In faking or feinting, the more exaggerated the movement, the more likely it will be effective. Don't worry about how the move looks as long as it confuses your man. Remember, the head and shoulders are most important in faking out a man.
5. Don't freeze in the pivot. Move unless you are setting a screen. Pivotmen should work on their men. Other players should cut off the pivot. Basketball is a game of motion on offense and defense.

6. Study the defense and figure what you can do to beat it. Study your man and determine how you can exploit his defensive weaknesses.

7. If a teammate sets a screen, be prepared to run your opponent into it.

8. Work on using the change of direction to set up "backdoor" plays against a defense that overplays.

9. You can create your own situations by moving without the ball. You can force the defense to make mistakes.

10. Develop a working rapport with some teammate. We used to call it "the buddy system" when I played in college. There was always one player who knew your moves so well, you could work with him without wasting any time thinking.

CHAPTER

4

INDIVIDUAL DEFENSE

Anyone can identify the player who created the greatest defensive impact on pro basketball. Yes, Bill Russell. He was not only good, he was shrewd. He played defense from the book but added a few chapters of his own.

He had the physical equipment. He had the mind. He had the knowledge. He had the ability to quickly analyze and react. He was the perfect blend of what it takes to play sound, fundamental defense.

He was pretty tricky. He would contest almost every shot until the Celtics would get too far in front to lose. Then he would let the other team drive in for layups. He would permit them to build their confidence when it did not matter and then jam shots when it did. He was a poolroom hustler on defense.

Russell was born with certain qualities that enabled him to apply the fundamentals of defense more naturally than those not equally endowed. But defense can be learned. Defense can be taught.

As strange as it might seem, defense is a problem for a pro basketball coach. How to play a man. The proper positioning. The proper stance. The proper footwork. How to handle a pick. When to overplay. Who to overplay. When to switch.

Defense always fascinated me. As a small man, it represented the greatest challenge in the game. It still does for many pros; Jo-Jo White of Boston, for example. That should surprise many people who consider him a shooter.

"I'd rather play defense," he says. "I like the idea of trying to stop my man from scoring." Individual defense may be approached from different directions by different players but the fundamentals are the same. I would say John Havlicek comes closest to playing ideal defense among all the pro players.

Havlicek is quick and aggressive. He attacks his man and is tough to shake. He fights through picks and has the speed to stay between his man and the basket. He has the quickness to recover if his man gets a step on him and the desire to keep challenging when beaten.

Walt Frazier not only has the mechanics but he knows how to play defense. He has a quick mind and maybe even quicker hands. Lennie Wilkens of Seattle is another with a quick mind and hands. Dick Barnett is the essence of concentration and a sound, fundamental defensive player.

Then there are the physical types. They know how to play defense but must compensate with muscle and desire for what they lack in speed. Dave DeBusschere and Dick Van Arsdale fall into this category. They play everyone body-to-body, nose-to-nose, eyeball-to-eyeball. They are worn out when a game is over but you can be sure their opponents feel just as bad.

DeBusschere always plays the tougher forward for the Knicks. Sometimes it creates awful mismatches. For example, when we play Phoenix and the Suns use seven-foot Mel Counts with Connie Hawkins. That means DeBusschere plays Hawkins and Bradley gets Counts. Size does not mean that much when you can play defense like Bradley.

BASIC DEFENSE

No matter what defense is employed by a team, it inevitably boils down to a 1-on-1 confrontation. Sometime, somewhere, one player winds up on another player and has to stop him from scoring. It doesn't matter if a team uses the zone, zone press, or whatever, it always boils down to one man against another and that is when a player must know what to do. In order to play good team defense, a player must know the intricacies of individual defense.

Defense is motion, constant motion. The worst thing a defensive player can do is relax or sneak a look at what is going on around him. A defensive player who does not concentrate on the job and the fundamentals will get into trouble. Sharp opponents will easily trick him.

Bill Sharman was great at decoying a man. He would move away from the ball and drop his hands, indicating he was out of the play. As soon as his man relaxed, or did not remain active, Sharman would break for the baseline. Russell would hit him with a pass for a short jumper and a basket.

Never rest on defense. If you are tired, learn to pace yourself by catching your breath while your team is changing over from defense to offense. If you are very tired, do not be afraid to ask the coach to take you out for a rest. If you are a Bill Russell or a Wilt Chamberlain or a Kareem Abdul-Jabbar you can rest by laying back after clearing a rebound and triggering a fast break for your team with a release pass.

On the Knicks, we like to pick up a man no further than midcourt, most times deeper, depending on the game situation. If we are fighting for time in a close game, we pick up the other team at the endline. The Boston Celtics do that. So does John Wooden at UCLA.

Some teams like to pressure the pass-in. Sometimes it winds up with a steal. At worst, it makes the other team work harder to bring the ball down, which can lead to turnovers. Some pro teams may double-team the pass receiver then have a man to pressure him all the way into front court.

We have assigned men but the players are instructed to pick up anyone in certain situations. If there is a fast break, Frazier, playing back, will not look for his man. He will take the man nearest him, even if it is Chamberlain, and expect each Knick to pick up the nearest opponent. That way someone is on someone. A team can always switch and pick up the right men but the first thing to do in an emergency is to leave no one open.

To avoid confusion, point at the man you are taking. Yell, if necessary. Don't be afraid to let your teammates know "I've got him!" A team's defense is only as good as the individual contribution and reaction.

If you are the man playing furthest back, make sure no one sneaks behind you. There is a tendency to fall into this trap on a fast break, when you might be distracted trying to direct your teammates on defensive assignments. I have seen a team send a player downcourt while shooting a foul and get a basket because the last man back was sloppy on defense.

Never mind what goes on ahead of you. Play that man nearest the basket. Don't let him take a pass over your head. Don't give him an open alley to the hoop if he should be given a pass on the side or in the corner.

As soon as your team loses the ball, check to see if anyone is behind you. If Dean Meminger is playing back and should spot Happy Hairston of Los Angeles breaking for the basket, he should race back and take him and switch only after help arrives. If Meminger should be stuck under the Knicks' basket and the Lakers break the other way, it is his responsibility to get back as fast as possible. He can't loaf; he has to get back in time to at least clog the middle. As long as he gets back on defense, he can help, even if the Lakers have broken too fast for the Knicks to pick up their assigned men. I have often seen a player trail a fast break and wind up "stealing" the ball because he arrived at the right spot just as the unsuspecting team was passing to it.

PICKING UP A MAN

If five individuals do their defensive jobs properly, a team can set up in front court and wait for the offense. Where a man meets his opponent depends on the type of defense. In using the full-court and half-court press, the guards will pick up their men at the endline, while at other times they will apply the pressure near midcourt.

Against the Lakers and other fast-breaking teams, the shift is quicker. You do not get much time to decide on what you would want to do. The idea is not to drop back too deeply. If you drop too deeply, the rest of the defense is confused as to what men to take. Always get back quickly to keep the other team from breaking someone behind the defense for an easy basket.

THE SCORING AREA

The closer a team moves the ball to the basket, the tighter the defense. You can give a man room on the outside but the space dwindles when he moves in. The amount of room you give a man depends on how much you need to react to any move he makes without fouling him.

Every player should be aware of where he is on the court at all times. He should protect the scoring lanes, which can be determined by the markings on the floor. He should be prepared to make a shooter go over him rather than let him drive for an easier basket. If a man is in the corner, it is wiser to make him drive toward the middle and traffic, rather than travel the shortest distance between two points along the endline.

THE DRIBBLER

Always protect against a man dribbling past you. As in all cases of fundamental defense, stay between your man and the basket. Don't reach for the ball; once you shift your weight forward, it is easier for the dribbler to get around you. Maintain a well-balanced position with your weight distributed evenly enough to match any move the dribbler makes.

If the dribbler stops, that is the time to close in. Be careful not to walk into a trap—where the dribbler gives off and cuts past. As long as the dribbler moves laterally, the man guarding him can maintain some spacing.

Pro teams invariably try to force the dribbler to the sidelines. It reduces the area of maneuverability and places him in a greater risk of being trapped. The guarding man should *never* yield the inside. If the dribbler goes down the sideline, force him into the corner but do not let him get around you. Try to break his rhythm by making some feinting moves as though you are trying to steal the ball. If he decides to drive for a layup, play to block the shot and not steal the dribble.

FLOOR POSITION

It is not always advantageous to stay between your man and the basket. Against a left-handed dribbler, try to make him dribble right. That means overplay his left hand. There are times when a team can play a floating defense, which means the forwards will gamble and cheat on their men to protect the middle. You do not have to guard a man that closely if he doesn't have the ball.

In any defense, it is up to the guard to cover as much territory as he can to close the passing lanes. He is responsible for his man when he is dribbling the ball, but he must also be alert and active enough to help out. If Jerry West is playing Jo-Jo White, who has the ball, Gail Goodrich, the other Laker guard, will drop off Don Chaney and cheat toward the passing lane nearest him. That might discourage White from giving the ball to a teammate who is somewhere in the vicinity of Goodrich.

REBOUNDING. Dave DeBusschere has established the inside position and is going as high as he can to get the missed shot. To protect it, he will pull the ball down and into his body with both hands.

Know where the ball is at all times so you can work on the passing lanes. Do not turn your head to look for the ball. Sneak a glance out of the corner of an eye but never lose sight of your man.

On rebounds, do not get caught too close to the basket. Judge the force of the shot by the distance it has to travel. Assume a rebounding position far enough away from the board to prevent the ball from bouncing over your head but close enough to prevent anyone from beating you to the ball.

Always think of defensive balance on offense. On the Knicks, we attempt to circulate so we do not get caught short in the backcourt. Sometimes, however, it is unavoidable. If Frazier drives for a jump shot along the baseline, Bradley or DeBusschere must be prepared to get out and protect against a fast break should the opposition clear the rebound quickly.

Use peripheral vision. Like a driver in an automobile, try to see more than the car in front of you. You use your side-view mirror, your rear-view mirror, and are alert to traffic on your weak side—but you never lose sight of the car in front. In basketball, you play your man first but you must know what is going on around you, which is where peripheral vision is necessary.

If you are two or more passes away from the ball, you can move one step closer to the middle to help clog the cutting and passing lanes. If you are one pass away, you must be close to or within one arm's length away from your opponent.

FOOTWORK AND STANCE

Balance is the key. The defensive man must be in position to react to the offensive man who has the advantage of making the first move. The feet should be fairly close—slightly less than the width of the shoulders. The weight is distributed evenly—not back in the heels or up in the toes.

No matter what happens, do not cross the legs. That is a fine way to trip yourself while the man goes around you. Slide left and right, according to the direction he is going. If he goes left, slide the right foot out and move that way. If he drives at you, a step backward will leave you in a secure, balanced position.

When guarding a man without the ball, crouch a little and be prepared for a fast start. When playing the man with the ball, do not go for the fake. Wait until he actually is in the act of shooting before leaving your feet in an attempt to block the shot. Some players key on the shooter's chest to avoid going for the head and shoulder fakes.

"Make the player commit himself," says Dave DeBusschere, who runs into the situation often in his role as an outstanding defensive player. "Make him show the shot, not just his head and shoulders. Always remember, the man with the ball must make the first move. The defense only has to react."

GOT YOU COVERED. Dick Barnett seems to be saying that to Jerry West in one of their frequent 1-on-1 confrontations. Barnett is prepared to go either way once West makes up his mind.

USE OF HANDS

Walt Frazier, Jerry West, and Lennie Wilkens have the fastest defensive hands in pro basketball. Make a mistake against them and you no longer have the ball. They have busy hands, which is the way it should be when playing defense.

Hands should be used to distract a shooter. In the first game of the Knicks' 1971–72 championship series with the Lakers, we were hot from outside. Jerry Lucas was hot from outside. Bill Sharman instructed Wilt Chamberlain to move further out on Luke in the second game with his hands up. It helped. Them, not us.

Chamberlain extends his arms on defense. I hope you can appreciate what that does to the passing lanes for a team trying to work the ball in close. It is wise to keep one hand high and the other extended when a man is driving at you. That way you can harass a shot and, possibly, impede a pass if your man is trying to give the ball to someone else.

(Overleaf) THE FASTEST HANDS. They belong to Walt Frazier, as you can see. Put the ball down near him and it can disappear.

USE OF EYES

"I watch a man's eyes a lot," says Frazier. It is extremely difficult to shoot, pass, or dribble without looking in the direction to be employed. That does not mean the defensive player should stare himself into trouble. Actually, if you are playing 1-on-1, the hips will tip off where your opponent is going better than anything.

Never lose sight of your man and never lose sight of the ball, either. If you are playing away from the ball, assume a position (or angle) between your man and the ball. Use peripheral vision to see both. That way you will be in a position to keep your man from sneaking off, and you can steal a pass or help a teammate.

SWITCHING

This is a technique that is generally employed in the pros, where man-to-man defense is emphasized. I always like to tie "switching" in when talking on defense. They go together.

A man switches because he is unable to keep up with his opponent on a play. He runs into a blind pick. He gets caught behind a screen. In some cases, when he has time to recognize what is developing, he should yell to a teammate to switch and take his man. The responsibility of yelling for the switch rests with the man closest to the basket, since he can see what is happening to his teammate.

I remember one game we won in the 1971–72 season. Bradley and DeBusschere kept running the same screen play after play because the other team wasn't switching. Bradley's man kept running into DeBusschere but no one yelled for help. So while the opposition stood flat-footed a few feet away, Bradley hit basket after basket and we won the game.

It is not necessary to switch unless the ball is involved and the defense gets into trouble. There is too much of a risk switching off a big man unless it is absolutely necessary to stop another player driving for the basket. Switching is not too difficult when used in a team defense against screening because switching is generally automatic under those conditions. The thing to remember is to try and switch back to your man if you get caught in a mismatch you cannot handle.

You must be prepared to switch to another opponent when you get picked off. For example, if Frazier pressures West in the backcourt, two

SWITCH. Walt Frazier has driven the hoop but finds someone in his way. Elmore Smith of Buffalo has dropped off Jerry Lucas to protect the basket and menace Frazier.

things can happen: (1) Los Angeles might clear out and let Jerry work on Clyde alone or (2) the Lakers might attempt to run Frazier into a pick to free West.

If the Lakers decide on a pick, Gail Goodrich will come over and West will run Frazier into him. That means Earl Monroe, our other guard, must be alert enough to pick up West. If Earl is not in a good position, then DeBusschere or Bradley must come out and help. That is why you can discuss individual and team defense but it is difficult to separate them.

SPACING

How close you play an opponent depends on him. Never play far enough off a man to permit him an easy shot. It is a good idea to determine a shooter's range and play him accordingly.

In the pros, if we find an opponent who does not hit from outside, we drop off and help protect the more vulnerable inside area. On the other hand, you would not do that against Jack Marin, Dave DeBusschere, John Havlicek, or Jerry Lucas. They must be played tightly.

A good gauge would be to stay within three feet of an opponent on the outside when he does not have the ball. As soon as he gets it, close in to a position that enables you to respond to any direction he decides to take. The Knicks play a lot of 1-on-1 after the regular workouts to drill themselves in defensive reactions.

MAN WITHOUT THE BALL

Determine everyone's strength, then act accordingly. If the man you play is not a good outside shooter, you can float until he gets the ball in close. If the man is the playmaker, you must play him closer. If he is an excellent shooter, play as tightly as possible and attempt to discourage getting the ball to him.

A player, any player, becomes more dangerous with the ball but you still must be careful of those players without it. If you drop off and float, keep your hands and body busy to make sure he has no clear passing lane. It is possible to be caught a little too far away when your man gets the ball. In that case, don't rush right at him. Close in and keep your center of gravity low should he try and drive around you. You will be able to change direction faster that way.

MAN WITH THE BALL

Don't try to out-guess him. He knows where he is going. If he is not a good outside shooter, he is more inclined to drive on you. Retreat a little before he moves, then pressure him when he goes. The idea is to try and force a bad percentage shot or cause him to pass off.

Of course, when you play an Elgin Baylor there is no such thing as a bad percentage shot. He used to throw them in from all angles. All you can do with a player such as that is give him the outside shot or force him away from the basket when he drives.

OUT-OF-BOUNDS PLAYER

Always assume a position on the side of the pass-in so you can see what is going on around you. The man out of bounds is not dangerous until he comes onto the court. John Wooden, most times, tells his players to forget about the player passing the ball in and double up on the potential receiver.

The one time we really play face-to-face with the out-of-bounds player is when we are pressing. When we are fighting the clock and pressuring, the pass-in is extremely important. Otherwise, we have our man play sideways, so he can avoid someone sneaking behind him for a block.

PIVOTMAN

Anyone who wants an education in how to play a big man in the pivot should watch Jerry Lucas against Wilt Chamberlain and Kareem Abdul-Jabbar, two distinctly different centers.

Wilt is the stationary pivot who depends upon ballhandling and muscle. Kareem is the moving pivot with the speed and shooting finesse of a forward. Kareem will move from side-to-side in the foul area—pivoting, turning, and being as deceptive as possible. Wilt gets the ball and uses his weight.

That means Lucas has to play them differently. He does not play directly behind Wilt. He overplays him on the side where the ball is moving. He will bother him with his hands by waving them in the passing lane to discourage Jerry West or Gail Goodrich from throwing it in. He will move in front of Wilt whenever possible. Always keeping in mind, when a shot is taken, that he must be in position to box out Chamberlain on the rebound.

Abdul-Jabbar presents another problem. He moves too quickly for Lucas to employ the same tactics he uses against Wilt. In addition, Kareem's reach is too long for Luke to front him and hope to intercept a pass or play on the side and hope to deflect one. He has to concentrate on staying between Kareem and the basket. He must block Kareem's path and force him to take a sweeping hook, rather than an easier roll-in. He cannot afford to ease off from behind because Abdul-Jabbar has a little jump shot that can be troublesome. Pivotmen must be played closely all the time when they are good scorers.

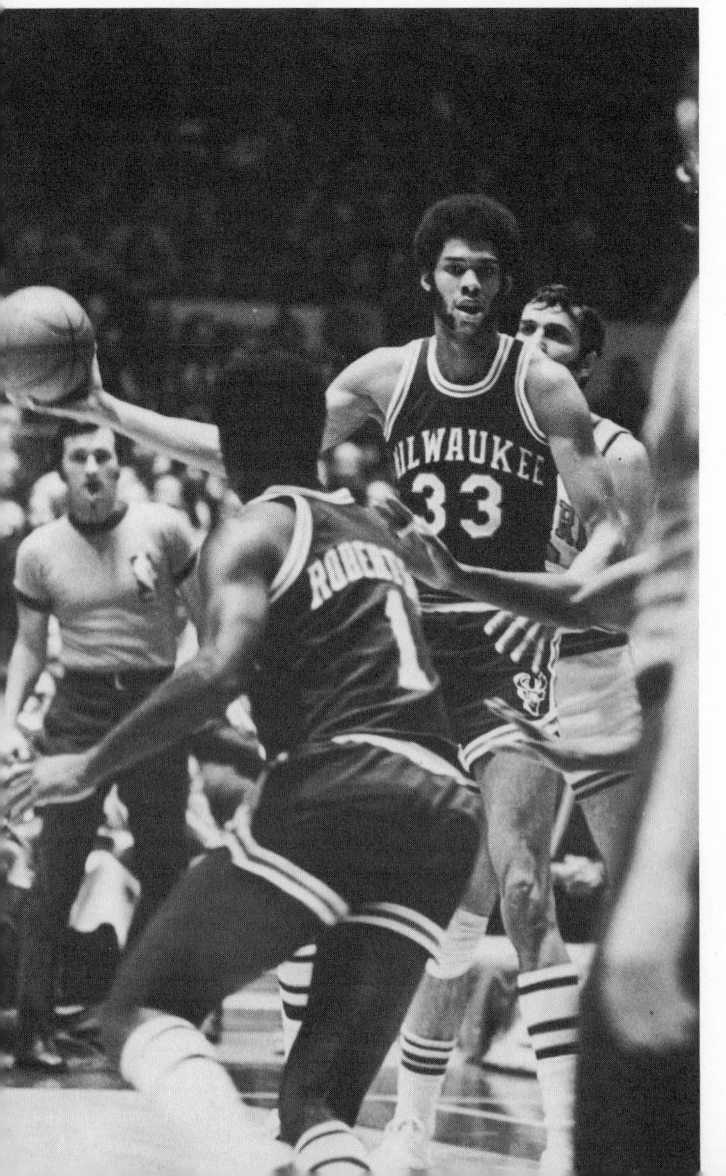

WHERE TO GO? Jerry Lucas waits behind Kareem Abdul-Jabbar for the play to develop. Luke is in a perfect position to keep the Milwaukee center from rolling to the basket or to switch and pick up Oscar Robertson should he take a handoff.

There are times when no one man can do the job, when Lucas needs help. In most cases, we rely on Luke to do whatever he can, when he can. This type of matchup places a premium on intelligence, which, somehow, never is the total answer when you are as big and talented as Chamberlain and Abdul-Jabbar.

TALKING

The voice is important on defense. I don't know why, but it seems as though the toughest thing to get across to a player is talking on defense. Always letting a teammate know what is going on if he gets into a blind position.

Defense does not begin and end with individuality. An individual may think his responsibility is fulfilling his own assignment, but he is only one part of a machine. It is nice to know that a player has been letter perfect against his own opponent, yet he should never forget his teammates. There are times when they need help, as there will be times when he will need it.

If someone on the Knicks sees the ball lost suddenly, he alerts his teammates by yelling: "Back! Back!" If someone on the Knicks steals the ball or comes up with it in a scramble, he yells: "Ball! Ball!" Anyway, he should.

Then there are the responsibilities at the defensive end, where most of the trouble occurs. Players get picked off or are run behind screens. This calls for a switch, and fast, but how many times do you hear anyone yell "Switch!"

We work on that. We have our defense talking all the time. On everything. Before a play even develops. Frazier, for example, cannot see what is going on behind him while trying to keep West from backing him up. Chamberlain might be moving in to set a pick on Clyde from behind.

It is Lucas' responsibility to alert Frazier. "Left, Clyde!" Jerry will shout, if Wilt has come out high to pick Frazier on his left side. Little things like that win or lose games. It is just as important for players to alert teammates on defense as it is to score.

Know where the ball is at all times. I would be a rich man if I had a dollar for every time I had to remind the Knicks to "See the ball." We had a little out-of-bounds trick we worked in the schoolyard when I was a youngster against an opponent who turned his head or back on the ball.

I think it happened once in an NBA game but I'm not sure. Assume

Oscar Robertson takes the ball out under his basket. The defense scrambles to set up. Oscar's man turns to see what is going on or to pick up anyone cutting to the hoop. The "Big O" bounces the ball off his opponent's back, steps onto the court for the loose ball and puts it in for two points.

Basketball is a game where the use of the mind, body, and voice are equally important. If it means helping your team win—and it often does—talk.

REBOUNDING

Position is the most important consideration. Boxing out is the secret. Jerry Lucas is one of the finest rebounders the pro game has known, considering the results and his size. When he gets position, it is virtually impossible for much taller players to get the ball unless it bounces over his head.

When a shot goes up, the defensive rebounder must first determine where his man is before looking for the ball. Lucas will turn directly into his man, boxing him out, then look for the rebound.

While Lucas is waiting for the rebound, he takes up as much room as possible. He keeps his man as far away from the board as he can and concentrates on not letting him escape the trap. He leans into his man but is ready to time his jump when the ball comes off the board.

Dave DeBusschere is another outstanding example of what can be accomplished by someone who has mastered the technique. He knows how to use his weight and body. He is only six-foot-six, but there are few players who can beat him to a defensive rebound once he is in position. He knows how to use his body to keep his man off-balance until he launches for the ball.

Winning teams usually control the rebounds. It certainly makes it more difficult to win if you let the other team get two, three, or four shots at a time because someone on your team does not know how to rebound.

The idea is to leap as high as you can. Get the arms up as high as possible. Grab the ball with two hands and bring it into the body for protection. Do not wave the ball out in front of you or over your head. It is too easy to steal that way.

Stay as low as possible after rebounding until you are sure you have control. Now turn and look to pass to a deep man or a teammate alongside. Teammates breaking downcourt should always be alert to the possibility of having to come back and help a rebounder if he gets into trouble.

TAP PLAYS

Never let your man sneak behind you on jump ball situations. Always keep him between you and the basket. Never concede a tap. Try to anticipate where the tap is going by studying the positions on the floor and you might steal it once in a while.

If Chamberlain were to jump against Frazier at the Los Angeles foul line, we would make sure to double up on anyone getting the tap inside. The forwards must be prepared to help each other should Wilt tap the ball forward to Jim McMillian or Happy Hairston. We might even have Frazier break in and help as the jump ball is conducted.

If that happens, Clyde, or someone else, has to be conscious of Frazier's man. Someone has to pick him up or he will be able to cut for the basket and take a pass for an easy shot.

On jump balls in the defensive area, each man is played closely and aggressively, with the emphasis on the inside men if the other team figures to get the tap. At your offensive end, if the other team figures to get the tap, protect against long tap plays where an opponent breaks for the basket.

Things to remember:

1. Stay between your opponent and the basket at all times.
2. Stay down, with knees flexed so you can react. Do not stand flat-footed and straight up. Keep center of gravity low in defensive stance.
3. Make the ballhandler or shooter commit himself. Do not go for the fake. Remember, the offense must make the move, the defense must react.
4. Learn to cover quickly on a turnover. Do not waste time thinking. Know what you should do before anything happens.
5. Get back on a fast break. Do not worry about matchups. Pick up the man nearest to you. Switch to your man only if your teammates can get set.
6. See the ball. Know where it is at all times.
7. Do not turn your head. Assume an angle where you can see the ball and your opponent. Keep both in view so your man cannot sneak away while your head is turned.
8. Don't be lazy. Play your opponent aggressively whether or not he has the ball. Attack on defense. Loosen up only if you are playing a poor shooter from outside.

9. Be prepared to switch at all times and let your teammates know by yelling.

10. Talk on defense. Communicate everything to teammates who cannot see what is developing. If you are the back man, let your teammate know where they are setting a pick on him.

11. Don't leave the backcourt uncovered after your team shoots. Someone must protect against an opponent sneaking away for an easy basket.

12. Don't play the ball unless you have good defensive teammates, or a Bill Russell, to cover for you.

13. Try and move your man laterally—away from the basket. Try and force dribblers along the sidelines and into the corners. Don't let an opponent drive the baseline. Force everything to the outside.

14. Keep your hands busy. Use them to distract the ballhandler and shooter. Extend them into the passing lanes.

15. Play a pivotman on the side where the ball will be coming to him. If he is much bigger and stronger, and takes you inside, get in front of him. Pressure all big men to move away from the basket for poorer percentage shots. Work from the basket up toward the foul line.

16. When an opponent shoots, box out your man first. Know where he is and turn into him before you look for the rebound.

17. Pick up your man as soon as possible. Don't let him move unmolested to the area on the floor he desires. Annoy him.

18. Go with the dribbler, don't slap at him. Don't reach for the ball. Maintain defensive balance at all times so you can move in any direction without wasting motion.

CHAPTER

5

TEAM DEFENSE

"DEE—fense! DEE—fense!" They were on their feet and screaming. There were 19,500 fans in Madison Square Garden and the Knicks had a serious problem. Willis Reed was hurt. It was the fifth game of the 1969–70 championship series with the Los Angeles Lakers, which was tied at two games each.

Willis had attempted to drive around Wilt Chamberlain, and, suddenly, there was Reed on the floor, holding his right hip in obvious pain. I ran onto the court with Danny Whelan, our trainer. Reed left the game, through for the night.

We wound up thirteen points behind at the half, with no Reed to handle Chamberlain. We had no one on the bench physically capable of matching Wilt, who might very well be the strongest man in the world. We had to adjust. We wound up using Nate Bowman, Dave DeBusschere, and Dave Stallworth—each a defensive risk in a 1-on-1 confrontation with Chamberlain.

The Knicks went on to win that pivotal fifth game and eventually capture their first championship in NBA history, 4–3. The reason why the Knicks survived may be attributed chiefly to its team defense. There was no way we could have won that series, with Reed's condition, if we had not spent so much time preparing our defense for just such an emergency.

Without Willis, we had to put more pressure on the Lakers. We had to be more aggressive. We made it difficult for Wilt to get the ball in close or where he wanted it. We had Stallworth and DeBusschere front him and the other players drop off to help. We pressed Jerry West, Elgin Baylor, and Happy Hairston and managed to steal the ball often enough to disrupt their offense.

We did the same things under the extraordinary pressures of a championship game we had done in practice and throughout the regular season of eighty-two games. We were defense oriented and everyone knew it. We held opponents under 100 points 27 times that season, or in one-third of our games. Though we never stressed individualism, three Knicks were selected to the All-Star defensive team. Walt Frazier, Reed, and DeBusschere were selected because they were the heart of a team defense that took many man-hours to create.

When the 1968–69 season ended in the playoffs in Boston, the players vowed to make the next season pay off. They came to our training camp determined to work for a championship. We got off on an eighteen-game winning streak that was a record until Milwaukee made it twenty and then the Lakers put together thirty-three victories in a row—one of the incredible accomplishments in professional sports.

Our eighteen-game winning streak did more to create a general awareness of our defensive concept than anything else. More people began talking of the Knicks and recognizing the value of team defense. Reed was the only one ever found among the league's leading scorers, yet we were winning more games than anyone.

We had good shooters, very good shooters. As a team, maybe the best outside shooters in the game. There were not many better than Bill Bradley, Dick Barnett, DeBusschere, Frazier, Reed, and our super sixth man, Cazzie Russell. We could handle the ball and hit the open man and convert our share of percentage opportunities.

We lacked two things on that team: size and rebounding. We were outrebounded most of the time. We had to find other ways to get the ball. We compensated with team defense. We pressured teams into bad shots. We stole the ball by funneling the offense into trap situations. Some steals are lucky. On the Knicks, we work on it. We set up defensive positions that forced and exploited mistakes. We believe that a team defense should create some offense.

A team that plays good team defense can stay in a game when the offense is not working. The Knicks sincerely believed it was impossible for them to be crushed in any game because their team defense kept them close all the time. There was a time, in the NBA, when a team could score as many as 140 points and still lose. The Knicks once scored 147 and lost by 22!

That game is in the record book. It was played against the Philadelphia Warriors in Hershey, Pa., on March 2, 1962, and Wilt Chamberlain scored 100 points all by himself. The Warriors wound up with 169. And how about the San Diego Rockets, when they scored 151 points on March 12, 1970, and still lost by 14 because the Cincinnati Royals scored 165.

Many things have changed. For one thing, the Rockets have moved to Houston and the Royals found a new home in Kansas City. For another, the teams in the NBA have become more conscious about team defense. In pro basketball, the defense, to some extent, is aided by the ten-second and twenty-four-second rules. The offense must move the ball across midcourt within ten seconds and must shoot within twenty-four seconds or lose possession.

Under the twenty-four-second rule, a shot must touch some part of the basket or backboard within the time limit or it is a violation. A foul shot also causes the twenty-four-second clock to be re-set. It is different in high school and college basketball, where the ten-second rule exists but not the twenty-four-second clock.

In high school and college basketball, there is no time limit on shooting, so they have more time to develop plays—which puts a greater strain on the defense. The defending team has to chase the offense within a longer reference of time, whereas the pros know they have to apply pressure for a maximum of twenty-four seconds.

Pro basketball devised its rules to eliminate stalling tactics that many felt slowed down the game. High school and college basketball have a modified stalling rule. Teams must move the ball within twenty-eight feet of the basket every thirty seconds if they are not closely guarded. There are many outstanding college coaches, such as John Wooden, who do not think it is enough. They would prefer a twenty-four-second clock or even the thirty-second clock used under international rules.

International basketball, which includes Olympic competition, is slightly different from the game we play here in high school, college, and the pros. It has a ten-second rule that applies only in the last three minutes of a game. Otherwise, a team may take its time bringing the ball over midcourt.

However, the thirty-second clock makes international basketball much like the pro game in the United States in that it forces a team to shoot and not hold the ball endlessly.

There are differences in rules and techniques but the playing fundamentals are the same in all versions of basketball. A defense that is successful in pro basketball, will be just as successful for high school, college, and international players.

The defensive concepts in pro basketball mainly are man-to-man. We do employ zone presses within the framework of the rules that prohibit pure zones. There are times when a switching man-to-man looks like a zone defense because there is a thin line of demarcation. The officials are responsible for calling any zone defense violations—with first a warning to the offender and then a technical if necessary.

PHILOSOPHY

Shooting is enjoyable; defense is hard work. Team defense is as good as the desire of the players. Most young athletes grow up with the idea that defense is not fun. The Boston Celtics changed that in the Bill Russell era by making defense popular and enjoyable because it was so clearly related to their fabulous run of eleven championships in thirteen seasons.

The Knicks have established a similar pride in their defense. They became more receptive to the hard work that is demanded when they realized how much it meant to winning. They discovered it was fun to keep the other team under 100 points. So did the Garden fans, who would root for it to happen and boo any player on the other team who had the audacity to make the basket that ruined things.

From a team viewpoint, a player must approach the situation with a determination to stop his man while being prepared to help a teammate. It takes the proper attitude to sometimes sacrifice a desire to hold an opponent scoreless when it is more important to contribute to the team defense. There are times when Bill Bradley may be playing a good shooter such as Jim McMillian but has to drop off and help Jerry Lucas with Wilt Chamberlain.

Jerry West is another example. In the first three games of the Knicks' championship series with the Lakers in the 1971–72 playoffs, he had a serious problem with his shooting. Yet, he caused us a lot of trouble with his defense. The way he switched to help cover for Chamberlain when

Wilt dropped off Lucas to protect the inside. The way he stole passes by closing the lanes when it appeared as though we could get the ball through.

Players such as West and Frazier make the all-defensive team because they are team players. They enjoy playing defense. They play aggressively and force their opponents to hurry their passes and shots. They have developed a keen sense of anticipation which enables them to attack on offense as well as recognize the danger signs when the team defense needs help.

A strong defensive team generates a brand of confidence that rubs off on the rest of the game. It takes outstanding teamwork to blend individual skills into a unit that instinctively reacts to every move by the opponents. This requires a balance that needs fine tuning. The ability to be in the right place at the right time with the necessary equipment. The application of delicate movements to protect the areas of vulnerability.

It is much like a game of chess. Each chesspiece is a weapon used to block the attack on the "king" by the opponent. In basketball, the "king" is the basket and the players are the pawns. By sliding one piece over, a player manages to impede the progress, as well as the strategy, of his opponent.

In recent years, the offense *vs.* the defense in the NBA has become an even greater game of wits. With the defense catching up, the offense has acquired a larger burden, much the same as what happened in pro football a few years ago.

Now coaches are trying to devise more subtle ways of setting up screens and picks to free a player for a shot. This puts a greater responsibility on the defensive player and his ability to slide and switch. A player must rotate against his opponents in order for the team to maintain defensive balance and not permit too many easy shots.

MATCHUPS

There was a time when matchups were dictated by size. It is not entirely that way anymore, not in professional basketball. You do match your center against the other team's center because they are the biggest men on each side. But the 1971–72 Knicks proved a team can operate with a high degree of success with a six-foot-eight Jerry Lucas playing seven-footers like Wilt Chamberlain and Kareem Abdul-Jabbar.

Our formula in regard to matchups is quite simple. Dave DeBusschere always plays the most dangerous forward on the other team and Bill Bradley is assigned to the second forward. DeBusschere is stronger and is better equipped than Bradley to absorb the physical stresses of rebounding and other areas of contact.

Yet, there is no rule of thumb. It depends on the situation; in the final analysis, the assignments are influenced by what is good for the team. Thus, when we play the Lakers, we find Jim McMillian is physically stronger than Bradley, but we want DeBusschere on Happy Hairston, to keep him away from the boards.

Chicago presents a different problem. Bob Love is the top scorer and DeBusschere ordinarily would play him. But Chet Walker, another dangerous shooter, is more aggressive off the boards, so we prefer to put Dave on him and let Bradley play Love. Against Milwaukee, we always had DeBusschere on Bob Dandridge; that was when Greg Smith, a smaller forward, was with the Bucks. Then when Smith was traded to Houston for Curtis Perry, a bigger and stronger forward, DeBusschere and Bradley switched assignments, with Dave playing Perry and Bill handling Dandridge.

The same approach applies at guard. The Knicks are fortunate to have smart defensive players in Frazier, Dick Barnett, Earl Monroe, and Dean Meminger. They are interchangeable because they have the intelligence to play any guard in the league. Clyde is a little quicker so we are more inclined to use him against speed, though we are not locked to a pattern.

Generally speaking, coaches know the habits of the other team and prefer to match height with height, speed with speed, scoring with scoring. That is the safest way. But there are times when certain situations call for adjustments.

For example, when the Knicks play the Lakers, the natural thing would be to allow Frazier to play West. We prefer to put Barnett on Jerry. For one thing, Dick is an outstanding defensive player, and he makes West work hard. For another, the harder West works, the more tired he figures to become at the other end of the floor, where he plays Frazier on defense. It also keeps Clyde fresher because a player can become awfully weary chasing West around.

While the assignments are made on an individual basis, the ultimate consideration is the value to the team. We meet in the dressing room before each game and go over the opponents. We watch a film in order to help the players relax and get their minds on the game coming up. We designate the individual assignments, but every player on the Knicks talks and thinks in terms of team defense.

BIG JERRY VS. LITTLE DEAN. Size is not the key consideration in a matchup. The Knicks will use Dean Meminger on Jerry West because little Dean has speed and quickness which compensates for what he gives away in height.

There was a sign in our dressing room for a long time that indicated what everyone considered the most important matchup. It read: "Pride and good defense."

In general, matchups are determined by a study of the defensive problems that will be facing a team. It is customary to put the best defensive forward on the best offensive forward and so forth. Strategy is only as good as the way it works.

Sometimes a well-conceived set of matchups is effective. Other times, it might not accomplish a thing. The fundamental requirement is for a team to be flexible so that it is prepared to do anything to disrupt the other team's offense.

SWITCHING

Switching, sliding, and shifting fall into the same defensive category. They represent the moves players must be prepared to make to handle the tricks of the offense. Most of the trouble is created by screens and picks. A defensive player cannot always keep up with his man. Frazier, West, and DeBusschere—the best defensive players—run into problems. The Boston Celtics have a perpetual motion offense designed to get the defense in trouble. They want to get someone picked off or caught in a screen. There is no escape in the NBA.

Most pro coaches prefer their players to fight through screens and challenge the shooter. In other words, if John Havlicek, perpetual motion himself, moves around a screen set by Dave Cowens, the defensive player should fight between them—not pass behind Cowens.

The reason is obvious. If Havlicek's defensive opponent moves behind Cowens, all John has to do is stop and he has an uncontested shot while using his center as a screen. If the defensive man goes between Havlicek and Cowens, the danger is minimized. There is no screen.

What happens if the defensive man finds no room between Havlicek and Cowens? That is where the team defense enters. Someone on the defensive team has to be alert enough to switch and help out. A switch in time will prevent Havlicek from breaking into the open.

When a team plays together for any period of time, such a switch should be automatic. It is wise for players to alert each other until that type of instantaneous reaction is attained. By simply yelling "Switch,"

GET HIM! Steve Kuberski fights through a screen to pressure Dean Meminger and prevent an easy shot. Kuberski has stepped in front of Dave DeBusschere (screened out) to help Jo-Jo White—playing Meminger—who got caught in traffic.

defensive players can escape some embarrassing explanations as to why they did not switch when the move was obvious.

Basically, it is important for a defensive player to play his own man and not worry about switching until it is necessary. Too much switching causes confusion. We do not switch on the Knicks unless someone cannot fight through a screen or there is a loose man floating around somewhere that must be picked up.

Switching to pick up a loose man is a matter of circumstances. A team must be alert when it faces an opponent who figures to control the boards and will trigger a fast break. Whenever the Knicks play the Lakers, we must watch Happy Hairston carefully because he might "sneak" away on a shot by us, figuring Wilt Chamberlain will get the rebound.

DeBusschere and Lucas, or Reed, will go to the boards when we shoot. Hairston, seeing DeBusschere leave him, will not fight for the offensive rebound. He will hang outside and then break downcourt as soon as he sees Chamberlain control the ball. That means someone on the Knicks has to switch and pick up Happy because DeBusschere is out of position.

In another situation, we might have one of our guards driving for a layup. Frazier or Monroe might have their momentum carry them out of bounds and be in no position to get back on defense quickly. Someone has to switch and pick up the guard's man in the backcourt while the guard switches to the first man he can reach.

We like our players to hold their defensive positions against their own men when they get close to the basket. Yet, there are times when our center must gamble and leave his man to prevent another opponent from driving an open alley to the basket. Should Lucas leave Nate Thurmond to pick up Jeff Mullins on a drive, this leaves the Warrior center wide open for a handoff, so the closest Knick has the responsibility of switching to Thurmond as soon as he sees the play develop.

FLOATING

This is a risky thing in professional basketball because everyone can shoot. Floating is more essential to zone defenses that are used in high school and college ball, where the risk of dropping off a man is not that great.

On occasion, pro teams will float a man to help jam the middle. The weakside forward, the one away from the ball, will drop off and float around the foul lane. Or the weakside guard will fall back into the middle if his man is outside and moving away from the ball.

FUNNELING, TRAPPING

Some of the things that happen to an offense are no accident. Part of what teams practice and attempt to do in a game is direct the ball where they would like to see it go. They want to funnel a dribbler away from his strength and toward the strength of the defense.

This is all part of pressure defense. It is impossible to steer an opponent if he is played loosely. That is why you will see many pro teams pressing the ballhandler as he moves downcourt. The defense, by applying pressure, is attempting to make the ballhandler move around and not penetrate.

Every man on the defense must know why the pressure is being applied and where the ball is at all times. Each defensive players assumes a position between his man and the basket. The deep men play loosely until the ball gets into the attacking zone, then they close the gaps. The closer the ball to the basket, the tighter the defensive player makes the passing lanes.

Team movement depends on where the ball goes. That is why it is important to funnel the ballhandler in a desired direction. A team with a big, mobile center has an advantage in this respect. The defense can let the ballhandler slide through certain openings if it knows it has a big man around to close the trap.

The Boston Celtics practically built their defense around Bill Russell because he was so quick and aware. They would actually allow a ballhandler to dribble to certain spots on the floor as long as it was away from the basket. Sometimes K. C. Jones or Bob Cousy would bait their men by playing them loosely and giving them the drive, only to have the ballhandler come face-to-face with Russell.

That is fine if a team has someone as big and talented as Russell to act as a traffic cop. It is best to prepare yourself to be more careful. Concentrate on a five-man effort that is designed to move ballhandlers into traps as well as control the passing angles.

This calls for overplaying on defense. In a most subtle way, the defense should try to set up its overplaying in a manner that will enable it to steal the ball. It requires movement and precision teamwork. By overplaying a good shooting forward, the defense can reduce his chances of getting the ball unless it comes off the side.

There are dangers in this type of defense. It is vulnerable to backdoor plays. A Spencer Haywood can fake out of the corner toward Lennie Wilkens, the ballhandler, and then double back along the baseline behind his defensive opponent. A simple pass from a good ballhandler like Wilkens and there is an easy basket.

Thus, when a team attempts to funnel the ball into a trap, it must be prepared if it does not work. It must know what to do if its defensive forward pays the penalty for overplaying and Haywood gets behind him. The other defensive players must know what is happening in order to be in position to cover and help out.

They cannot know if they have no idea where the ball is located. They cannot know if they are staring at their own men and have their backs to the play. Someone, the other forward or the center, must switch and close the backdoor on Haywood.

WEAK SIDE

This is the area of a team defense that is expected to help out when trouble arises. An efficient team defense basically is a helping out defense. It should develop to the point where the players away from the ball are trained to help their teammates.

This is a situation where the man on the weak side must be conscious of his man but ready to move onto someone else. On the strong side, everyone will be playing his man closely. On the weak side, the defensive player can shift toward the scoring area without losing sight of his opponent. He assumes an angle between his man and the ball.

Obviously, if the offense tries to throw crosscourt, the weakside forward is in position to steal it if he has remained alert. If the offense attempts to cut through the middle, the weakside forward can choke it off by sliding over. He has to be careful about wandering too far because his man can sneak behind him for a pass.

These maneuvers are worth the risks involved. Overplaying places pressure on ballhandling and can disrupt superior offensive players—or, at least, make it more difficult for them to do what they want to do. Pro teams play each other that way because the more you make a team pass the ball around, the less time it has to beat the twenty-four-second clock. It is imperative that good shooters do not get the opportunity to maneuver into their favorite shooting areas as they please.

TRAPPED? Phoenix has set one for Walt Frazier. The Suns bring a big man out to help "pinch" Frazier but he escapes by pushing the ball through the opening.

The Baltimore Bullets always had good shooters—at the guards and forwards. Jack Marin, now with Houston, represents the typically dangerous 1-on-1 shooter you find in the NBA. Any team playing Marin knows it must concentrate on keeping him from getting the ball. They will overplay him and hope to force his teammates to look elsewhere for a safer pass.

There is no way a defense can stop superior players all the time. The thing a team should try to do is control the tempo of the game. Make the other team play your game, not vice versa. It can best be done, we think, by the application of an intelligent team defense. "Defense," says Dean Meminger, the Knicks' No. 1 draft pick out of Marquette University for the 1971–72 season, "is consistent. Offense is fickle." That just about says it.

DOUBLE TEAMING

Some steals produced by Frazier are accomplished through his initiative, some are the result of teamwork between the guards. Sometimes you must gamble and double-team Jerry West, Pete Maravich, Hal Greer, and Lou Hudson when they have the ball.

Frazier is slick at it. He has keen anticipation. He can read plays as they develop. It might possibly have something to do with the sense of awareness he developed as a quarterback in high school. The other teams are quite conscious of his intuition, coordination, and quick hands, which gives him a slight defensive edge because they might be worrying about him.

It is important in double teaming for the guards to know each other very well and work together. One guard's job is to pressure the ballhandler and keep him so busy he has no time to look around. That enables the other guard to set up the double team. Now if the ballhandler suddenly decides to turn back to avoid the pressure being applied by his man, he finds the other guard in position to block him or steal the ball.

The risk is obvious. Should the ballhandler escape the double teaming, he has a teammate wide open because one of the defensive guards has left his man. But it is worth the risk if used discreetly because the man with the ball is out of position, making it difficult for him to hit a free teammate. Also, it is wiser to force the ball away from the middle, where a guard can penetrate for an easier shot or pass off for a layup.

Double teaming the pivotman is frequent. This works in two ways. If Wes Unseld has to move in front of Nate Thurmond to keep him from

HELPING OUT. Walt Frazier drops off his man just enough to discourage a pass to Wilt Chamberlain but not too far in case the Laker with the ball attempts a shot.

LAKERS

getting a direct pass, then the weakside forward must drop off his man to cover a lead pass to Nate. Obviously, if Jeff Mullins should lob the ball over Unseld's head, there would be no way of stopping Thurmond from getting the ball for a stuff shot unless a defensive forward came over from behind to break it up.

Now if Unseld plays Abdul-Jabbar from behind, then Wes may need help in front. Someone should keep Kareem from getting the ball too easily because he has a sweeping hook shot that no one can stop. The forward in deep on the strong side (where the ball is) has to float off his man when necessary.

Milwaukee likes to run Bob Dandridge off Kareem in the pivot because he is a better outside shooter than Curtis Perry, the other forward. A defensive forward in a situation like that has a few things he has to consider. How far can he drop off Dandridge? Should he fake a move toward Abdul-Jabbar, hoping Oscar Robertson will not give him the ball? Should he indicate he is following Dandridge but then suddenly change direction, hoping to steal the ball should the "Big O" throw into Kareem?

There is a fine line between thinking and reacting or determining what the defensive forward does, or when he does it, in a double-teaming situation against the pivotman. Such refinements best explain what it takes to play team defense and why players and coaches spend so much time with it.

Pro teams also double up on the ball in other areas on the floor. On out-of-bounds pass plays, some teams will leave the passer alone and have their two guards pressure the receiver. On half-court and full-court presses, the objective is to trap the ball with two defensive men, hoping to steal it or get a jump ball.

PICK AND ROLL

This is a tough play for the defense. It requires alert switching and help from the weak side. Let's say Nate Thurmond and Jeff Mullins of Golden State are working it on Elvin Hayes and Archie Clark of Baltimore, which is bound to happen when those teams get together.

Nate will set a high pick, either at the top of the key or along the foul lane. Mullins will move across Thurmond with the ball, trying to run Clark into Nate. If Archie is picked off, Hayes, playing behind Thurmond, must move with Mullins to prevent him from getting an open shot.

Thurmond, with Hayes out of the way, now rolls to the basket on Clark, the smaller man. Mullins hits Nate with a pass, and that is where the other Bullets enter. This is where persistent practicing of team defense and experience pays off. That is, it will if the weakside forward, Unseld or John Tresvant, has watched the ball and seen the play develop. If they have assumed the proper defensive angle, between their men and the ball, one or the other should be able to drop off in time to cut off the lane on Thurmond or maybe even steal the pass or knock it away. At worst, they could force Nate to pull up sharply, or, possibly, commit a charging foul.

Clark could help prevent the complications. He could fight through the pick and stay with Mullins, or, if that fails, switch automatically and try to cut Thurmond off at the pass by himself. Sometimes Hayes and Clark might gamble and leave Nate alone to double up on Mullins, hoping to steal the ball or trap him so he cannot pass to Nate.

Unseld or Tresvant must make a move to help out as soon as they see the pick and roll developing. They cannot wait to see what Clark and Hayes will do. The double-teaming maneuver has a fringe benefit for the defense if you look at it as another opportunity to pressure the offense into giving up the ball.

The steal or forced turnover is as effective as the rebound for getting possession and creating an easy basket. Some of the best 2-on-1 and 3-on-1 opportunities come off mistakes created by such defensive pressures as double teaming.

High school and college coaches are not limited to man-to-man defenses and zone presses, as we are in the NBA. Half-court zone presses become strict under the basket in our league. We may use Phil Jackson and his long reach to pressure the ballhandler entering the attacking zone, and he can double team the ball. But the other players must satisfy the officials that they are playing a man.

In other words, Jerry Lucas cannot hang around the basket and protect the middle while his man wanders far away. The rule in the NBA requires him to be within eight feet of some player. High school and college teams may use zone defenses at anytime and anywhere. They are prohibited in the NBA.

Actually, there is a thin line between a switching man-to-man defense and a zone. The zone started out as a stationary defense. Now virtually all zones are shifting. It takes a sharply trained eye to determine the difference between a zone and switching man-to-man at certain times.

Joe Mullaney, the coach of the Lakers during the 1969–70 season, grew up in the schoolyards of New York. While he was the coach at Providence he introduced a few tricks that helped bring national prominence to that school. His record there led to his being signed by Los Angeles, where he coached two seasons before moving to the Kentucky Colonels of the ABA.

During one game against the Lakers, in the Garden, the Knicks managed to build a big lead. We were playing tough defense. Mullaney called a time-out to talk to his players. When the game resumed, the Lakers went into a strange formation.

Jerry West took the ball and, once he got past midcourt, dribbled along the sideline. The other four Lakers cleared out to the opposite corner. That left West 1-on-1 against Dick Barnett. Twice Jerry hit with jump shots.

We made the obvious adjustment. We had some of our players drop off into the middle to protect against West driving, which enabled Barnett to concentrate on playing Jerry closer. The officials charged us with a technical. They informed us we had to play within eight feet of a man or it was illegal under the rules of the NBA.

In other words, it was a zone defense. High school and college teams do not have to worry about that. They are permitted to use zones. The 1-3-1 was perfected by Clair Bee of Long Island University to be used against high-scoring pivotmen. Bee placed a man in front of the pivotman and one behind him in a pincer movement. The idea was for the front man to cut off the pass and the back man to limit the pivotman's freedom around the basket.

The 2-3 was designed to help a team with rebounding and neutralize an opponent that had strong shooters from the sides and corners. The 3-2 was predicated on its ability to handle a team that had long shooters and strong ballhandlers.

Restructuring the thinking, defense begins at the moment the ball is turned over to the opponent and not at the half-court "Maginot Line." The building blocks of defense will involve proper conditioning of players, instant pressure, proper awareness of the position of the ball, knowing the passing lanes that the offense most often uses in its attack patterns and cutting off those lanes, double teaming the ball, adjustments by the defensive men away from the ball to clog the passing lanes to compensate for the double teaming, and the setting of traps to force a pass or intercept one.

Basketball is such a quick-moving game, the defense is required to react with lightning speed. It also places a tremendous demand for awareness on the defense so it can counter the rapidity of the offense and be effective in getting off shots behind screens. Further, if the offense should elude the pressure up front on any given situation, the defenders up front must have secondary assignments to help them create effective positioning downcourt.

The top evaluation of an all-league defensive player in football is his mobility in making plays in the flow away from his area. They call it pursuit—when the left or middle linebacker can make the play to stop a sweep on the far right side of the field. You know there is no substitute for that type of competitive hustle. Similarly, when a front defender on a full-court press can intercept a pass in the foul lane area under his basket, then the coach and the player, no doubt, have set up secondary positioning. The player must be graded highly for his hustle in making the play far from his original assignment.

Modern spectators generally prefer to see high scoring contests. However, there is a growing awareness and a significant appreciation developing for the defensive aspects of every sport. Since Joe Page of the New York Yankees glorified the bullpen, relief pitchers are better appreciated while getting paid more and more for the number of saves they make over the course of a season.

Defensive units in professional football are given standing ovations by fans who have become more conscious of the importance defense plays in every game. We on the New York Knickerbockers recognize the necessity for defensive balance in basketball. Defense and defensive strategy may equalize the great offensive burst in the 1950s and 1960s. The name of the game in the 1970s may be defense.

CHAPTER

6

PRESSURE DEFENSE

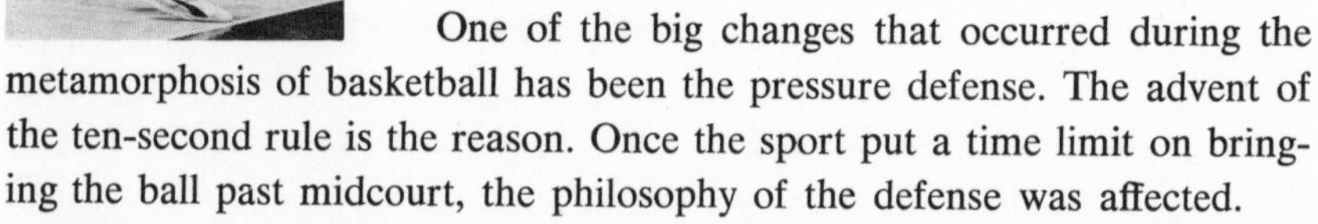

One of the big changes that occurred during the metamorphosis of basketball has been the pressure defense. The advent of the ten-second rule is the reason. Once the sport put a time limit on bringing the ball past midcourt, the philosophy of the defense was affected.

In the old days, before the ten-second rule, the only time a ballhandler was pressed in the backcourt was to break up a stall. A good dribbler could kill a lot of time with the full court available for a freeze in a tight game where the clock was important.

It reached the ridiculous many times in the early days of the NBA. On November 22, 1950, the Ft. Wayne Pistons played the Minneapolis Lakers in Minneapolis and won, 19-18. The Pistons led by a point entering the final quarter and then went off on a tremendous scoring burst—they outscored the Lakers, 3–1, for the quarter.

High scorer for the Lakers was George Mikan—he managed fifteen of the eighteen points. The remainder went to Bob Harrison, now coach at Harvard, on a field goal and to Jim Pollard on a free throw. The Lakers took eighteen shots, eleven by Mikan, and the Pistons, a well distributed thirteen.

PRESSURING PASS-IN. Phil Jackson is in the process of making it difficult for Milwaukee to pass the ball in-bounds. The pressure man should be tall and active whether it is a full-court or half-court press.

That was the lowest scoring game in league history. There was another game in which the stalling tactics were made to look even more ridiculous. One player actually took a newspaper and sat on the floor reading it while his teammates held the ball, and the other team refused to come and get it.

Today, the players do not get enough time to read the numbers on their backs. Everything is accelerated. There is no lead that is safe because of the pressure defenses. You learn that quickly in the NBA.

There was this game with the St. Louis Hawks in the Garden back in the 1967–68 season. I was scouting for the Knicks and was there as a spectator. I will never forget it because it was Bill Bradley's first game back after being out of action for a few weeks—he had been hit by a small sports car on Eighth Avenue near the old Garden.

I will never forget it for another reason. The Knicks were ahead by seventeen points with six and a half minutes to go but wound up losing in overtime. Richie Guerin, the coach, ordered a full court press because the Hawks were in a desperate situation. Lennie Wilkens, Zelmo Beaty, Joe Caldwell, Paul Silas, and Bill Bridges did the rest.

FULL-COURT PRESS

This is a 3-1-1 zone type formation as used by the Hawks (in the above game) and other pro teams. Caldwell was the middle man up front because he was active and quick. Joe was flanked by Wilkens and Silas, with the jobs of the front three based on trapping the ball once it was passed in.

Caldwell played the passer tightly, hoping to create a five-second violation or steal the ball. Once the ball moved in-bounds, Joe headed for the ballhandler and helped double team him. If Wilkens' man got the ball, then Silas moved in on the player who passed the ball in hopes of stealing the return pass (see diagram 6-1).

Meanwhile, Bridges, playing short safety between the foul line and midcourt, floated around, and looked to intercept an outlet pass. Beaty was the deep safety and he protected the territory from the midcourt line to the basket. Bridges and Beaty positioned themselves in accordance with the pressure being applied to the ballhandler and where on the court it was taking place.

The object of the Hawks was to force a long, hurried pass they could intercept. They were looking for the Knicks to waste a man behind Beaty

Diagram 6-1 Full-Court Zone Defense

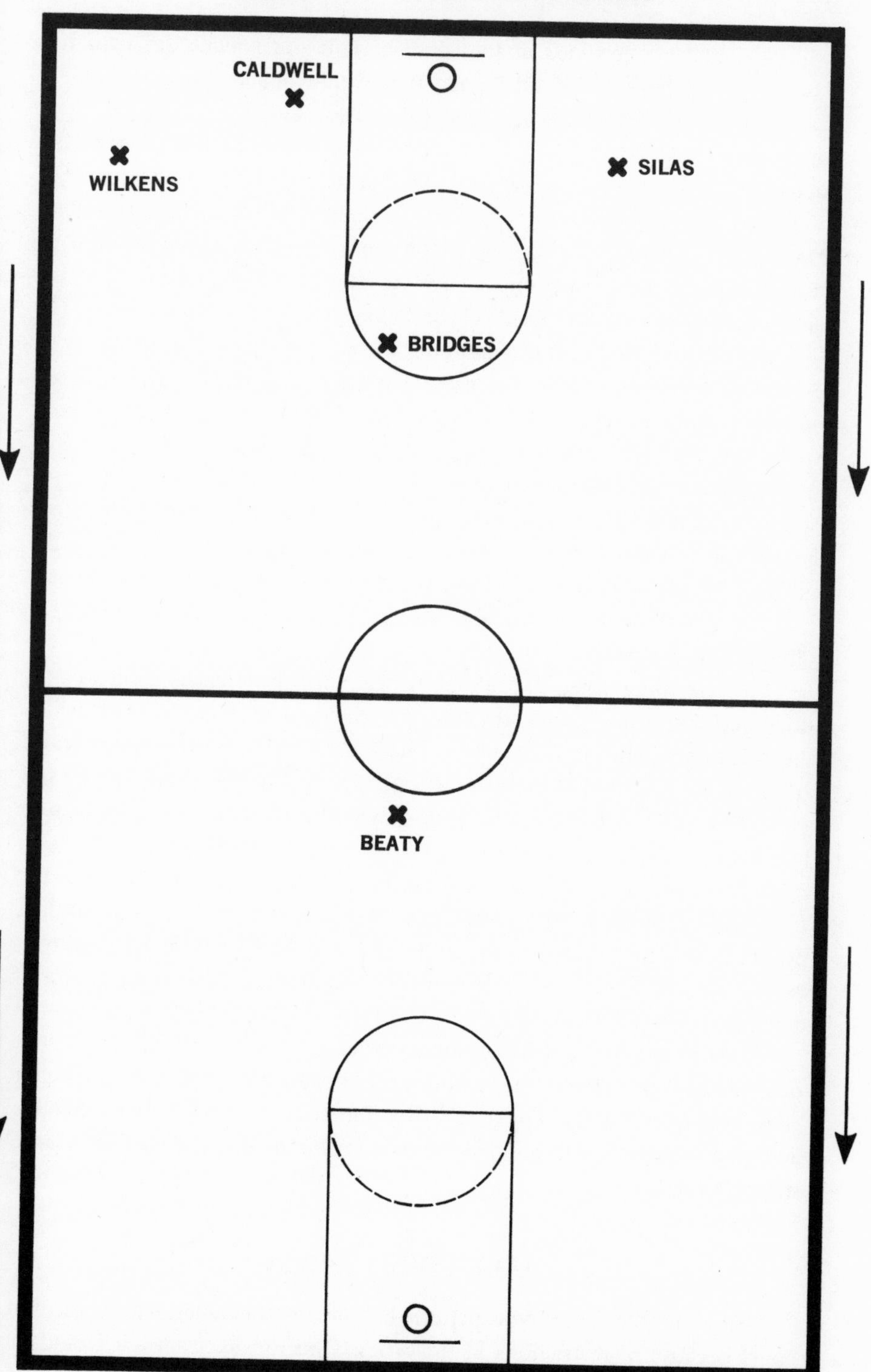

while the ball was trapped at the other end. If the Knicks did that, the Hawks would have a 5-4 advantage that would enable them to gamble more and play the ball. Bridges and Beaty operated as free safeties. It is the same philosophy employed in football, where the linemen pressure the quarterback, hoping to rush a pass that the defensive backs can pick off.

Things changed as soon as the Knicks escaped the trap. When the ball reached an outlet man, and headed up court, Bridges and Beaty had to hustle and cover the deep men. Now the other team figured to have the advantage once it escaped Caldwell, Wilkens, and Silas.

Someone on the Hawks figured to be caught downcourt, creating a 3-on-2 disadvantage for the defense. That is the vulnerable part of a full-court press—the calculated risk a team takes when all values are considered. Beaty and Bridges might have to defend against three opponents until they got help within four seconds.

The full-court press is mostly effective against a team that does not handle the ball well. By accelerating the tempo, the defense can rattle the offense. By forcing the other team to overreact and speed things abnormally, a defense can increase the percentage opportunities of having the offense lose the ball.

There are times when the full-court press may be used as a surprise to break up the other team's rhythm. A coach might find it beneficial to throw an opponent off stride when things are not going well for his team. In the NBA, most teams use it to get back into a game—usually late in the game when they are fighting the clock. It is a gambling defense by nature that can be hurt by a smart, ballhandling team that retains its poise.

Eddie Donovan, when he was coaching at St. Bonaventure, used the full-court press the entire game. Under those conditions it is a demanding defense. A team has to be in superb condition. Most pro teams employ it as a strategic weapon when in trouble because a game of superstars is demanding enough by itself.

The full-court press starts primarily after a team scores, on a foul shot or a basket—preferably after a foul shot because the defense has a better chance to set up. It is kept on all over the court as long as it is effective and accomplishes its purpose. If the other team breaks it, there is no sense staying in it.

HALF-COURT PRESS

This is another zone type pattern but not as unadulterated as the full court because of restrictions in the NBA. Once again, Caldwell would be the key man for the Hawks, since he is the one used to chase the ball. He would set up at the midcourt line and wait for the ballhandler to reach him. Joe would be the middle man, flanked by Wilkens and the weakside forward, each prepared to double-up on the ball as soon as Caldwell attacked.

It was Caldwell's responsibility to pressure the ballhandler as soon as he reached the attacking zone and force him toward Wilkens or the weakside forward. In the meantime Beaty and the other forward overplayed their men. They were ready to switch and pick up the open man if the ballhandler escaped the pressure up front and managed to get a pass in deep (see diagram 6-2).

High school and college players and coaches will recognize the similarity to regular zone techniques. What the pros start with in the half-court press is a 3-1-1 or 3-2 zone, but they are not allowed to stay with it. Once the ball escaped the Hawks' front line, they were obligated to go into a man-to-man defense or risk a technical foul.

In all respects, most pro teams treat defense as an attacking weapon. Defensive pressure should begin when the opponent gets the ball. There is no logical reason for allowing the other team to bring the ball across mid-court as it pleases. No matter the kind of defense, it should be aggressive, with the intention of destroying the offense, not delaying it.

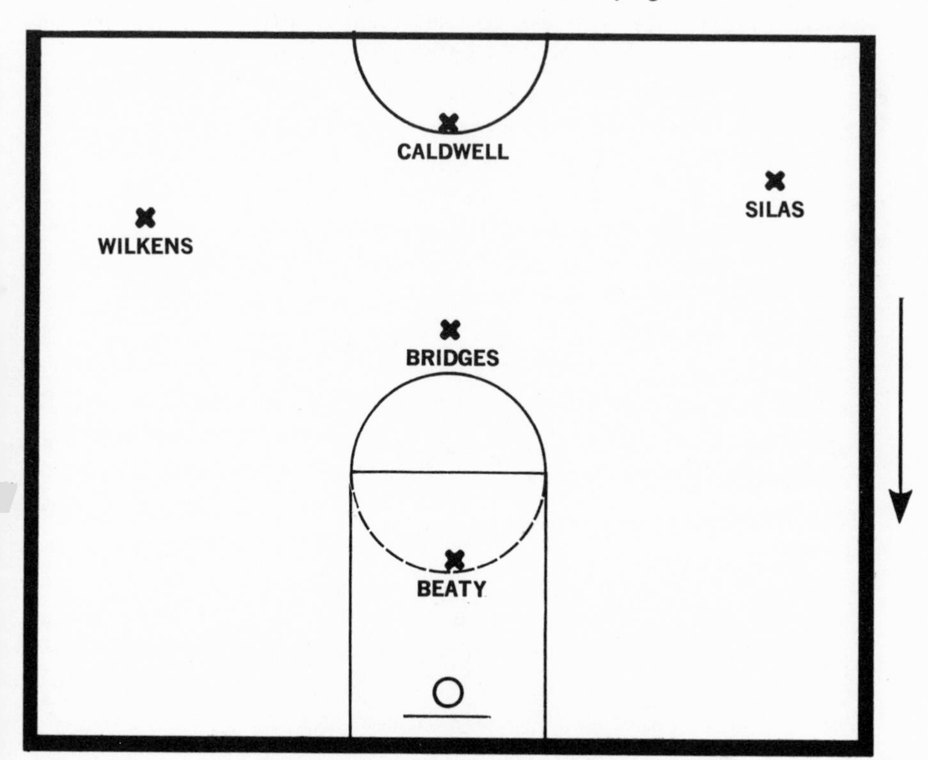

Diagram 6-2 Half-Court Press

The middleman's role in the half-court press is typical: He must attack. He must not let the dribbler drive past. He must wave his arms and pressure the ball. And, he must avoid fouling while doing all those things.

Each defensive man has the same responsibility once the ball moves in his direction. They all are working to prevent the opposition from escaping along the sidelines or through the middle. They prefer to make the other team shoot from outside if they cannot steal the ball.

Caldwell was the wild card for the Hawks. He would drop off and help out if the ball moved in deep. The Hawks were not concerned with leaving the weakside man open. If the ball moved away from Wilkens, for example, he dropped off toward the middle to help cut off the passing lane. He still had time to get back to his man if there was a return pass.

Beaty and the weakside forward floated. Zelmo's territory was the middle and the weakside area Caldwell left open while fulfilling his duties as ball chaser. Bridges had to protect his side of the court while being prepared to slide to the middle if Beaty had to move over to the opposite side to pick up a man.

Every Hawk player was prepared to fall back into a regular man-to-man if the press was broken. They did not waste time looking for assigned opponents. They picked up the nearest man and fell into a normal defensive pattern. They switched to their regular men when they had the opportunity—not when it made them more vulnerable to a basket.

In every press, the idea is to keep the ball in front of the first three men. Double team the ball as soon as it is passed in. Try to force a dribble or a long pass. Keep the ball along the sidelines if possible because it is easier to trap a man there. Once the ball gets to the middle of the floor, there is more room for the offense to maneuver.

BREAKING FULL-COURT PRESS

Your opponent has just scored. As you prepare to make the in-bounds pass, you are confronted with a full-court press. This is the attacking defense employed so successfully by many teams. There is a defensive man waving his hands like a windmill and all your teammates are being closely guarded by their defenders.

You have five seconds to get the ball in-bounds or you lose possession—automatically. You now are faced with the first requirement for breaking the press—making a successful pass-in. The Los Angeles Lakers, or any top basketball team, are familiar with these defensive tactics because they confront them as often as anyone.

To cope with the situation, the Lakers can set up play situations which will free a receiver for the pass-in. Gail Goodrich might try and free himself by using feints, sudden starts and stops, and various moves designed to shake loose (see diagram 6-3).

The pivot man, Wilt Chamberlain, will not break downcourt. He will come to the ball and help relieve the pressure. On the weak side, Happy Hairston might set a screen for Jim McMillian, the other forward, uncovering Jim so he can double back for the pass. Hairston, after the screen, can now break downcourt in order to give Jerry West (the passer) a target for a long, release pass if the defenders have packed too tightly.

If West decides to hit McMillian with the pass, Jerry heads for Jim and slices around him. This puts West in position to take a return pass on the move or draw off the defense and permit McMillian to escape. West can clear out by using Chamberlain as a screen and heading for the sidelines.

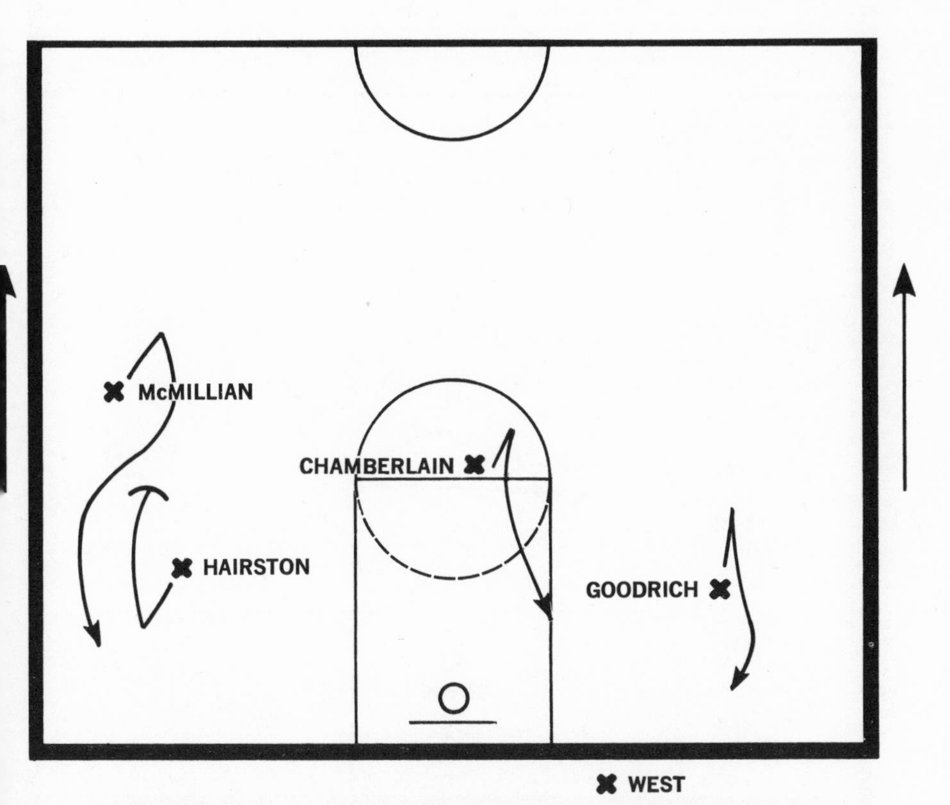

Diagram 6-3 In-Bounds Play Against Full-Court Press

Diagram 6-4 Attacking a 1-2-2 Full-Court Press

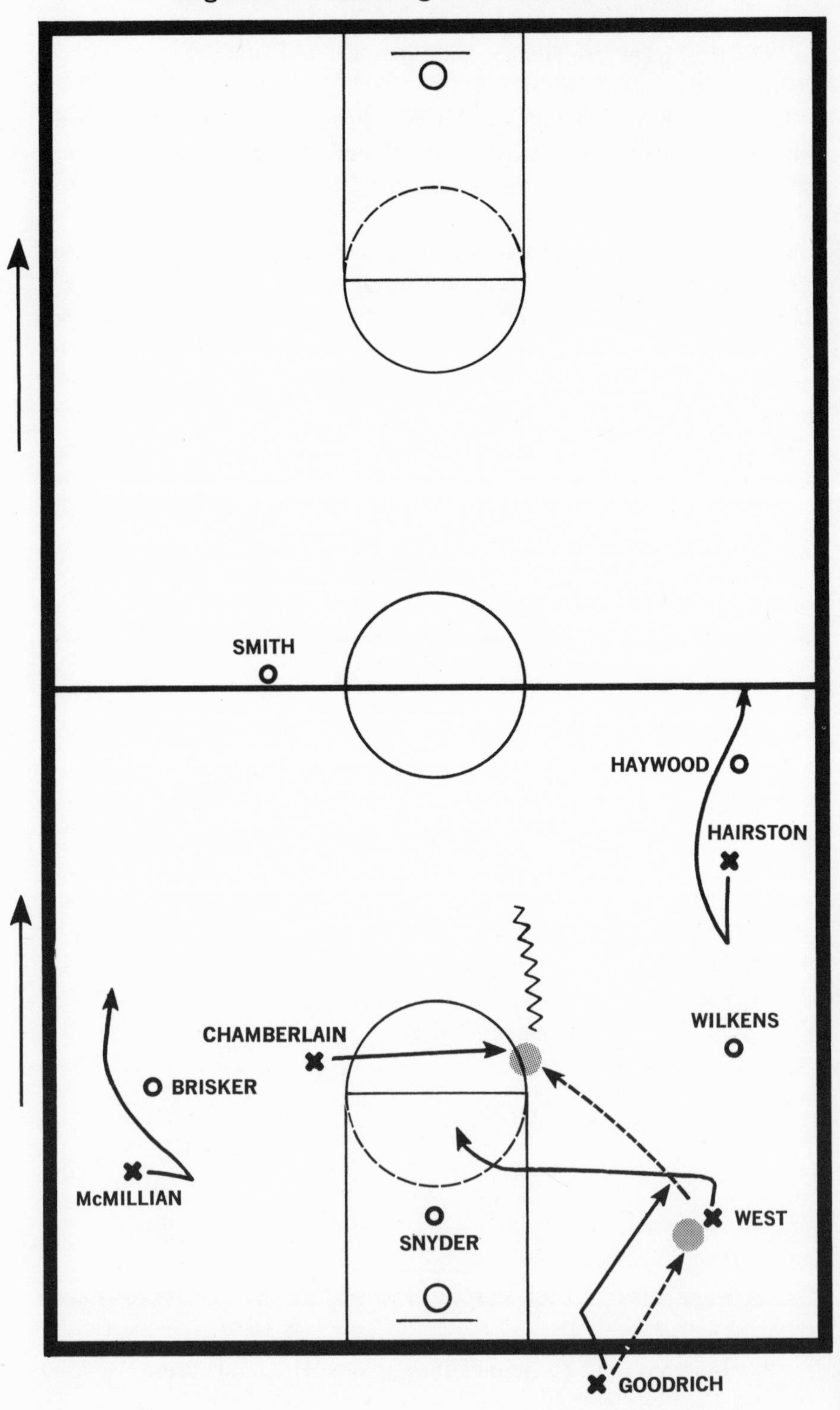

Now McMillian can turn up court on the dribble or pass to West or Goodrich and convert the pressing situation into a fast break. The thing to remember is the less dribbling, the better. The defense wants you to put the ball down because it is easier to steal. The give-and-go is an ideal weapon. If trapped, it is better to settle for a jump ball than throw the ball aimlessly and let the defense steal it for a cheap basket.

There are times in professional basketball when a team has a fine dribbler, such as Walt Frazier, Lennie Wilkens, Oscar Robertson, or Archie Clark. There are times when a dribbler of that caliber might be able to escape all by himself, but the percentages are against it. Avoid dribbling until the ball escapes the trap.

Once West, for example, gets the ball with room to maneuver, it is permissible for him to dribble his way forward—always keeping in mind that there is a ten-second rule. The defense is vulnerable if the offense can escape the trap quickly. Hairston has released downcourt and heads for the corner. McMillian has swung back to take a release pass.

The defense, by using three front men to try and trap the ball in the backcourt, has left itself at a disadvantage. It only has two men back to protect against the break and one is either in the backcourt or around midcourt. Thus, a fast break situation presents itself to the offense if it is capable of moving the ball swiftly enough to exploit the gambling nature of the full-court press.

In college basketball, where zone presses are in greater vogue than man-to-man pressure tactics, the offense may have to employ a variety of attacking weapons. For example, should the Seattle SuperSonics use a 1-2-2 full-court press, the Lakers might try to attack through the middle (see diagram 6-4).

Where the defense on the full-court press permits the first pass in-bounds and then begins to apply pressure by attempting to double-team the ball, Goodrich will in-bounds to West. Then Jerry passes quickly to a moving McMillian, who will be cutting toward the open area of the zone. Jim, by pivoting quickly and moving down the middle, might convert the situation into a 3-on-2 fast break. Jim, flanked by Hairston and Chamberlain, will then attack Don Smith and Spencer Haywood, the two deep defenders.

In the event the Sonics use a 1-2-1-1 full-court zone or a 3-1-1 defensive pattern, the Lakers might be able to use a 2-2-1 attacking pattern (see diagram 6-5).

Goodrich in-bounds to West. As Dick Snyder and Lennie Wilkens, the guards, converge on Jerry, he returns the ball to Gail. Now Goodrich takes

Diagram 6-5 Attacking a 1-2-1-1 Full-Court Press

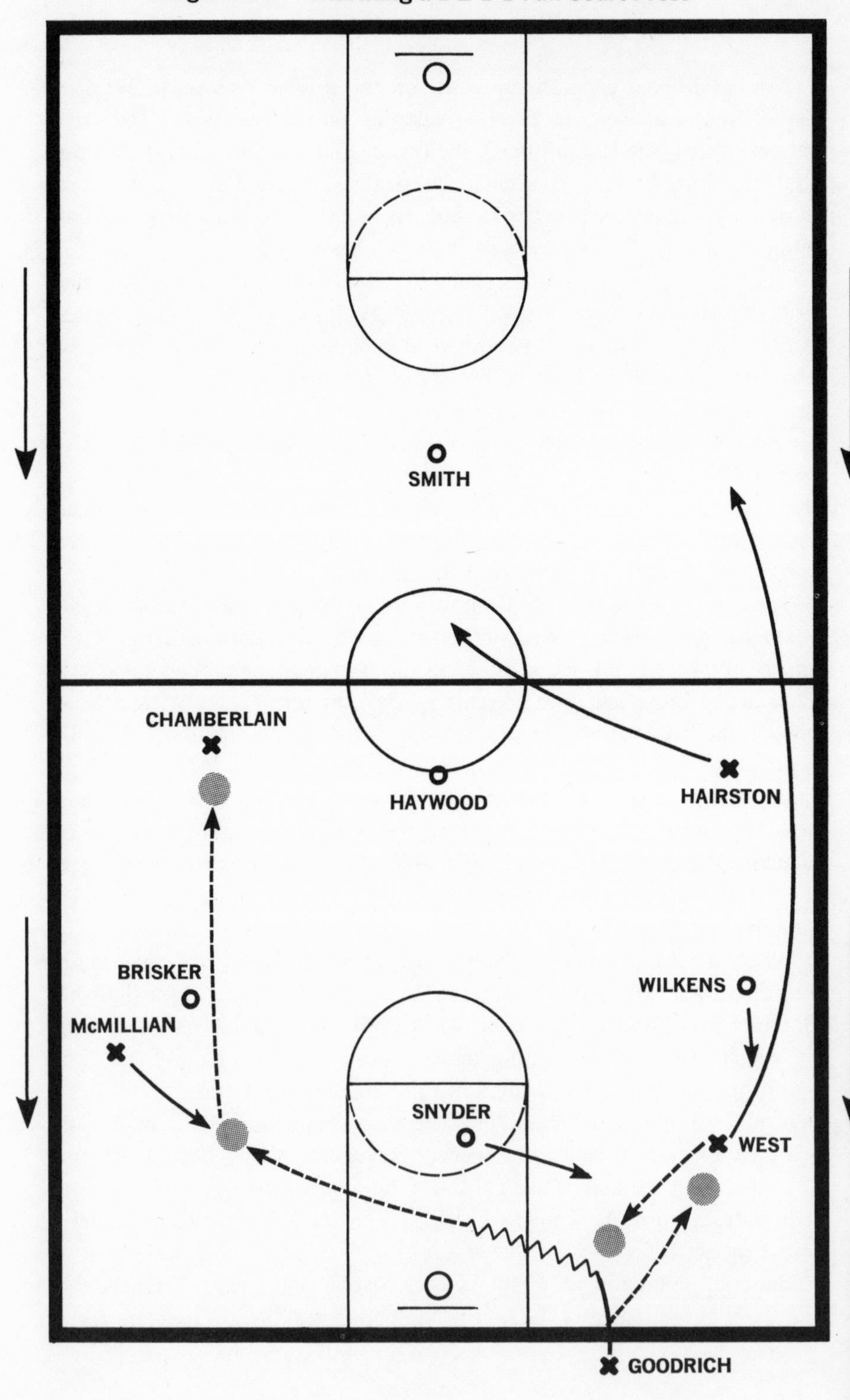

a dribble or two to his left and passes to McMillian, who quickly passes up ahead to Chamberlain. In the meantime, Hairston cuts toward the middle as West moves ahead and takes his place on the flank. The offense has moved into a fast break before the defense can regroup.

In attacking the full-court press, always use alert, crisp ballhandling to move the ball to the open man. The pivotman must be mobile in order to provide movements that will provide safe outlet passes to him. The ballhandler must be quick so he can take advantage of the escape situation when it becomes available.

There are a few weapons available in case the ballhandler is pressured too much at the endline while attempting to make the pass-in. For one thing, he is permitted, in the pros, to run along the baseline before passing in-bounds, as long as he does not exceed the five-second limit. Thus, should Goodrich feel trapped in the middle of the court at the endline (under the basket) he can run out-of-bounds toward West, flip the ball to him, then take a return pass on court for a quick, unexpected escape.

This is not permitted in college basketball. Once the official hands you the ball, you cannot move along the line. You must pass-in from the spot where you have taken the ball out.

There is another option that is permitted by pro rules. Goodrich may take the ball out and pass to West, who has stepped out of bounds across the endline. Jerry, thereby, is in a better position to make an unmolested pass-in.

If Goodrich, the passer, is really pinned down by a defender, Gail can gain time by bouncing the ball off the defender's leg and back out-of-bounds. This gives the offense five more seconds to make the pass. The ultimate, when trapped, is to call a time-out rather than give up the ball.

That is what happened the night the Knicks beat Cincinnati in Cleveland to set an NBA record of eighteen straight victories during the 1969–70 season. That achievement was surpassed by Milwaukee, when it won twenty in a row the next season, and Los Angeles in 1971–72, when the Lakers compiled an astounding thirty-three straight victories.

The Royals, that night in Cleveland, were trying to hold onto a five-point lead inside the final minute of the game. We had just scored and Bob Cousy took the ball out under his basket. We were in a full-court press. Cousy could not get the ball in, so he wisely called for a time-out rather than lose possession under the five-second rule.

What a player does depends on the situation. The thing to remember is that you must be prepared to do something.

BREAKING HALF-COURT PRESS

When the ball has been advanced beyond midcourt and has been knocked out-of-bounds by the defense, the NBA rules call for the pass-in to be made into the front court. Since the offensive team cannot pass into the backcourt, the defense can pick and apply the pressure with a half-court press.

It is important for the offensive team to be prepared to get the ball into play within the five-second limit and against the tighter defense. Some teams, on occasion, have made effective use of a formation where four players line up single file (see diagram 6-6).

If the Chicago Bulls, for example, are being pressured, Chet Walker moves out of the formation around Bob Love to the opposite side of the court and is ready to cut back toward Jerry Sloan if necessary. Love swings around Norm Van Lier—going through the area vacated by Walker.

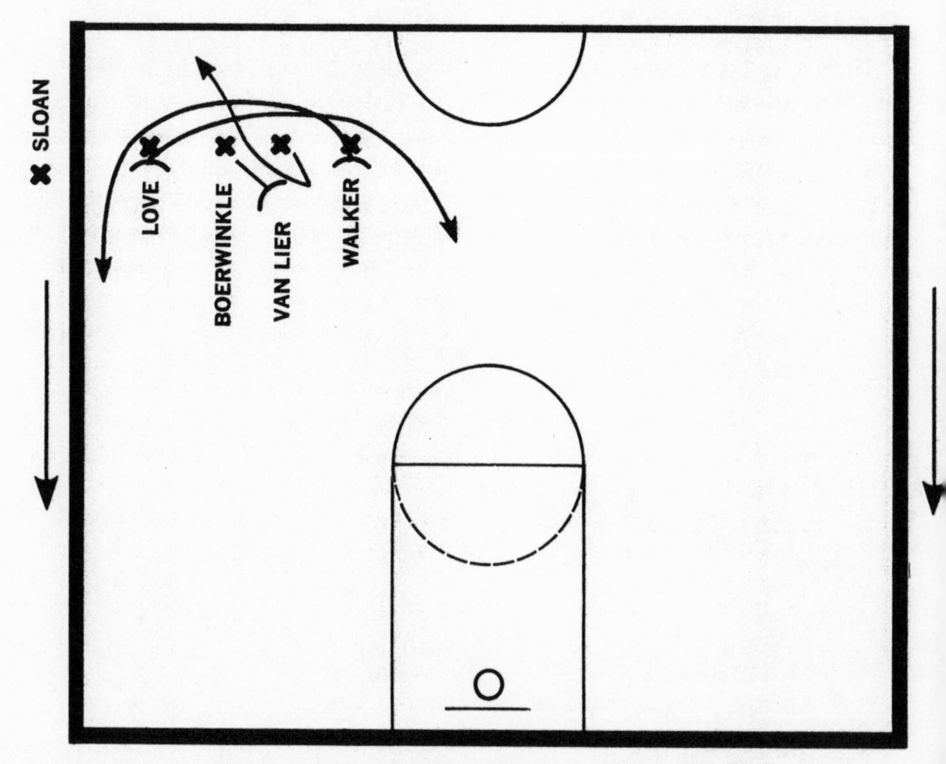

Diagram 6-6 Four-In-A-Line Out-of-Bounds Play

Tom Boerwinkle, the center, moves forward and sets a screen on Van Lier's man. Norm takes a step forward and then moves back behind the screen set by Boerwinkle.

That gives Sloan three possible receivers for his pass-in: Walker, Love, or Van Lier. Sometimes, everyone on defense may leave Boerwinkle wide open, so Tom is in a position to break for the basket and take an open pass. If the defense overreacts or fails to pick up a player, the Bulls may be able to pick up an easy basket. The objective, however, is possession—to get the ball into play against a pressure defense.

DEFENSING FAST BREAK

When your opponent employs the fast break as a major weapon, it becomes vital to defuse it. It is obvious that a team cannot break unless it has the ball. Thus, the best weapon against a fast-breaking team is aggressive rebounding off the offensive board. A team that can pull down the rebounds without being contested is in the ideal position to trigger fast breaks.

In the NBA, there are many great rebounders capable of igniting fast breaks—Wilt Chamberlain, Kareem Abdul-Jabbar, Wes Unseld, are only a few. It is not likely that a team can count on too many offensive rebounds against them. So you do the next best thing—you attack the rebounder and attempt to cause a turnover or create pressure.

Highly mobile players can double-team the rebounder or pressure him so that he cannot get the outlet pass off quickly. It is a calculated risk that is worth taking if you are being hurt by the fast break. It must be slowed down. Obviously, when you double up on the man with the ball, it leaves you vulnerable downcourt if the opponent is successful in getting the pitch-out to the outlet man.

The second possible area to concentrate on is the outlet man. If your opponent assigns a specific person to handle the pitchouts, then you may be able to attack him and prevent the completion of the outlet pass. It all depends on the habits of the other team.

Generally speaking, the outlet pass is made to that side of the floor where the ball is rebounded. Once you are clued in on the passing lane or to whom the release pass is going, have someone cut over into that area. By playing between your opponent and the passer, you are in a better position to pick off the pass—or at least see that the receiver does not get it unmolested. Sometimes, if you pop into the passing lane, the rebounder may be forced to hold up his pass. That serves the purpose of slowing down the fast break.

In order to prepare players for these specific defensive assignments, your offense must have proper circulation and spacing. You cannot afford to clog up one area. An offense should move and rotate so that it's reasonably spread out and can convert quickly to defense if the situation changes suddenly. The outside players should always be conscious of the fast break and drop back as soon as the ball changes hands.

In the event the opponent succeeds in breaking two men down court against a lone defender, it is important for every player to know how to play defensively against two opponents. The defender must play between the two men—feinting constantly with hands, head, and body at the man with the ball but never permitting the man without the ball to get too far behind him. The idea is to protect against the deep man while trying to pressure the man with the ball and getting him to commit himself.

The defender should never leave the defensive foul lane area unprotected. He should try and stop the man with the ball near the foul line. Do not let him penetrate deeper. Try and force him to shoot from outside and then head for the man underneath and box him out on the rebound.

In every instance, the defender should try to pressure the two offensive men long enough for his teammates to get back and help. Nate Thurmond is an efficient defender in this type of predicament. He tries to cut off the passing lane between the two offensive men. He tries to read the eyes of the man with the ball in order to anticipate the direction of the pass. He has the quick hands to pick up the ball in flight or react to the jump shot that might take place in his area (see diagram 6-7).

The center should not commit himself to the man with the ball, otherwise he will leave his flank open for a bounce pass and a layup. He must not allow himself to be backed up too deeply; this would enable the man with the ball to drive to the basket. Thurmond must maintain his poise and position, concentrating on trying to delay the offense long enough for help, or, if possible, force a poor percentage shot from outside.

At times, the offense may be able to fast break with three men and catch only two defenders back. In a 2-on-3 situation, the two Golden State defenders might try to play it in tandem fashion. They might prefer to have the two men back line up behind each other, rather than spread out—one placing himself in front of the foul line, picking up the ball-handler, the other behind the foul line, reacting in either direction (see diagram 6-8).

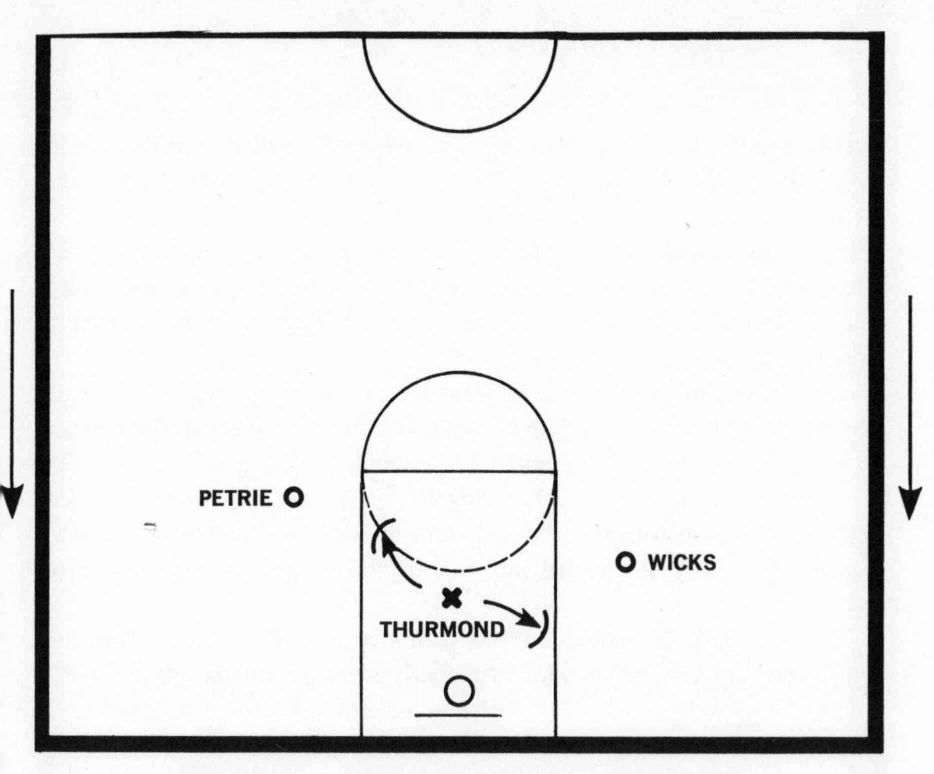

Diagram 6-7 Playing Defense: One Against Two

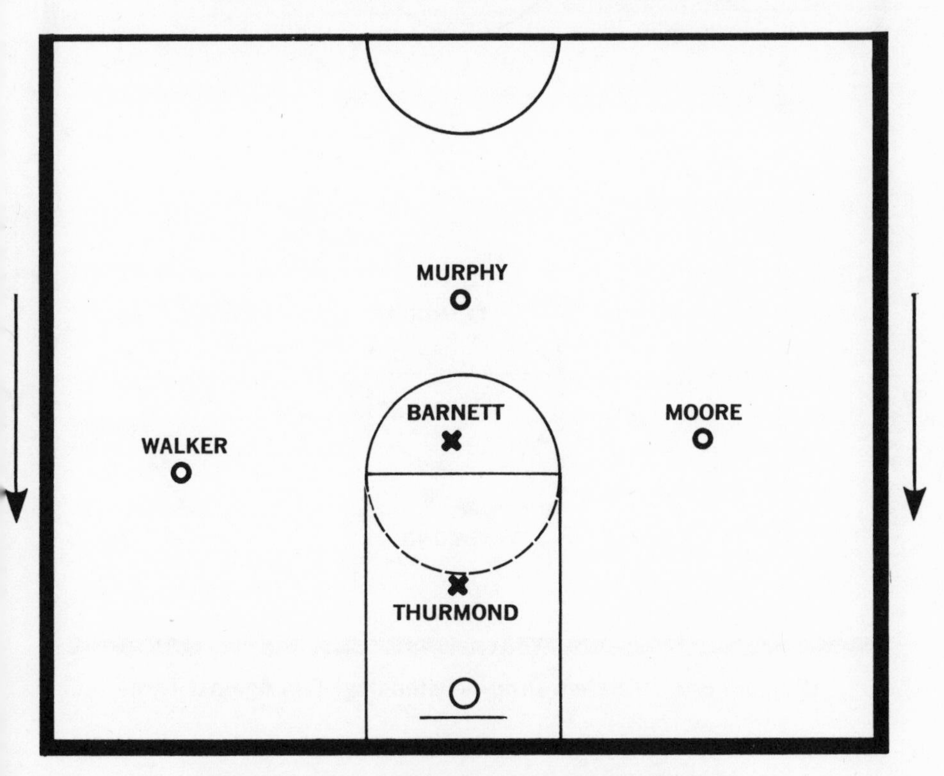

Diagram 6-8 Defensing: Two Against Three

If Jim Barnett can stop Cal Murphy, the middle man on the Houston break, then Thurmond moves to the side where the ball is passed. Barnett takes the tandem drop to cut off the passing lane from Jim Walker, the other Rocket guard, to Otto Moore, the center. Walker doubles back to Murphy for the pass. Barnett feints up ahead and tries to stall the offense until help arrives. If Murphy takes a shot, Barnett and Thurmond drop back and protect against the rebound by getting inside position on Walker and Moore (see diagram 6-9).

In all cases, every player must head for the defensive area right away. No one should hang back just because all five offensive players are not in on the attack. Wilt Chamberlain, for example, might prefer to stay back on defense once he triggers a Los Angeles fast break. Bill Russell did that often when he was with the Boston Celtics in order to pace himself. It gave him a little rest that enabled him to play forty-eight minutes whenever necessary.

The team with the ball can afford such a luxury. The team without the ball, especially one caught in a fast break, must get all the players back

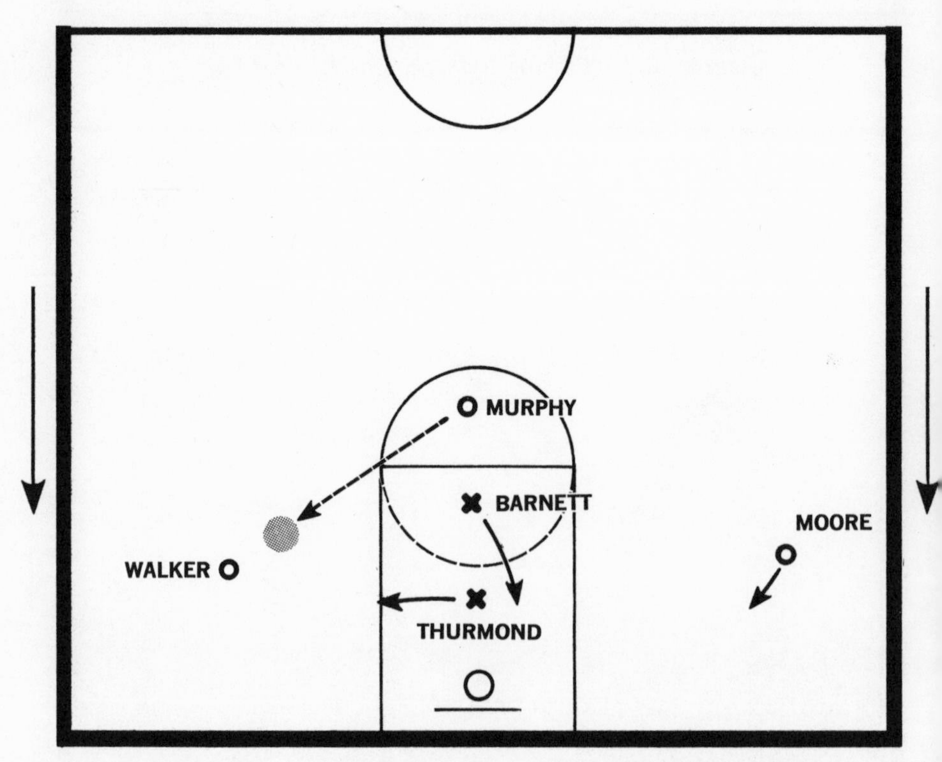

Diagram 6-9 Tandem Drop—Defensing: Two Against Three

NEVER GIVE UP. Fred Carter, then with Baltimore, is about to sweep Dick Barnett's shot away in the 1969–70 playoffs. Carter chased the play and provided an excellent example of how hustle pays off.

as fast as possible. With a fast break geared to cover the distance between two baskets in approximately four seconds, the offense must convert to defense in less than four seconds or pay the penalty.

There is no excuse for malingering. The most annoying thing for a coach is to watch a player "bleed" over a turnover while the play goes the other way. Every player must get back or he will leave his teammates at a disadvantage. Never give up on a play.

I will never forget one impossible defensive play Fred Carter, at that time with Baltimore, now with the Philadelphia 76ers, made against the Knicks in the 1969–70 playoffs. We had Dick Barnett break away for what would have been the winning basket in overtime but Carter never gave up. He came from behind—and out of nowhere—to block the layup and sweep it away. We won in the second overtime but Carter made a defensive play that was a dream. Purely through hustle, he got back and blocked the shot.

DEFENSING SCREEN AND CROSSOVER

In a man-to-man defense, you may run into the problem of an opponent who likes to move behind a screen in search of an unmolested shot. In the ordinary crossover of two opponents, the defensive players try to slide through—especially where there is no ball involved and the distance from the basket is greater than eighteen feet (see diagram 6-10).

You try to prevent the offensive player from running one defensive player into his teammate, as Stu Lantz of the Detroit Pistons might run Oscar Robertson of the Milwaukee Bucks into Lucius Allen if they crossed over. If Allen moved over, Dave Bing could drive toward the basket, trapping Lucius on Lantz. The correct play on the crossover is to have Allen move between Lantz and Robertson and continue his defensive position on Bing.

However, Allen and Robertson may double-team Lantz in an effort to steal the ball or tie it up for a jump. If Bing should be dribbling around Lantz, then Oscar would step forward and try to force Dave to reverse his direction. As Bing turns, Allen is in position to pinch or steal the ball.

When the opponent moves behind the man setting the screen, looking for a shot, and the distance is within eighteen feet, Allen would be required to fight over the top of the screen. He must get at the shooter behind the screen. The shooting skills in the NBA are so superior, it is

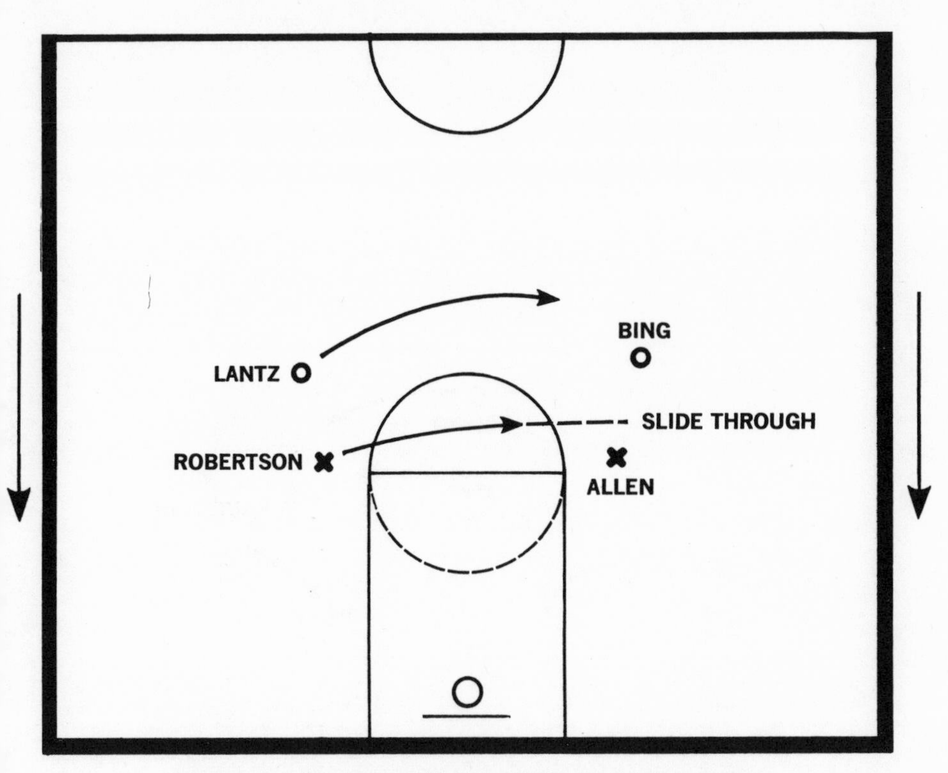

Diagram 6-10 Defensing the Screen and Crossover

necessary to contest every shooting possibility. Every effort must be made to force a poor shot or pressure the man with the ball into passing off.

If the Bucks were playing the Buffalo Braves, Allen, in order to get at Walt Hazzard, would have to fight over the top of the screen set by forward Bob Kauffman. Kauffman must maintain his position without moving into Lucius to avoid an offensive foul, thus permitting Curtis Perry, the Milwaukee forward, to half play Bob and half help Allen with Hazzard (see diagram 6-11).

Perry does not over-commit. He plants his left foot between Kauffman's legs and moves his right foot alongside Bob's left leg—keeping his right hand high to pressure a shot from behind the screen. If Kauffman decided to use the pick and roll, Perry is in position to move with him—fronting the Buffalo forward and watching the ball. By delaying the shot, the defense, with the aid of the twenty-four-second clock, can minimize or take away the screen for shooters.

Most teams try to play man-to-man with a minimum of switching. The less switching, the less opportunity for mistakes, though a team does a lot

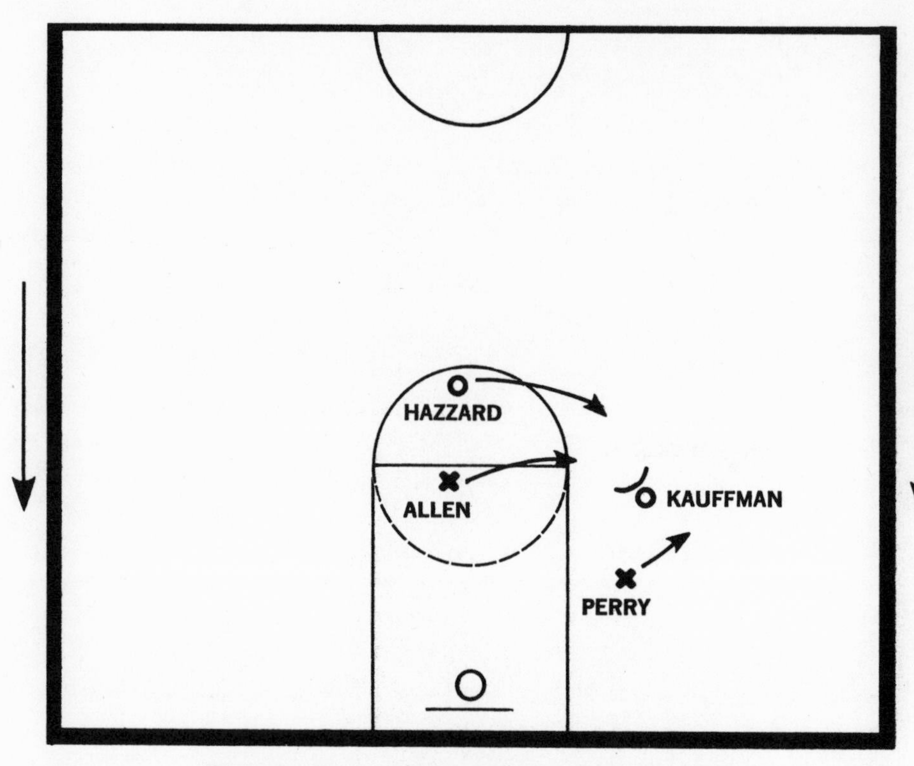

Diagram 6-11 Defensing Screen by Forward

of talking on defense. A switching team leaves itself exposed to mismatches. We prefer to fight or slide through screens and switch only as a last resort. A switching defense is the only weapon against picks. If Nate Thurmond puts his body against Barnett, for example, there is nothing that can be done other than have Lucas switch and pick up Dick's man, while Barnett is stuck with Nate. In that event, the defense must remain alert enough to switch back as soon as possible, if possible.

A lot of what I am saying may be repetitious but that is the way we work on the Knicks. When we are confronted with a problem, we take it to practice and attack it from the start. We assume nothing. We solve the problem by reviewing the fundamentals and then working on the solution.

By now, you would assume most pro teams would know how to apply a press and how to handle one. Yet there are times when something happens to the mechanism. So back to the drawing board for a refresher course.

At the beginning, when the Knicks were working toward their first championship, I am sure some of the players became bored by the repetition. How many times can a professional basketball player listen to someone remind him about watching the ball, not turning the head, when to switch, when not to switch, and so forth without getting a little annoyed?

But a basketball team is no different than the car Peter Revson drives at the Indianapolis classic, other than it is made of flesh and blood and has emotions. The motor of Revson's car must be finely tuned. They keep working on that engine over and over until it is as perfect as humanly possible.

Things to remember about team defense:

1. Hustle at all times. Do not give up if an opponent steals the ball and has a breakaway. I have seen such great players as Jerry West, John Havlicek, Cazzie Russell, and Walt Frazier miss layups. I have seen seven footers go up for a dunk shot and miss. Team defense starts with everyone's desire to challenge over every inch of the court.

2. Make the other team pass as much as possible. The more an offense handles the ball, the more likely a turnover or the chances of it losing patience and taking a poor percentage shot.

3. Be prepared to sacrifice and help out. Cooperation is teamwork. A team that plays together, thinks together, and talks together will win together. An unselfish attitude on defense helps establish an unselfish attitude on offense.

4. Each man must be careful not to drop too far off his man while overplaying, otherwise he will not be able to get back in time on a return pass.

5. Each man must be conscious of his floor position, that there is a calculated team balance. He must play his own position fundamentally sound so an opponent cannot drive around and provide extraordinary pressure on his teammates. It is better to allow an opponent to shoot from the outside.

6. In fast-breaking situations, the defensive team should always attempt to force the dribbler to stop above the foul line. Try to induce the ballhandler to shoot from outside, then turn, and go for the rebound.

7. Each man should know the habits of his opponent: Is he a good shooter from outside? Does he prefer to drive? Is he a good ballhandler? Such bits of information are valuable when a defensive team has to make a split-second decision.

8. In the press, the front three do the switching, while the back two retreat and protect the area around the foul lane.

9. Challenge all offensive rebounds. An opponent that can clear a rebound quickly, without pressure, will be in position to fast break. Try to

tie up the ball or, at least, do something to prevent a quick outlet pass.

10. Most fast breaks are organized. They consist of an outlet pass and a series of short passes and some dribbling. Study an opponent's pattern and try to anticipate where the outlet pass is going.

11. Do not concern yourself with the other team's fast break so much that it affects your game. Be prepared to react when it happens, but do not worry about it when you are on offense. If the other team can get you to keep two men back at all times, it has gained an advantage. A good team defense reacts to any situation and does not have to waste time or opportunities thinking or adjusting.

12. Fight through screens; don't drop behind them. Switch when a teammate gets trapped. Jump out and show yourself at a shooter even if he is wide open and it is impossible for you to get close enough to block his shot. Box out after a shot. Do not give up a second shooting opportunity to the opponent.

CHAPTER

7

TEAM OFFENSE

Basketball is a thinking man's game and the more minds the better. Never lose sight of the fact that basketball is a team game and everyone on the squad should be involved. Everyone and everything is important.

By being receptive to suggestions from the players, a coach will establish a greater feeling of involvement. A player gets to feel it is "our" team, an attitude that pays off in many ways. Such as the fifth game of the 1969–70 championship series with the Lakers after the Knicks lost Willis Reed with an injured hip.

We went to the dressing room losing by fifteen points at halftime. We discussed the situation. We knew what had to be done on defense. We had only Nate Bowman, Dave DeBusschere, and Dave Stallworth available to play Wilt Chamberlain.

What about the offense? What were we going to do about Chamberlain jamming the middle and hanging around the boards? How could we prevent him from destroying our attack all by himself? We engaged in an open discussion while Willis was in the trainer's room, stretched on the table in pain.

Bill Bradley had a suggestion. Why not try the 1-3-1? Bradley would play the high post, flanked by Dick Barnett and Dave Stallworth. We would send Dave DeBusschere in deep to roam around and, hopefully, get some shots from the side should Chamberlain hang around underneath the basket.

If Wilt dropped off to help on DeBusschere, the foul lane would open up. If Wilt came out, DeBusschere would clear and let his teammates drive on Chamberlain. It worked beautifully. I can still see Stallworth driving on Wilt along the baseline and scoring.

Even if it had not been successful, the use of the strategy had its fringe value. It established further that the players and coach were working together. That I do not think I know all the answers. A coach's job is to keep an open mind on ideas and suggestions, but retain, primarily, the right to make the decision.

There has to be some respect for authority. Yet, a coach has to earn that respect by the manner with which he encourages team contribution and, of course, how successful are his methods. Some players are better than others but there are no special privileges or rules on the Knicks. Everyone and every situation is treated with equal importance.

The way we give fouls on the Knicks is a good example. We figured it was poor percentage basketball to have a starter add to his normal load by giving a foul. In professional basketball, a team is limited to four team fouls in a quarter, with a penalty shot awarded for any additional. It is better to give the spare foul than risk having a basket scored.

Therefore, we decided it was better to have someone on the bench enter the game to give the foul, rather than risk a personal on a regular. It is something for high school and college coaches to consider when they are involved in a tight game. Give a foul when it will help your team but do not have a serviceable player give it.

I recall a game the Knicks played against Cincinnati in the 1969–70 season where the Royals paid a severe penalty for not having someone on the bench give a foul. It was the night, in Cleveland, when we came from five points behind in the final twenty seconds or so to win our eighteenth straight.

Oscar Robertson, then with the Royals, had given two fouls early in the game. They did not seem like much at the time, yet, he wound up fouling out. It was good strategy to give the fouls but you never know what is going to happen in a basketball game. You should always play the percentages as best you can, conceding it might be impossible at times.

Bob Cousy, the coach, had just activated himself. Without the "Big O" to handle the ball, Cousy inserted himself. It was an extremely difficult situation. Tremendous pressure for Bob, a pressure player throughout his career, who, nevertheless, had been away long enough to make him more of a risk under the existing conditions than Oscar Robertson.

We capitalized on some of Cincinnati's confusion for a couple of steals and won, 106–105, on two free throws by Walt Frazier near the buzzer. There is no saying the same thing would not have happened if the "Big O" had not fouled out. But on the Knicks, we like to play it safe. We like to have our bench give the fouls.

We handed the assignment to Mike Riordan. That is all he did for a long time. He was our specialist. The fans laughed at the beginning. Then they began to applaud Mike when they recognized the significance of his contribution.

Was he embarrassed? Never. Riordan never considered it menial. That is the way it should be with everything. If a player is used to give a foul, he should treat it with importance. If he has to sit on the bench, he should be just as emotionally and intellectually involved in the team's welfare as the superstar who plays forty-eight minutes a game.

It may seem as though I have wandered far from the subject of team offense—not at all. There can be no significant team offense if the players are not prepared to consider themselves as part of the whole structure. The entire philosophy of team defense is based on each player sacrificing to produce maximum efficiency from everyone.

Basketball has made amazing strides since I learned it in the schoolyards of Brooklyn. The players are bigger, faster, and stronger. The game has accelerated to the point of ultimate speed. The one-hand shot has placed a premium on defense. The defense had to become tougher to stay with the offense.

Yet, with all the progress, I still think there is a tendency to complicate basketball. There is an inclination to overcoach. Too much time is spent on teaching the razzle-dazzle. I prefer the simple approach to team offense. Work for the best percentage shots with the use of fundamentally sound principles.

Every team must organize its offense. It must determine the strength of its material and install a pattern that serves as a foundation on which everything is built. Each player must familiarize himself with what he can do for the team and where on the floor he can best penetrate a defense. A team then develops various options and creates freelance opportunities in relation to the basic offense it has established.

In professional basketball, the offense is confronted with a man-to-man defense. Although half-court and full-court zone presses are employed more and more, the basic defense a coach must attack in preparing a team offense is the man-to-man. It has been that way since the days of George Mikan and the Minneapolis Lakers, the first powerhouse in the NBA.

Virtually all teams still emulate the Lakers' basic 2-3 offense—two guards out and three big men inside. John Kundla, the coach, built his attack around a powerful front line of Mikan, Vern Mikkelsen, and Jim Pollard, with Slater Martin, Whitey Skoog, and Arnie Ferrin handling the backcourt.

What is important is that a team needs a starting point or system, though it is obvious the approach will be different on different teams. The Chicago Bulls, under Dick Motta, preferred control basketball and started from there. The Boston Celtics always leaned to the fast break. The Los Angeles Lakers, the Milwaukee Bucks, and the Golden State Warriors build their offense around a strong pivotman because of Wilt Chamberlain, Kareem Abdul-Jabbar, and Nate Thurmond.

There are others. The Philadelphia 76ers, once they traded Chamberlain and Luke Jackson suffered a serious tear of an Achilles tendon, relied heavily on forwards and guards who could cut and shoot behind screens.

SET PLAYS

Set plays are generally related to control basketball, which, really, is fundamental basketball. That is the way I learned to play the game before it was revolutionized by the fast break. Errors are minimized in a controlled game. The ball handling is better. The passing is better.

It is percentage basketball, and it offers more opportunities for success in high school and college ball than in the pros, where there is a twenty-four-second time limit. All pro teams are equipped to utilize any type of offense. The ideal situation is to be flexible enough to exploit any development.

For example, the Boston Celtics, normally a fast breaking team, may find it advisable to play control ball simply to slow down an opponent. Or a deliberate team, such as the Chicago Bulls, might be faced with a situation where the opponent is slowing things down. As a matter of strategy, or change of pace, the Bulls would want to start fast breaking to interrupt the other team's pattern.

The old Minneapolis Lakers were devastating with their 2-3 set offense.

It is a flexible approach that lends itself to many variations. Every team in pro basketball today uses some version, such as slicing the guards around the high post.

Jeff Mullins will hit Nate Thurmond in the pivot and then crisscross with Fritz Williams, each driving for the hoop. Nate can give the ball to either guard or, if his opponent switches to protect against the cutting Mullins or Williams, fake the handoff and go up with a jumper from the foul line (see diagram 7-1).

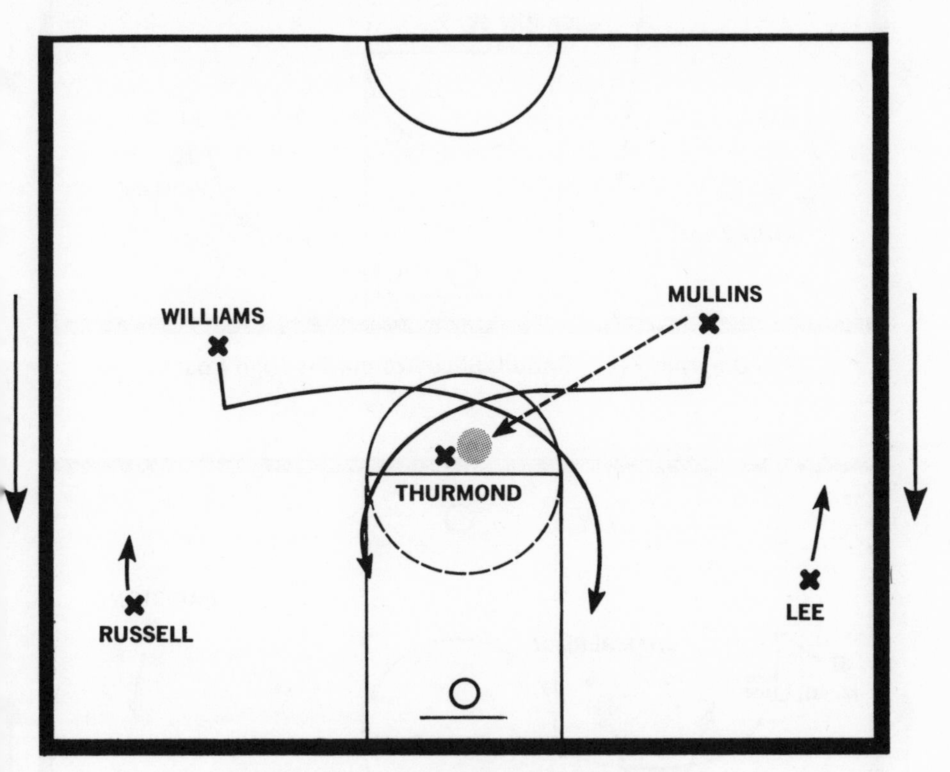

Diagram 7-1 Slice Around the High Post

Philadelphia used an interesting variation of the slice with Hal Greer. When the ball is passed to Luke Jackson in the high pivot, Kevin Loughery fakes as though the slice is on. Greer breaks directly for the basket, receiving a bounce pass from Jackson for a layup (see diagram 7-2).

The slice also can be set up by a guard and forward. In the 1971–72 championship playoffs, the Lakers often used it against us. Jerry West flipped the ball to Wilt Chamberlain on the side of the foul lane. West

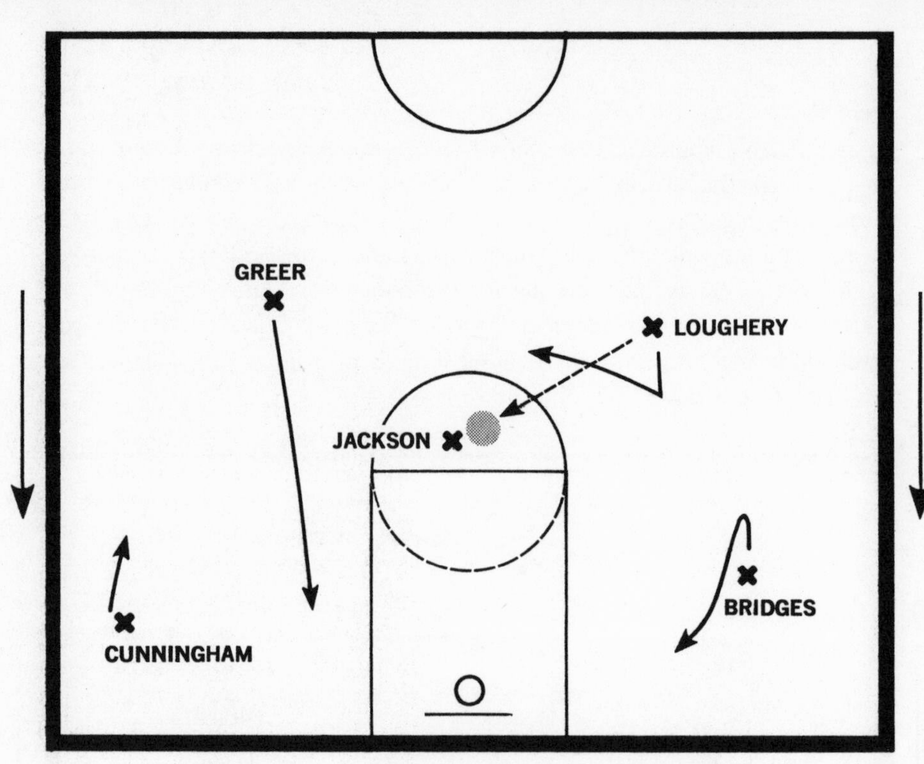

Diagram 7-2 Option: Slice Around the High Post

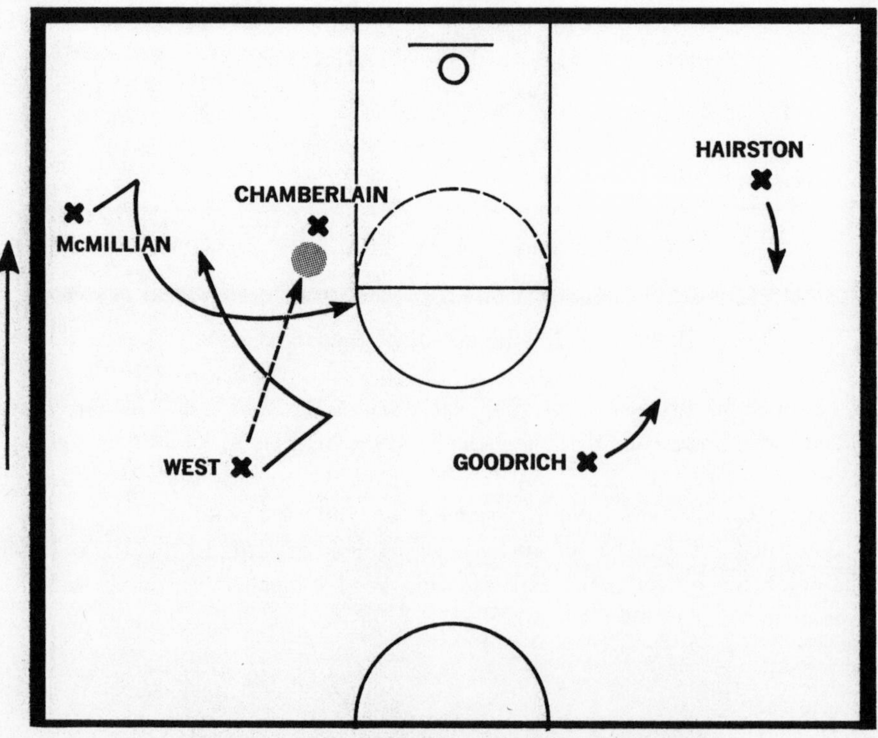

Diagram 7-3 Slice Play: Guard and Forward

and Jim McMillian then crisscrossed around Wilt, with McMillian getting a jumper (see diagram 7-3).

On a variation, West would pass to McMillian, who flipped to Chamberlain and broke toward him. West sliced around McMillian and went to the corner for a pass from Wilt and a jump shot (see diagram 7-4).

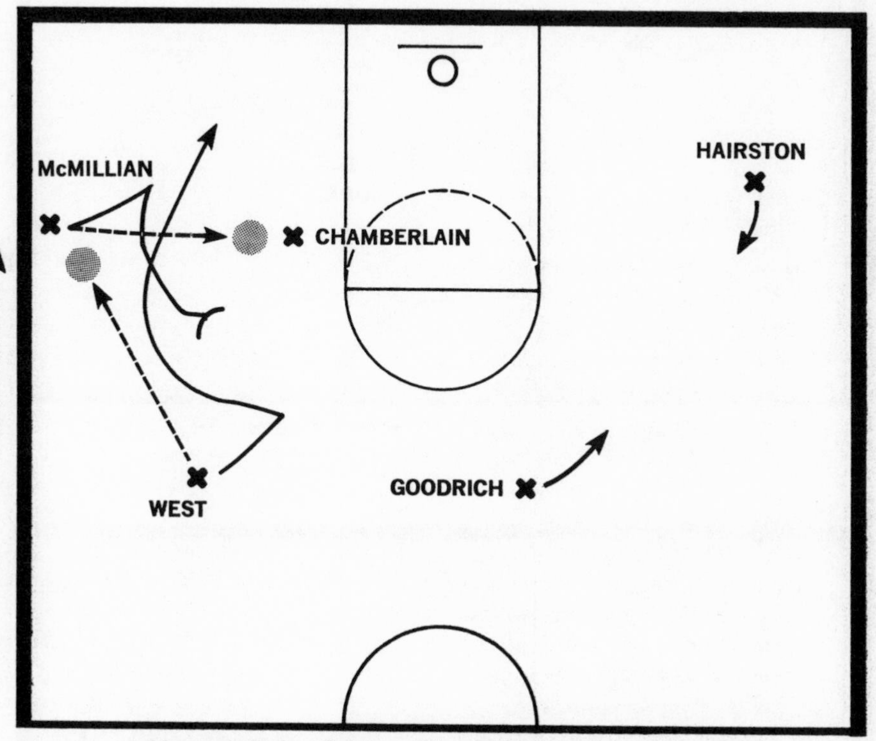

Diagram 7-4 Option: Slice Play Guard and Forward

The Boston Celtics, in the championship era of Bill Russell, set up a double screen for their forwards. John Havlicek passed to Russell, on a high post along the foul lane, and broke to a spot near the center. Tommy Heinsohn swung out behind Havlicek and Russell for an open shot (see diagram 7-5).

Occasionally, a "backdoor" variation was utilized to beat an opponent who might be overplaying a forward too much. Heinsohn faked to the baseline, then out, and drove behind his man. Meanwhile, Havlicek had given the ball to Russell and headed for Heinsohn as though setting up a double screen. Tommy drove through the open door along the baseline to take a pass from Russell for a layup (see diagram 7-6).

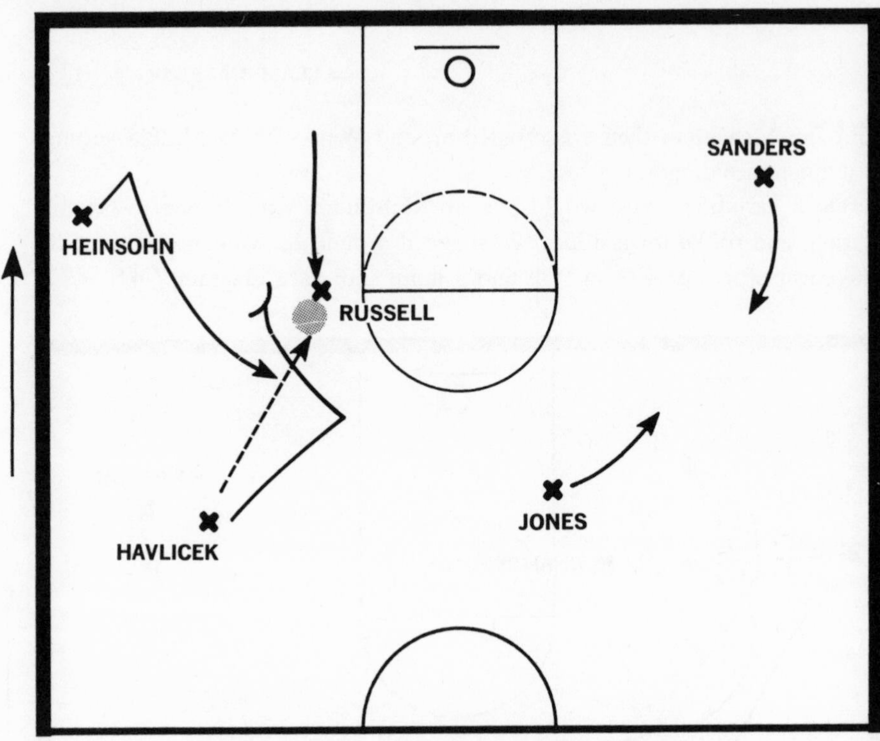

Diagram 7-5 Double Screen for Forward

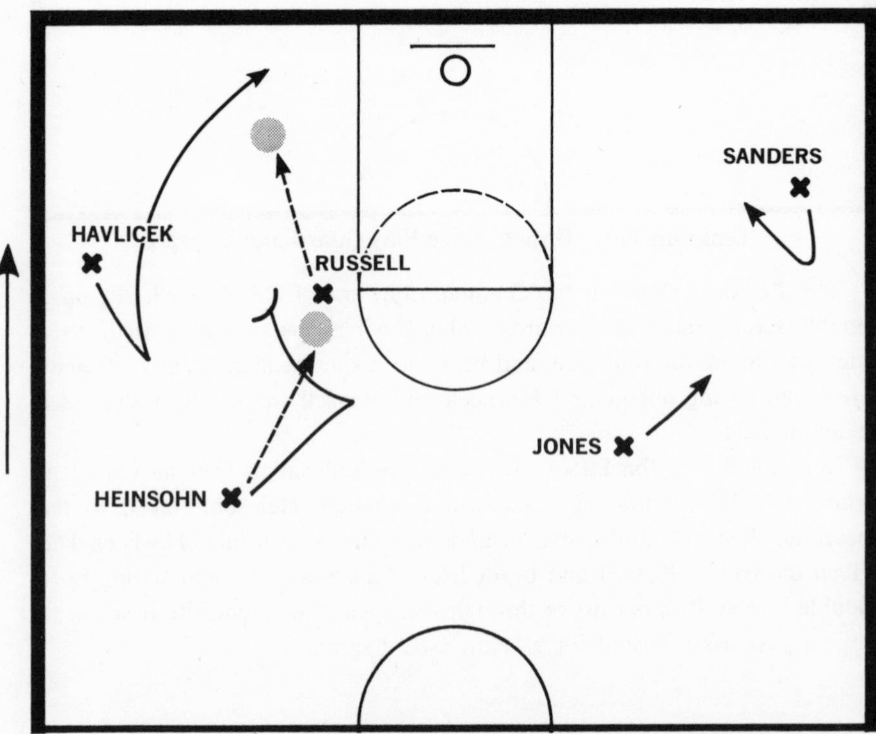

Diagram 7-6 Option: Back door Variation on Double Screen

The 2-3 may be used with corner clear-outs to create moves into vital scoring areas. Teams use their forwards to clear out an area and allow a guard and the center to set up two-man plays, such as the pick-and-roll. Lennie Wilkens of Seattle, for example, might pass the ball to Spencer Haywood and then head toward him for a return pass. Spencer moves and runs his man into Don Smith, the center, and goes to the foul line.

Now Wilkens has a number of options: he can give the ball to Haywood for a shot; he can fake a dribble to his right, reverse to the left, and go up for a jumper; or he can pass to Smith, who has rolled to the basket (see diagram 7-7).

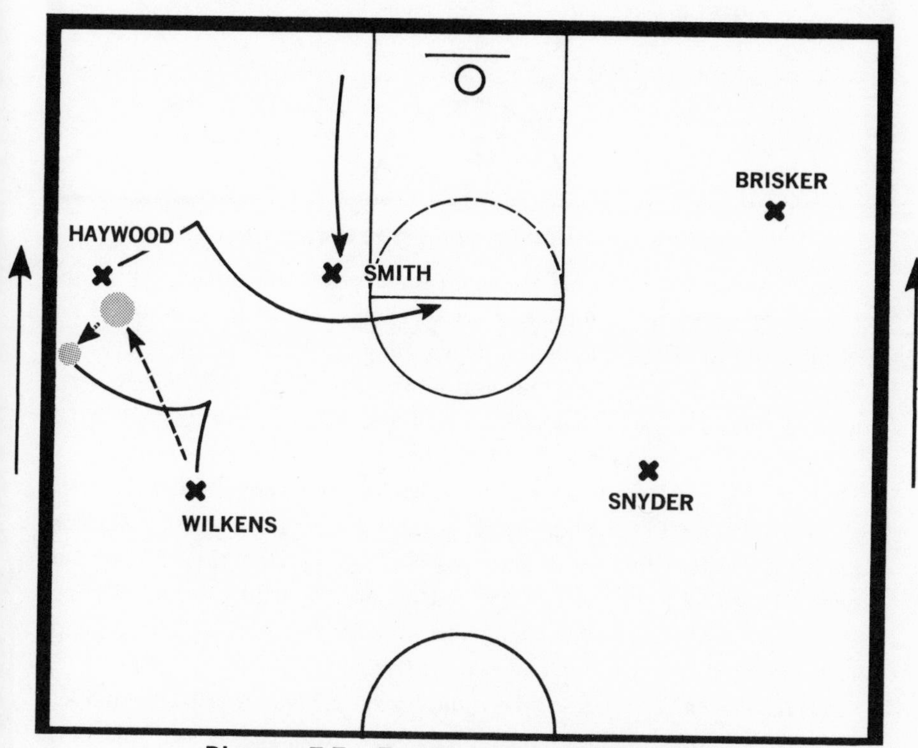

Diagram 7-7 Two-Three Corner Clear Out

The 76ers had a version they used to set up Billy Cunningham behind a screen by Jackson. As Cunningham cleared from the side to the foul line, Jackson executed a half-turn to the inside of the court after taking a pass from Greer. Then Cunningham swung back and took a bounce pass from Luke for the shot (see diagram 7-8).

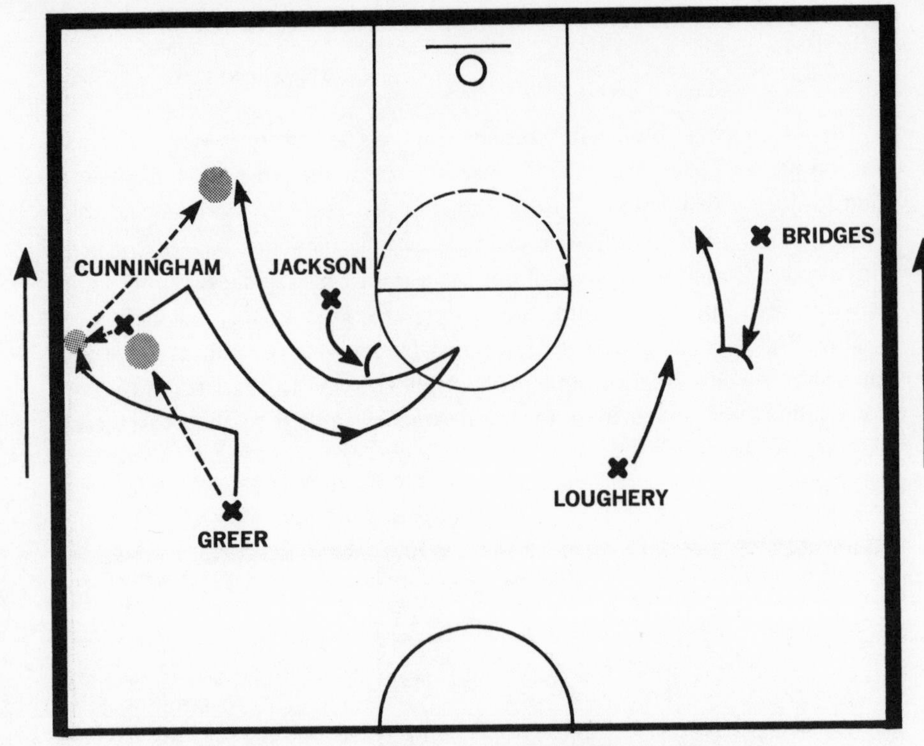

Diagram 7-8 Option: Two-Three Corner Clear Out

The clear-out may be used to screen for a pivotman moving out of the low post. It is good for a mobile, scoring center, such as Bob Lanier of the Detroit Pistons. The ballhandler, Dave Bing, dribbles to the side. The forward, Curtis Rowe, clears out and moves across the foul lane to set a screen. Lanier swings out toward the ball and takes a pass from Bing for a turnaround jumper or hook shot (see diagram 7-9).

The Milwaukee Bucks use Abdul-Jabbar to set a screen away from the ball. This enables Bob Dandridge to go underneath for a pass or Kareem to roll off the foul line for a pass and shot. After Dandridge clears out, Oscar Robertson is in position to feed him on the move or hit Kareem with the pass. The Bucks also work this play for Jon McGlocklin, a guard and sometimes forward (see diagram 7-10).

There could be a variation where the forwards slice or crisscross underneath to set up a double screen for a shot from above the foul line. Abdul-Jabbar can be in the low post and Perry runs past as though heading for the basket. Dandridge swings across from the weak side and sets a double screen with Kareem, who has moved out. Perry reverses and doubles back to take a pass from Robertson for a jumper (see diagram 7-11).

Pro basketball coaches developed many interesting options, depending on certain players. They are suitable for high school and college teams

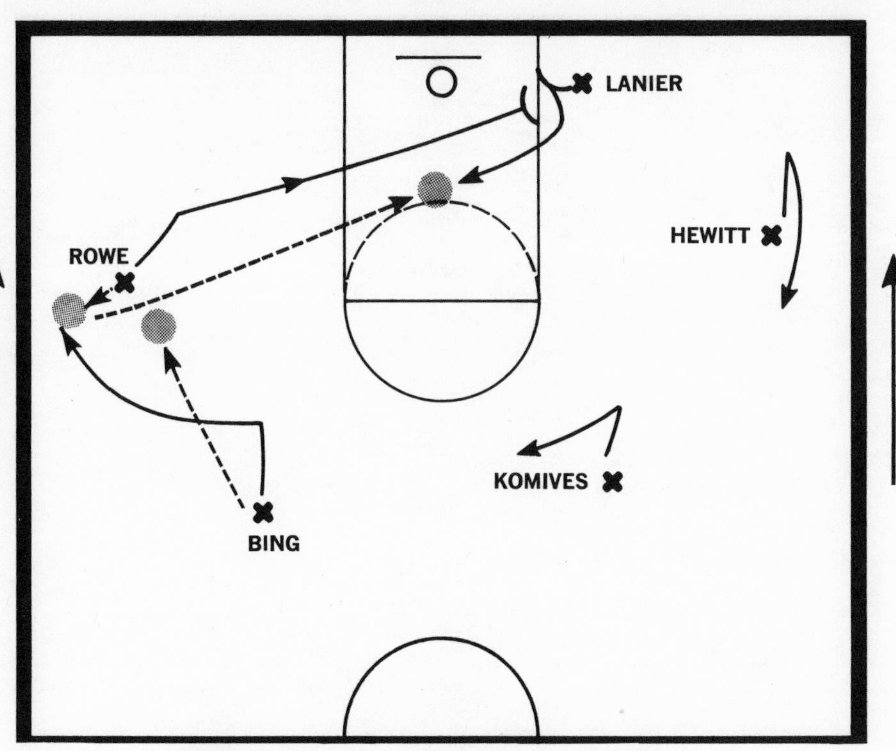

Diagram 7-9 Clear Out to Screen for Pivot

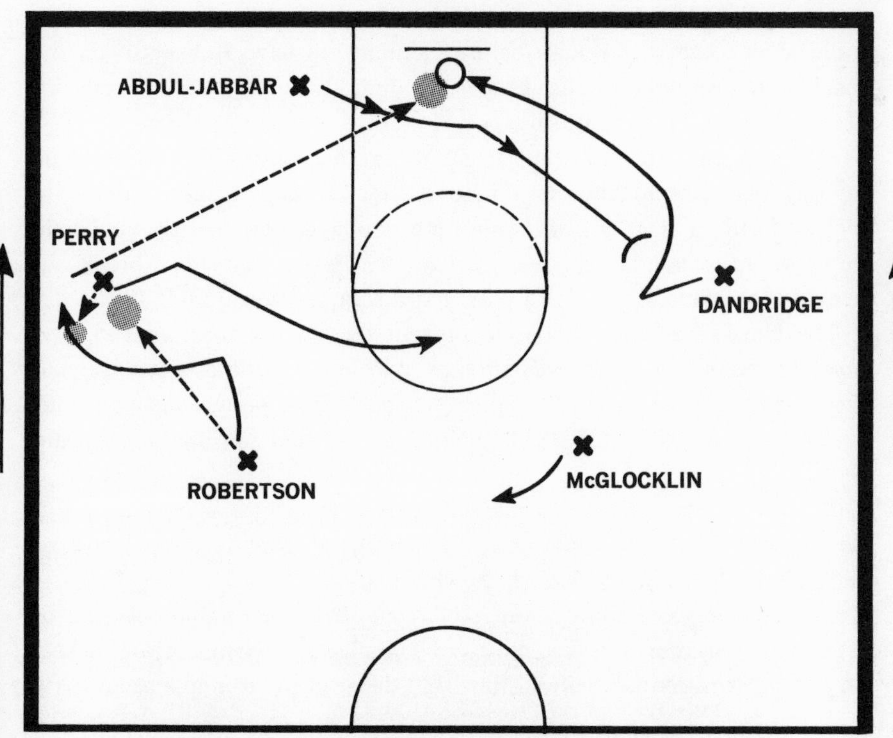

Diagram 7-10 Screen for Opposite Forward

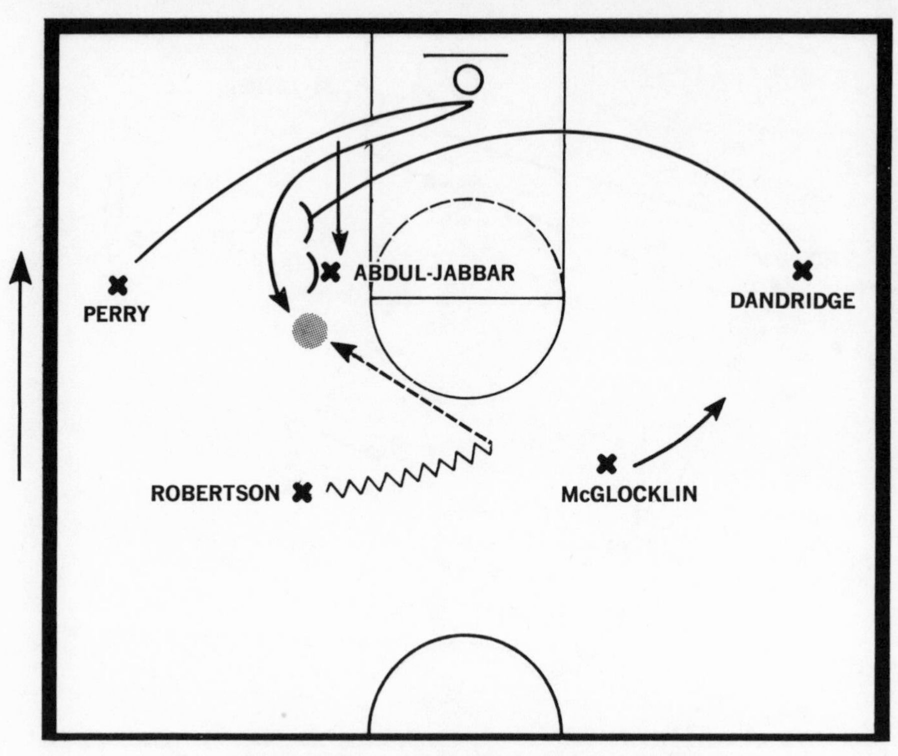

Diagram 7-11 Double Screen for Forward

if a coach has the proper personnel. When Alex Hannum was coach of the NBA champion St. Louis Hawks (1957–58), he had the good fortune, as I did as coach of the Hawks before Hannum, to have Bob Pettit on the team. Pettit was one of the all-time shooters, with an accurate range of about twenty feet on jump shots.

Hannum used the 2-3 extensively to exploit Pettit's fine touch. One favorite play was to have Clyde Lovellette, the huge center, work with Slater Martin, a small guard, to set up a double screen near the foul line. Pettit would jockey his opponent toward the baseline and then break out behind the double screen for a pass and a shot (see diagram 7-12).

The Hawks had two options to prevent the defense from cheating too much on Pettit. On one, Lovellette moved around Martin as Pettit went to the baseline. If the defensive center dropped off to protect against Pettit getting a pass inside, Lovellette jumped to the foul line for a pass and shot (see diagram 7-13).

If the defensive guard dropped off to protect against a pass to Pettit, the Hawks had Martin move around Lovellette. That released Slater to get a shot off behind the big center (see diagram 7-14).

One advantageous thing about the 2-3 is that it is easily converted to a 1-3-1 for variation and flexibility. No complicated adjustments are necessary. The transition is a natural flow. We did it in the championship series

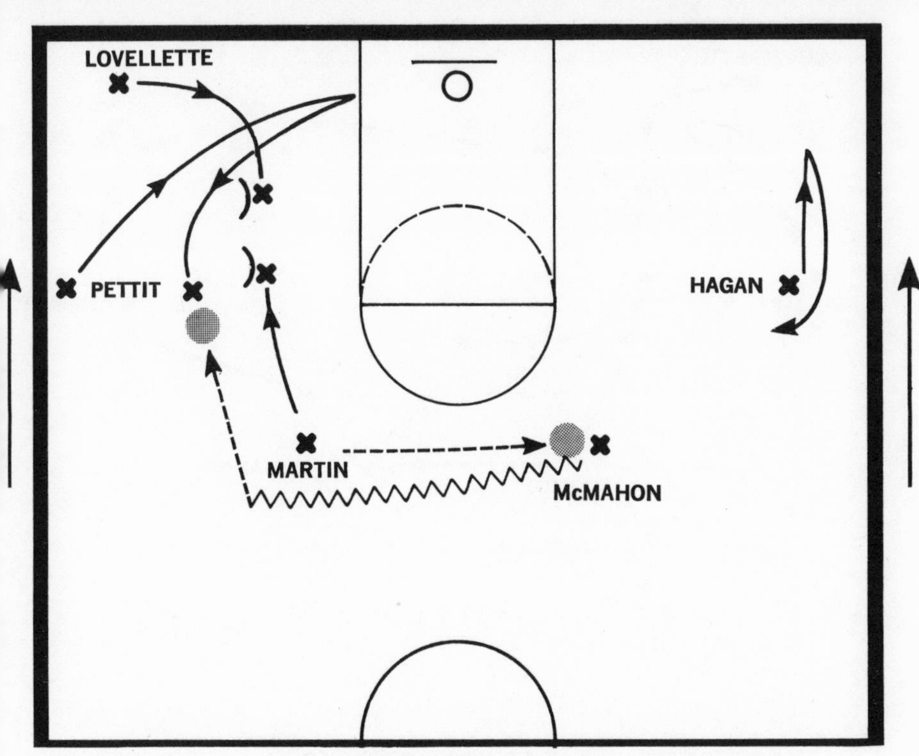

Diagram 7-12 Forward Behind Double Screen—Pivot and Guard

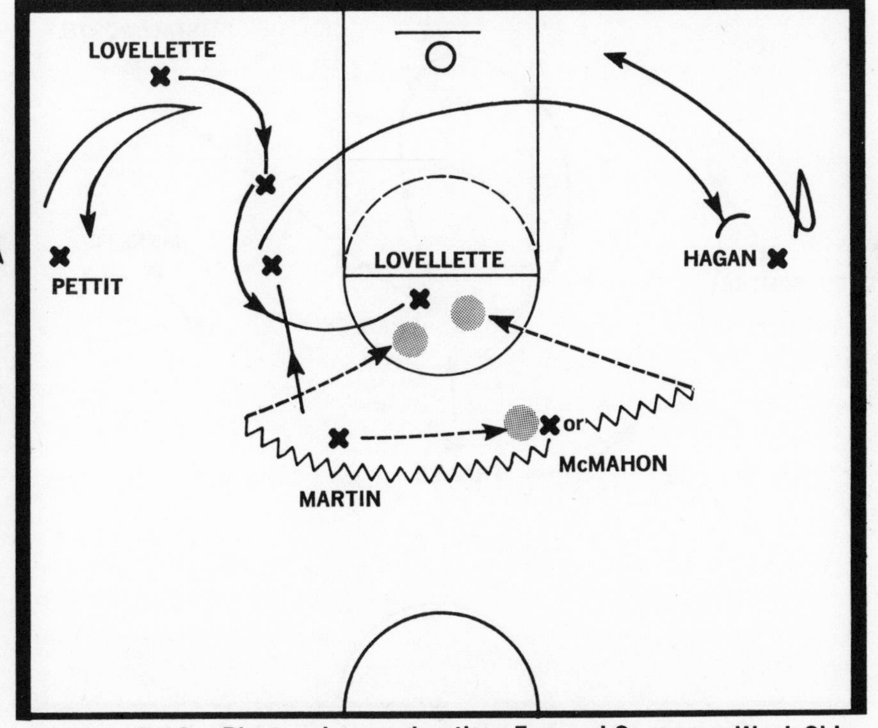

Diagram 7-13 Pivot and second option: Forward Screen on Weak Side

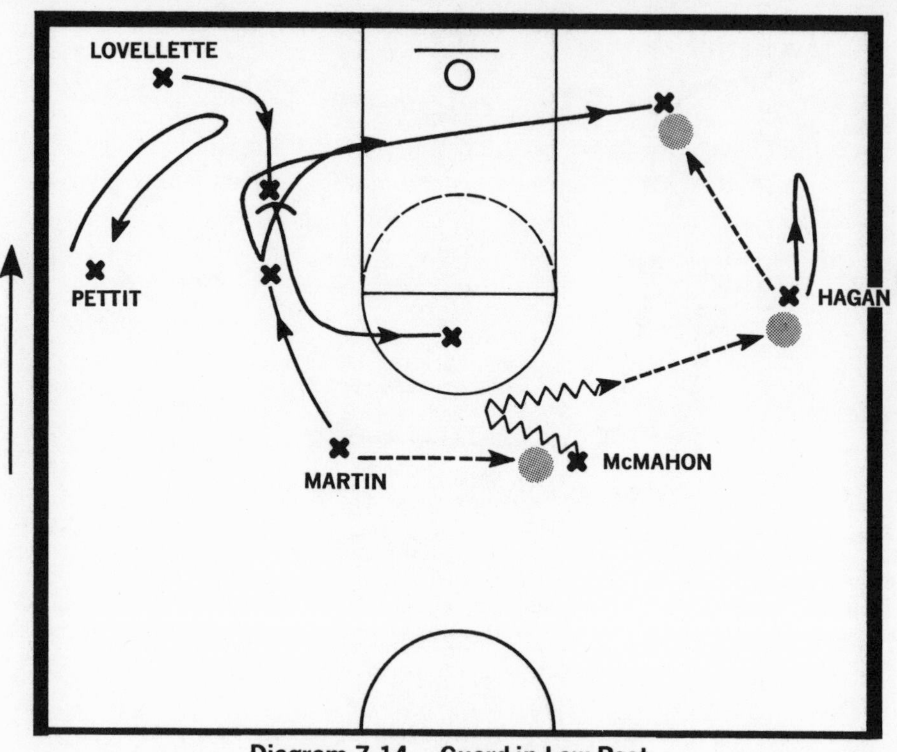

Diagram 7-14 Guard in Low Post

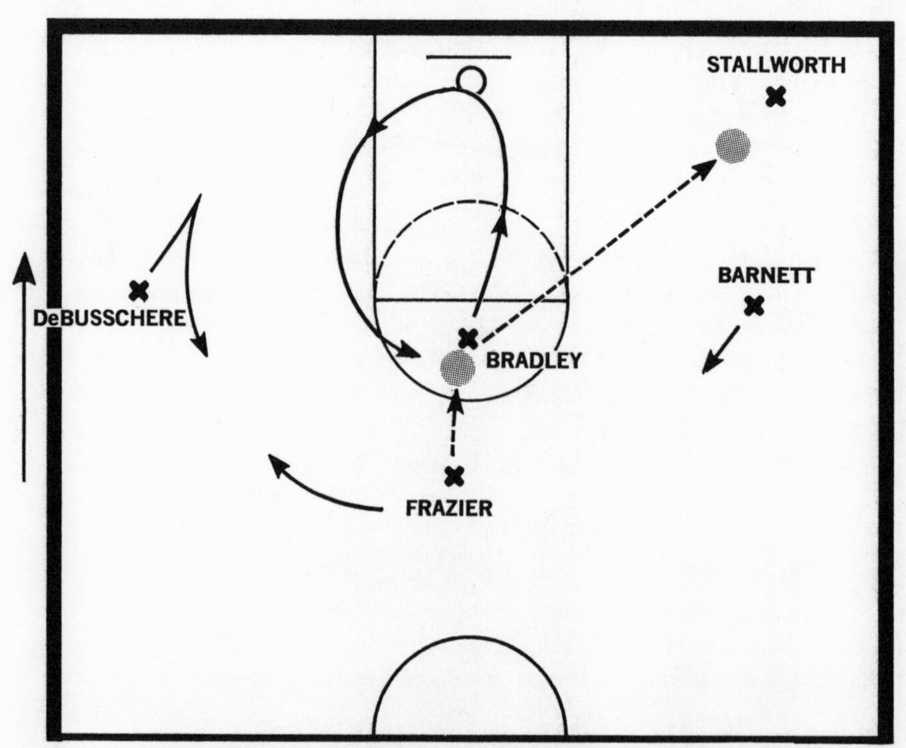

Diagram 7-15 1-3-1 Formation: Bradley to Stallworth

with the Lakers. We didn't need any time to detail everything. We were prepared for the switch. They were natural moves that experienced players make instinctively against defenses. The ideal situation would be to have a team composed of players who do not have to call out plays—they do things automatically.

When Bradley took a pass from Frazier and hit Stallworth in the corner, Stalls was able to go 1-on-1 along the baseline because the Lakers were drawn away from the basket. When Bradley's man moved to help out, Stallworth hit Bill with a return pass for an easy shot from the foul line (see diagram 7-15).

The 1-3-1 formation can be effective against many defensive variations but especially against zones. High school and college players should remember that crisp movement and ballhandling are basic requirements. A simple "revolve" can be organized within the 1-3-1 that will penetrate vital areas.

Atlanta, for example, might have Pete Maravich pass to Don Adams, with the ball then going to Lou Hudson in the corner. Hudson is a good outside shooter and must be respected. If the defense does not cover him, he has a percentage shot along the baseline (see diagram 7-16).

Adams also can cut through the lower part of the defense on a straight give-and-go. If the defense does not react, Don can take a return pass for a layup. If there is no return pass, Adams can swing all the way through and head away from Jim Washington, the other forward, on a clear out.

Now Maravich moves to the spot vacated by Adams and Washington heads for the spot Pete left. That way, the 1-3-1 formation remains intact and is in position to work, again, on the defense because of the revolving of players.

Let's assume the defense sloughs off to clog the passing lane between Hudson and Adams. That is where Walt Bellamy, the center, begins a second move. He will cut into the opening created by the defense's desire to protect against Adams' pass and cut (see diagram 7-17).

Hudson, with the ball in the corner, has the option of passing to Bellamy if he has good scoring position. If not, Lou can move the ball out to Maravich, who has swung into position for the pass through the natural movement of the "revolve." Pete can reverse it to Washington and Bellamy can continue across the lane to set a screen for Adams, who will take a pass from Washington for a shot (see diagram 7-18).

In the rapid movement of Adams and Bellamy, as they cut into the defense, the other team will tend to shift toward the strong side—where the ball is. By moving Adams and Bellamy to the weak side quickly, the

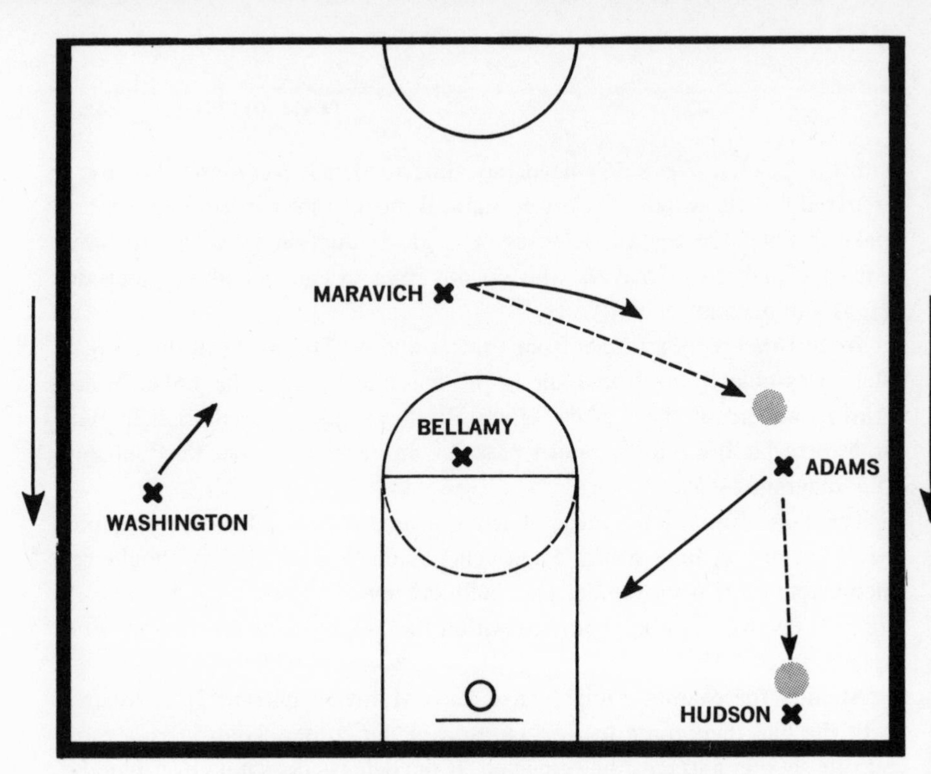

Diagram 7-16 1-3-1 Revolve: First Move

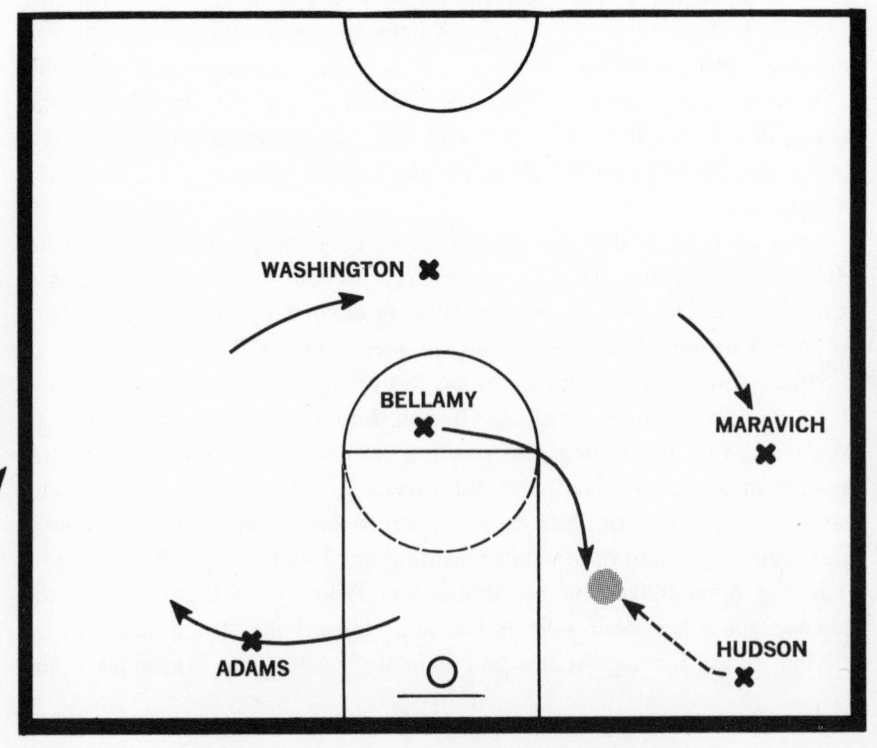

Diagram 7-17 1-3-1 Revolve: Second Move

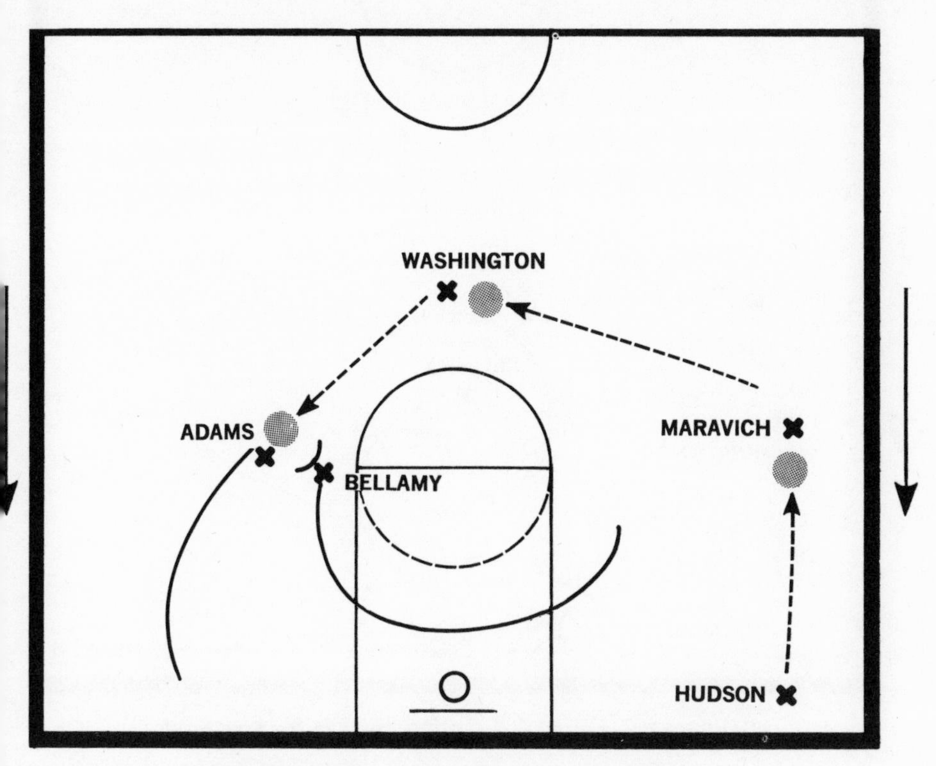

Diagram 7-18 1-3-1 Revolve: Third Move

Hawks can create a good shot no further than fifteen to eighteen feet from the basket.

Optional moves may be added to the "revolve" to compensate for changes the defense might make to protect the vulnerable areas. With the ball on the side, Bellamy, on a high post, can exchange and screen Hudson, on the low post, to create a short jump shot (see diagram 7-19).

When Maravich passes to Adams, the Hawks can slide Bellamy in low toward Hudson, playing near the baseline. Lou will swing around Bellamy and take a pass from Adams for a short turnaround jumper in the middle, near the basket.

Atlanta might employ a shuffle option, allowing Bellamy to move over and screen for Adams cutting around him. Don will head for the basket while Hudson clears out to the corner. The ball moves from Maravich to Washington to Adams (see diagram 7-20).

There are many formations which a coach and his players may use in organizing an offense and making it productive. The importance of any formation is to serve as a starting point from which to operate. How well the fundamentals are executed and how quickly the offense exploits defensive weaknesses will determine the degree of success.

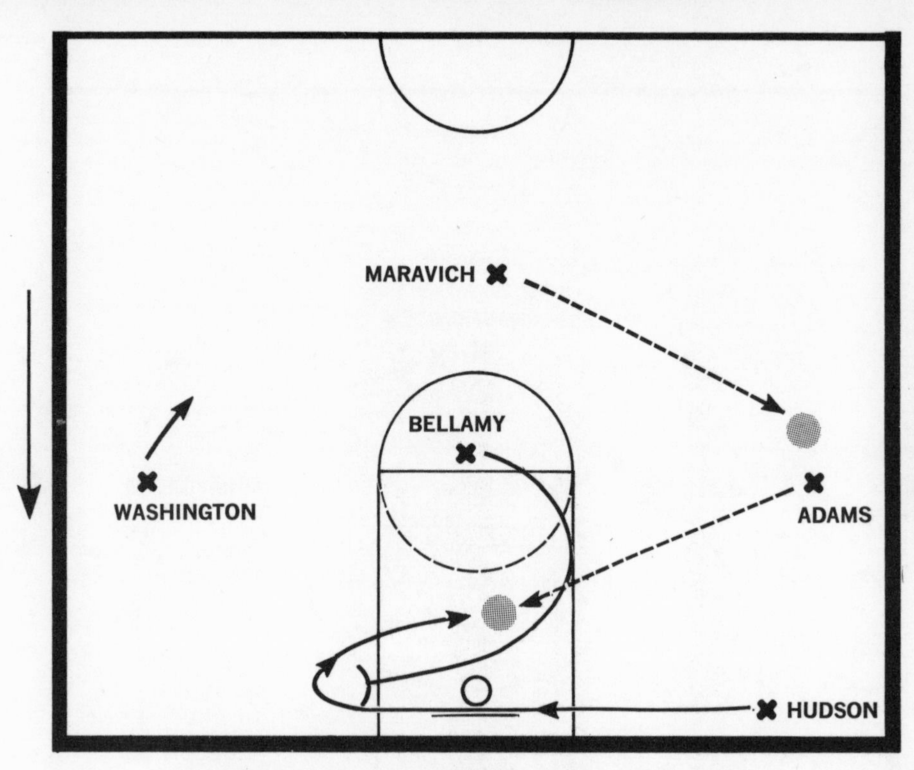

Diagram 7-19 1-3-1 Option: Screen for Low Post

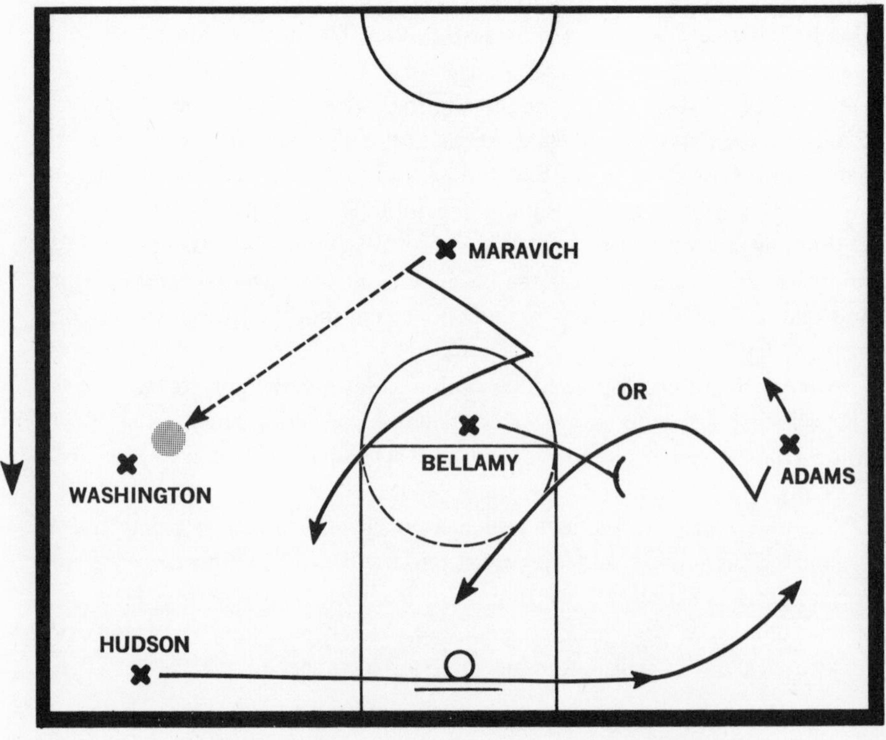

Diagram 7-20 1-3-1 Revolve: Shuffle Options

Teams may reverse the 2-3 and play a 3-2, or even three guards and two under. The three-guard offense provides more mobility and quickness in a situation where a team must do something to alter the pace of a game.

Baltimore has been known to employ the three-guard offense on those occasions when the other team was doing too well. A forward and center, acting as deep men, can set flash pivots or keep the middle open. This will accelerate the offense and, while it might be a gamble from the viewpoint of rebounding, it can, under certain conditions, be an effective, strategic weapon. It opens the game more and can force the defense to adjust, sometimes to the point where the other coach has to bring in a quicker, smaller man to match the offense.

The three-guard offense can generate freelance scoring though the concept remains within the scope of a set pattern. Thus, Archie Clark of the Bullets might bring the ball into the attacking zone, pass to Phil Chenier, take a return pass while moving behind a screen by Mike Riordan, the third guard, and then feed Wes Unseld in a side pivot (see diagram 7-21).

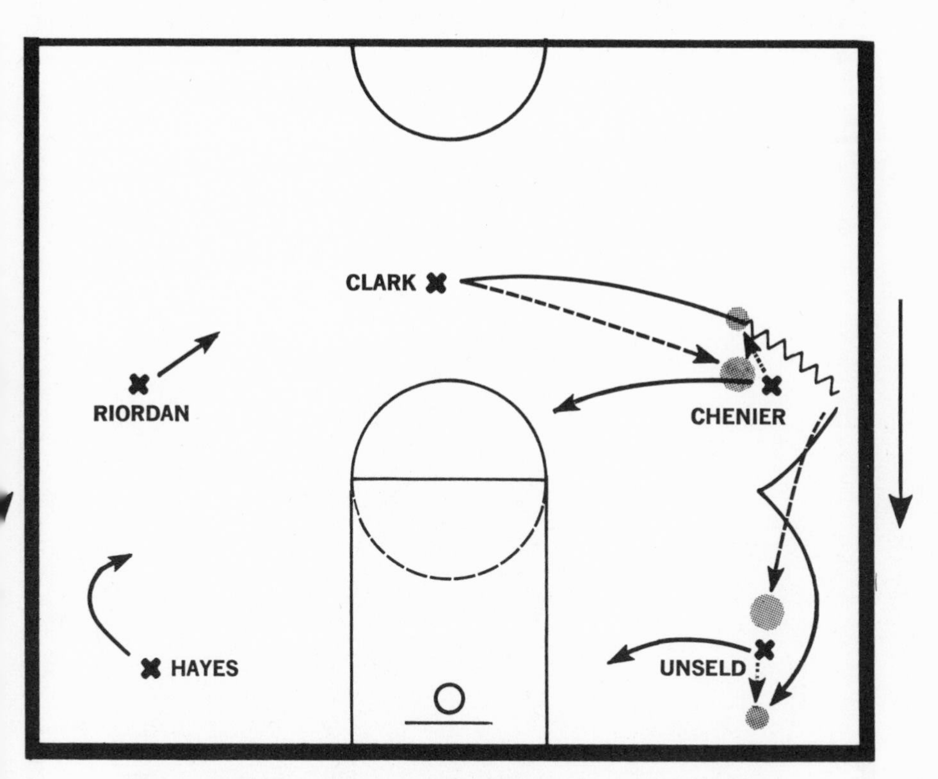

Diagram 7-21 Three Guard Offense: Guard to Forward

That establishes an immediate two-man play between Clark and Unseld, with Archie going baseline and Wes rolling to the basket after giving him the ball. Unseld might even fake the handoff to Clark and drive to the foul line for a short jump shot. Or he might drive toward the middle with the ball and set a screen for John Tresvant, who moves behind Wes for a pass and jump shot.

On another play, the Bullets might spring Riordan for a shot around a screen set by Chenier, swinging across the floor from the side. Clark will feed Unseld in deep and near the sideline. Riordan, a lefthanded shooter, will move around Chenier and through the lane to his strong side and take a pass from Unseld for the shot (see diagram 7-22).

Baltimore might mix it up by starting the play in the same manner but with a different purpose in mind. Clark will pass to Chenier this time and move behind him for a return pass. Archie will feed Unseld, while Chenier releases and cuts across the lane to set a double screen with Riordan for Tresvant (see diagram 7-23).

Tresvant can slip behind the screen or go backdoor along the baseline. If John decides to go backdoor without the ball, Riordan can roll out to the foul line and set up as a secondary outlet for a pass from Unseld.

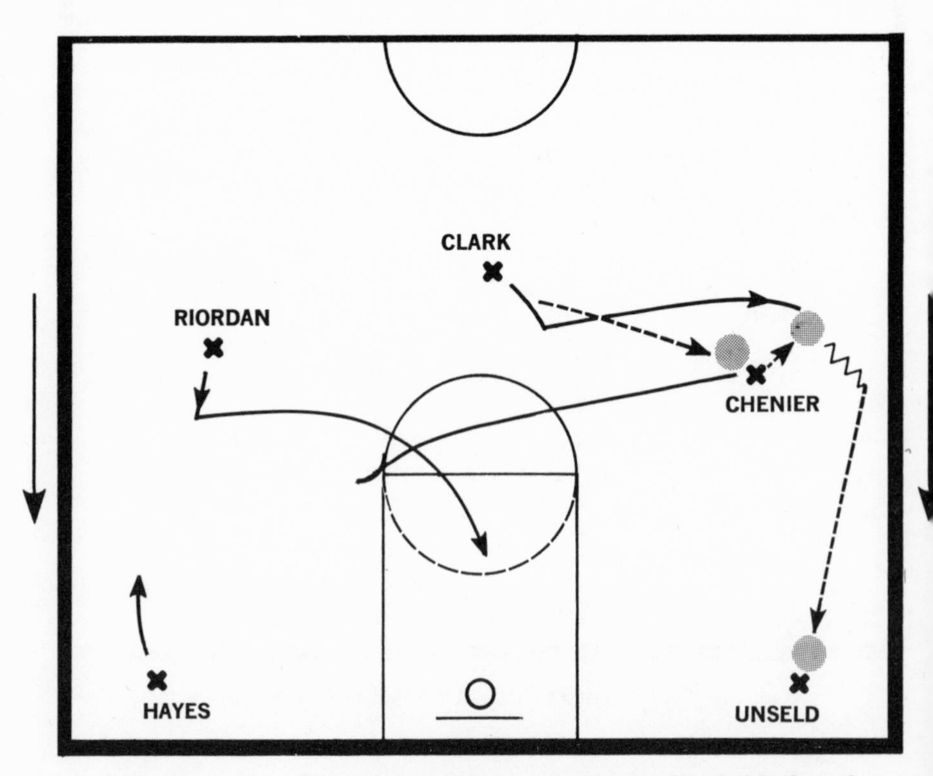

Diagram 7-22 Three Guard Offense: Screen for Weakside Guard

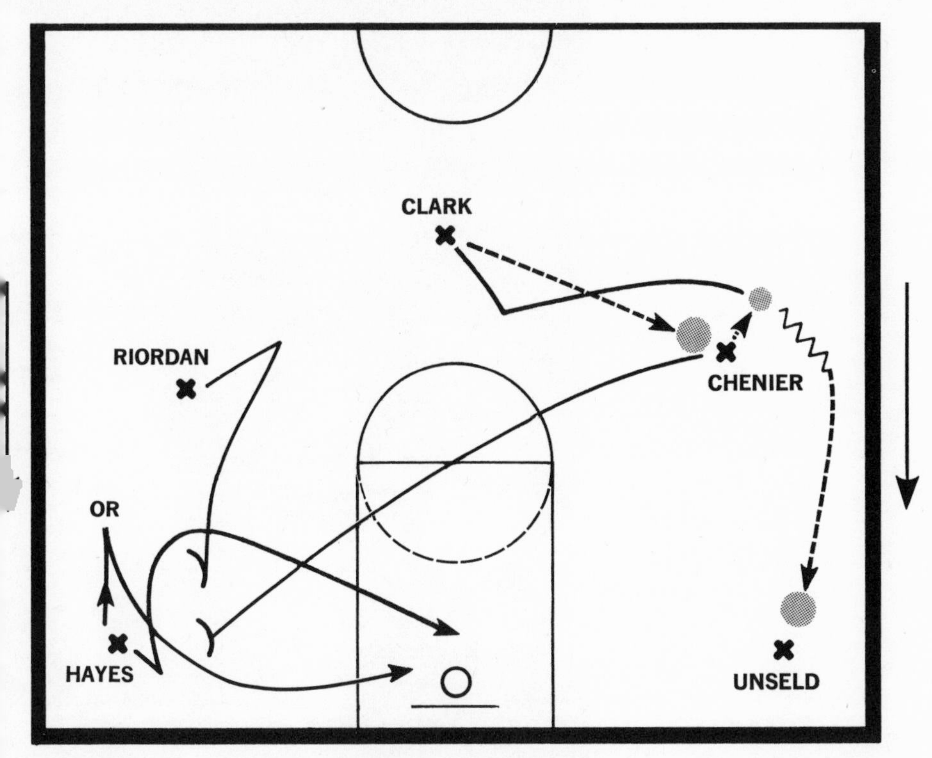

Diagram 7-23 Three Guard Offense: Double Screen for Weakside Forward

In a three-guard offense, players such as Clark and Chenier can create many 1-on-1 opportunities. If the middle is open, Chenier can fake a return pass to Clark and drive on his opponent. If the defensive players switch to help out, Phil has an open man in Unseld or Tresvant.

The main requirements are good ballhandling and moves with and without the ball. Also a fair amount of success in rebounding because the offense is using a guard as forward, therefore giving something away off the boards. The Knicks have used the three-guard offense with some degree of success, while we have seen it work against us at times.

We do not leave our offense to guesswork. Our set plays are labeled. They may be called "2-1F" or "Bailey Howell" or "San Francisco" for identification. We do not use play books, though many coaches do. We practice our plays and expect the players to know them.

We use set plays if the defensive team keeps us from fast breaking. Set offenses generally operate best when a team has a tall and strong player to set picks and screens and pass the ball. If the offense is designed to free players behind a single post, then the big man does not have to be an outstanding ballhandler.

We use Reed and Lucas for everything because they are equipped to screen, shoot, pass, and rebound. Most teams in high school and college

32

QUARTERBACKING. Walt Frazier is in the process of trying to make the defense react. He has moved around a screen by Jerry Lucas. What he does now depends on what the Seattle players do.

build around a big man and have him create situations around the foul lane. On the Knicks, we concentrate on a five-man moving game.

Each man has a certain area to protect in the set offense. Corner men should play deep. The pivotman locates in the foul lane area, while the guards work the backcourt. This alignment is important. The idea is to spread the defense and give the offense more room to operate. If the corner men play deep, there is a better chance to develop scoring opportunities within a shorter shooting range.

The guards advance as far as possible without jeopardizing possession. On the Knicks, we use Frazier to apply ballhandling pressure on the defense. He is the quarterback. He must determine if he can penetrate (get around his man) and force the defense to switch, if he should pass off or if he should shoot.

Clyde is uniquely endowed with the ability to analyze quickly what is taking place. He never takes his eyes off the defense. He dribbles without looking at the ball. He works everything in conjunction with the big men. All guards should do that. The function of the little man in pro ball is to get the ball to the big men and work off them.

An effective attack, whether it is set or spontaneous, must have balance. Part of that balance is related to being in a position to switch to defense when the ball changes hands. Some guards like to hit the boards after a shot is taken by their side. That is dangerous.

Offensive rebounding is for big men, though little Dean Meminger has an uncanny knack of getting his hands on our missed shots. We like aggressive basketball and there are times when Meminger should follow his or anyone's shots. In that case, someone has to cover for him in the backcourt should there be a fast break.

If Frazier or Barnett drive inside for a shot, it is up to the corner men to remain alert for the fast break. DeBusschere and Bradley are as good at it as anyone in the league. They not only know when to release and get back on defense, but they are not afraid to expend the extra effort it demands.

Finesse plays an important part in the success of any offense. Players must have the timing for pattern movement. They must know when to pass, cut, change direction, use screens, and set up posts. They must understand why certain moves are made and where they should be made.

We prefer Barnett and Frazier, our guards, to drive the hoop straightaway and not from an angle. It enables our team to respond smoothly. Screens are easier to set up, and Reed can time his moves better.

The forwards create the motion inside. They apply the pressure to the defense by not letting it get set if they keep moving. Bradley weaves in and out, from corner to corner, or reversing if his man chokes him off. Sometimes Bill will scoot back behind a screen for a shot from the corner. Sometimes he will swing all the way around and clear his man out to the backcourt and open it up for Frazier to go backdoor or for Reed to get a jumper.

Reed, our big man, or Lucas must follow the flow of our offense. Depending on the position of the ball, they swing across the foul lane. We like to keep our big men active. They must be prepared to get the ball while they are maneuvering.

It may come from Frazier or Barnett. Sometimes it will come from Bradley or DeBusschere. Most times, if Lucas or Reed are in the pivot, we prefer the ball to come to them from the side where there is less chance of being intercepted—the side where there is less traffic.

THE WEAVE

We like to move the ball out of a weave. The Boston Celtics do it all the time. When I was at City College, the weave was one of Nat Holman's pet maneuvers, and we would spend hours meshing our movements until they flowed. The basic requirement is good ballhandling.

That does not mean dribbling. Holman preferred that we move without putting the ball down. We had drills where three, four, and five men would wheel and deal down the floor without a dribble.

That is what we try to accomplish on the Knicks. Our best game is when the ball moves three or four times without touching the floor. The passes zip around until the ball reaches the open man with the best shot. Every coach in the pros, I think, prefers to have his players move more and dribble less.

The weave puts pressure on the defense because it represents constant motion. It exposes weaknesses and enables the offense to exploit them. It is a good mechanism for a team that is looking for an easy jumper or driving basket. Everything is done on the move.

Players move and screen without the ball. They learn to pass and react quickly in a defensive situation they have created. There are five-man weaves, four-man weaves off a high post, and all sorts of setups off movement.

The weave can create problems for the offensive team. Since it moves so fast, and the players must know where the ball is at all times, it places a strain on spacing and balance. They must keep their heads up to avoid charging their opponents.

It is not extremely difficult to defend against the weave. That is why the offense must avoid passing down the middle, and pass away from an opponent to protect the ball. Change direction on a shifting defense and use the bounce pass. If the defense moves behind a screen, stop and take a jumper. If an opponent plays closely, run him off the pivot or a screen.

GIVE-AND-GO

This was another technique I learned from Nat Holman. He was a firm believer in the instinctive reactions of a player that would enable him to exploit a defense quickly. Give-and-go, or smart basketball, is designed to cut down on mistakes and provide maximum efficiency.

It assumes different forms but the purpose is the same—to work together as a team and set each other up for a scoring opportunity, to operate spontaneously and create purposeful movement. It starts with one player giving the ball to another and going in a direction that has a distinct bearing on what his team is trying to accomplish.

If Frazier should discover his man is turning his head or dropping off too much, he will pass to Bradley and cut for the basket and a return pass. If West thinks he can run his man into a pick, he will give to Wilt and then go for an open spot and the shot. It is a tactic of constant motion with the offense probing for weaknesses.

We blend a lot of give-and-go into our offense. It takes quick reflexes, alert players, good ballhandling, and a keen knowledge of floor position. The ball and the players keep moving until someone gets a good percentage shot or a layup. Lucas made the Knicks an even more effective team in that respect. His addition to the team gave us, in effect, two guards and three forwards at all times. More importantly, it gave us five players on the court who were capable of spontaneous reactions or employing the give-and-go techniques that keep a defense from getting set.

Every man in our lineup is a good passer. Each is capable of hitting a cutting man or making the smart pass when needed. One of the things that makes the Knicks effective is that in Lucas, Bradley, and DeBusschere we think we have the best passing front line in the game. Guards are supposed to be ballhandlers but it is unusual when all your big men, if you will extend us the courtesy of considering the 6-5 Bradley a big man, can also handle the ball well.

This availability of good ballhandling makes a spontaneous style effective. The defense cannot zoom in on the ball without a risk. Each Knick knows how to feint, pass, shoot, and exploit a defensive weakness. They all are capable of doing the things that are necessary when one is stopped.

There was no better example than in the first game of the 1971–72 championship series with the Lakers in Los Angeles. No team ever shot better or moved the ball better or played better fundamental team offense than the Knicks in the first half of that game.

We had thirty-one baskets at the half and twenty-one assists. We kept moving the ball and hitting the open man and making our shots. We missed only one of our first nine shots and that was a block by West on Monroe. We were 16-for-21 at the quarter and 31-for-43 at the half—a .727 shooting percentage.

The Lakers said no team had a right to shoot that way. It was uncanny, unbelievable, and unwarranted. We preferred to think that, while we were hotter than any team had a right to be, we, at least, had done the things that resulted in the shots. Our spontaneous movement was responsible for shaking West, Chamberlain, McMillian, Happy Hairston, and Gail Goodrich on defense.

"We had good shots," explained Bradley, saying it for all the Knicks after we won that first game of the series, 114–92, on LA's court. "We moved the ball well. I thought we played a good, complete game. We took a minimum amount of poor shots and worked the ball."

Bill Sharman, the Laker coach, put it another way. "New York is a great shooting team," he said. "You cannot concentrate on any one man. We didn't react to their movement. We couldn't get to their shooters. New York is smart."

It doesn't always work out that way. We wound up losing the series, 4–1, because Chamberlain went wild and Goodrich did some outstanding shooting and McMillian hit when the Lakers needed it. Also, DeBusschere hurt his side in the second period of the second game and that had an effect on our offense and defense.

We were satisfied that we had played good team ball. Each player had been tuned in. We anticipated the defensive moves and set up our scoring opportunities. We played the kind of ball we had worked hard to perfect through the years. The kind of ball Bradley, DeBusschere, Barnett, Frazier, and Reed had used to win a championship. The kind of ball Lucas adjusted to when he came to the Knicks. Fundamentally, the kind of team ball that was made to order for Jerry's style.

We missed winning another title by only three victories. It was good enough to confirm our faith in our fundamental approach to the game as well as our application of those fundamentals. It was good enough for the Knicks to eliminate Baltimore and Boston on their way to the 1971–72 championship finals.

"Very poised and a very fluid offense and defense," John Havlicek was moved to say of the Knicks. "They never get rattled. They're winners. They have poise, smartness, and experience. If one thing doesn't happen, they make something else happen. They have continuity."

FAST BREAK

The aim of the fast break is to get to the basket before the defense sets up. It is a good weapon against a team that is bigger, stronger, and, possibly, better. In most instances, the fast break must be triggered by a good rebounder who can get the ball out quickly.

On the Knicks that would be Reed or Lucas. They clear the rebound and fire to the release man—either Frazier or Bradley, the middlemen on the break. The middleman must be a good ballhandler. It is his responsibility to bring the ball up court and make the play on the move when it develops.

When a shot is missed, Lucas, or any center, will get the rebound, turn, and look. He might find a teammate at the outer half of the foul circle, or he might see someone along the sideline, opposite the foul line, or near midcourt.

Once the pass is cleared, the man with the ball should come down the floor about eight feet from the sidelines and head for the middle. His teammates on the fast break should peel off to the wings. The rebounder can lay back in case a pass is stolen or, if he can beat his man downcourt, follow the play as a trailer.

The play should go rebound, middleman, wing, middleman, wing, middleman. There should be no wing-to-wing passes unless it is to a man cutting to the hoop for a basket. The less dribbling the better. Each man fills his own lane. The middleman should wind up with the ball and take it to the foul line. Assuming it is a 3-on-2 break, the middleman slows down and looks for his options: (1) hit the wingman who has the best scoring opportunity, (2) stop for a jumper, or (3) drive all the way.

AWAY HE GOES. Los Angeles has cleared the rebound and Jerry West is on his way downcourt. His eyes look straight ahead, and he is going as fast as he can to beat our defense and put it in a hole.

That is the most crucial part of the fast break. The middleman must exploit the opportunity and make sure he does not take the defense off the hook by ignoring his options. There is a tendency to shoot too soon or put your head down and drive or, the worst of all, go up in the air near the foul line, hoping to make the defender commit himself.

Bob Cousy had a problem with Nate Archibald in that respect. Nate, a dangerous man on the fast break, found it difficult to consider the options. He would make up his mind that he was going all the way because of his superior speed, which was easier for the defense to handle. Archibald, though, learned to mix it up. He acquired the knack of slowing down a little while approaching the foul line, giving his teammates a chance to exploit their advantages. He learned that when he was on a 3-on-2, and one defender came at him, that left a teammate open for a pass. Or, if both defenders laid back to protect against his teammates driving in close, he had an easy jumper from the foul line.

Cousy, of course, was in a great position to tell Archibald about what the middleman does on a fast break. He handled the job with outstanding success for the Boston Celtics. He managed to get Nate to work at controlled speed on the fast break and not limit himself as he came into the scoring zone.

The middleman, or the man with the ball, does the feeding, and he must keep that in mind and not look only to score. If Frazier, our middleman, should get tied up around the foul line, it is up to our wingmen, Barnett and Bradley, to swing back for a pass. While it is important that the wingmen fill their lanes all the way downcourt, they must be alert enough to help out if the defense jams the ballhandler.

This is where the trailer is valuable. The defense usually ignores the trailer, mainly because it is shorthanded and has enough trouble worrying about the ball. All it takes is hustle to trail a fast break and quite often it pays off with a basket.

The fast break can be used in any situation where possession changes quickly—even on missed foul shots. One player with the inside position steps away from the lane as his teammate goes for the rebound and taps the ball to him. Or an inside player can tap the rebound back to a guard near the sideline. In either case, the ball is clear and the defense is caught flatfooted by a baseball pass to the outlet man.

The secret is the quick outlet pass and the positioning of the release man to receive it. Lucas and Reed know they should look for Frazier or Bradley when they are triggering a fast break. Frazier handles the release pass 40 percent of the time for us and Bradley 30 percent. It is a good idea to establish the responsibilities of each player and work on them.

Here are a few things to remember: Proper defense positioning. Box out everyone to prevent offensive rebounding. Each player is to remain between his man and the basket—giving the team a chance to sweep the rebound cleanly in order to set up a quick outlet pass before the defense can recover.

It is a good idea to consider the rebounding percentages. Seven of ten shots taken from the left side, with a high trajectory, usually bounce to the right side of the court after hitting the rim, and vice versa. Shots from the side, with a low trajectory, figure to hit the rim and bounce back toward the shooter or rebound toward the middle. The bounce of the straightaway shot is determined by what side of the rim it hits.

Every rebound should be protected by pulling the ball into the body. The pitchout should be no more than fifteen or twenty feet, unless a teammate breaks open deeper than that. Hit the outlet man on the same side of the floor where the rebound is taken.

Keep the lanes well spread. Do not bunch and let the defense move in on the ball. Make the passes short and swift. Use the lob lead pass if a teammate has managed to get behind the defense. Someone should trail the play and someone should hang back in case the ball is stolen and the action suddenly goes the other way.

Fill in the open lanes but trail the play if you cannot find one. The two wingmen should remain slightly ahead of the middleman and cut sharply for the basket at a 45-degree angle as they approach the foul line. The middleman has the responsibility of opening the vital area around the foul lane.

We use the fast break extensively in our scrimmages. We not only learn to use it but, also, to handle it by employing it in our practice sessions. We concentrate on less dribbling and no long passes. We want the ball to move but not to be put on the floor because it slows everything down.

If you have a team at a disadvantage, it is better to pass the ball and keep the defense spread out and guessing. There is not much sense in trying to fast break if there is no advantage. Once the defense is set up, it is wise to go into a controlled offense. Slow things down and call plays.

It takes approximately four seconds to cover the ninety feet from one end of the court to the other. If a defender can hold off the offense on a 2-on-1 break for two to three seconds, he is assured of help from his teammates. By simulating game conditions and rotating defensive assignments, everyone on a squad can get a chance to react in fast-break situations.

We use 2-on-1 and 3-on-2 drills at times even though scrimmaging is more practical—the players have a better chance to react under game conditions. In the 2-on-1 drill, the two outside lanes are on offense and the middle lane is for the defender. We run the drill from one basket to the other in three-man teams, then back the other way.

In the 3-on-2 drill, we divide the court into five lanes. The first, third, and fifth lanes belong to the offense; the second and fourth to the defense. We rotate the players so they get familiar with the lanes and every phase of the fast break.

The Los Angeles Lakers used the fast break with tremendous success to help them win the 1971–72 NBA championship. Bill Sharman employed the tactics he learned as a player with the Boston Celtics and as a teammate of Bill Russell, an expert at the art of triggering the fast break.

Russell, a great rebounder, would wheel and sometimes peg the ball, it seemed, without looking. He knew where his teammates would be and it took only a glance to see if they were open. Sharman had Wilt Chamberlain do the same thing, though Wilt rarely threw to midcourt as often as Russell.

Most times, Chamberlain would get the outlet pass to West and we would find ourselves with Gail Goodrich on one side and Happy Hairston on the other. The fast break was the Lakers' most devastating weapon and it ruined many teams. "The Knicks," said John Havlicek after the playoffs were over, "did a good job against the Lakers' fast break. They did it with good floor balance."

We rotate on offense and always try to keep someone moving to an open spot for floor balance. That is one way of having some protection against the fast break. Floor balance and aggressive rebounding to slow down and pressure the outlet pass are the best weapons. One without the other minimizes the solution. If there is aggressive rebounding without floor balance, then the Lakers can sneak Hairston deep for a long pass and an easy basket. If there is floor balance without aggressive rebounding, then the Lakers can control the defensive board too easily.

The Knicks do not fast break all the time. We prefer to use it only when the opportunity occurs. Some teams use it to force a defense off balance. Some teams use it to accelerate things against an opponent that likes to slow things down.

We prefer a blend of controlled ball and the fast break. If we cannot gain an advantage by breaking across midcourt, we slow it down and begin looking to hit the open man. We do not try to go all the way if the opening is not there. A team has to be patient. If the quick scoring opportunity is not there, work until you can get a percentage shot.

SPECIAL SKILLS

It is fine if a coach can put together a team with balanced skills. I have been fortunate with the Knicks to have that type of player. We have worked on developing a balance that does not place emphasis on any one player.

Yet there are those situations where certain players have certain dominating skills, and they must be exploited. Milwaukee, for example, with Kareem Abdul-Jabbar. He has such offensive ability that the Bucks work almost everything off the pivot.

That doesn't mean Jabbar takes all the shots. He does, however, handle the ball most of the time. The Bucks use him as a screen to cut off for the basket or jump shots. He either passes off or wheels and shoots.

The pivot play was discovered by accident or through the resourcefulness of the Original Celtics. They were on a tour in the 1925–26 season and appeared in Chattanooga. They ran into an unusually tough defense. They floated a guard around the middle and made it difficult for the Celtics to penetrate their passes.

They called time to discuss the situation. "We'll have to get that guy out of there," said Johnny Beckman. "He's breaking up our passing game." There was a moment of silence as the players thought.

"How about me playing in front of him and blocking him away from the passes?" suggested Dutch Dehnert. "You can pass the ball to me and I'll pass back. That way he'll be busy guarding me and you guys can work your plays."

That did it. That added a dimension to basketball that helped the big man. The pivot play was born. It became sophisticated. Most pro teams use the high and low post. When we have Reed at center, we go to the low post more often because he is strong and a good shooter. We use Lucas on the high post more than Reed because Jerry is an excellent ballhandler and has outstanding shooting range.

A big man does not have to be a good shooter to play the pivot. Wilt Chamberlain is the best example. He knows how to handle the ball and sets an effective pick with his huge body. He led the league in assists the season (1966–67) the Philadelphia 76ers won the championship.

We like our pivot men to move. We do not concentrate on their scoring. We want them to maneuver the defense out of position and screen for their teammates. We want them to be a part of the offense not *The* offense.

Lucas sort of revolutionized our thinking after he joined the Knicks. The NBA was a league of towering centers and nobody really expected a team with a 6-9 center to attain any degree of success. Yet, we came so close to winning our second title with Lucas taking over when Reed could play only eleven games.

We did not build our offense around Jerry, but he handled the ball a lot both in the low and high post. His was an active pivot that added to our

3
EW YORK
10

motion. We used him in the championship series with the Lakers to pull Chamberlain away from the board. We did the same thing against Wes Unseld and Baltimore.

Dave Cowens of Boston was another thing. Cowens is a lot quicker and mobile than Chamberlain and Unseld, so he was able to come out and neutralize Lucas' shooting threat from outside. We sent Jerry inside more against the Celtics and had him pick and set screens for Bradley and DeBusschere.

Elvin Hayes is a different kind of pivot. He is mainly a shooter. When he was with the Houston Rockets, they played more of a freewheeling game because of him. They weaved and set screens and attempted to give the ball to Hayes in good scoring position for his turnaround jumper.

Nate Thurmond of the Golden State Warriors is another active pivot player who prefers to play the low post. He has a good turnaround jumper from the key or along the baseline. He also has a rolling hook that is dangerous if he is not pressed away from the basket. He knows how to handle the ball and use his body to help free his teammates.

Tom Boerwinkle is not a scorer in the Chicago Bulls' attack but is very effective in the pivot. Dick Motta, the coach, likes to play him in the high post above the foul line with the guards around him. Boerwinkle has the sizeable body that can move into the low post and screen for jumpers by Chet Walker and Bob Love. Big Tom is strong enough not to be moved out of a spot once he acquires it, making it easier for a team to work plays off him.

Bill Russell was not a good shooter but the Celtics built their offense around his play in the pivot. He was an exceptional ballhandler and intelligent player. He would handle the ball above the foul line and give it to the Celtic who came up with the best shot out of the weave they constantly used. He would move inside to exploit the defense and occasionally turn in for a hook shot but mostly to set screens and pass off.

It is fundamental that a pivot man should rely on plays if he is out of his shooting range. In that respect, he should always try to maneuver into his best position. He should not let the defense dictate where because it is concentrating on forcing him into a bad position. He should keep moving so that the defense cannot get set and block him out of the position he desires. A fake or two without the ball helps.

Most big men in the pivot prefer the hook shot; few in the NBA have good outside shots. Their range is limited. Reed and Lucas are exceptions.

A BIG PROBLEM. Wilt Chamberlain shows why it is difficult to play him in the pivot. There is no way Jerry Lucas can reach out and take the ball. Wilt can give it to Jim McMillian or some other Laker or keep it and roll in for a shot.

Don Smith of the Seattle SuperSonics can hit from about fifteen feet away because he is a forward who was converted to center.

The turnaround jumper has been the most dramatic shooting development for the big men in the NBA. Most of the players who work the pivot are capable of scoring with it from a range of about ten feet. Thurmond, Hayes, and Reed have the best range.

Chamberlain and the more powerful pivot players employ the roll in. Abdul-Jabbar has added a fake and reverse roll because of his quickness. Lucas can do the same thing against a defender who does not react quickly.

For years the Lakers took advantage of the special skills of Elgin Baylor and Jerry West. They built their offense around the shooting of these two, neither of whom was limited to shooting. One of the reasons why Los Angeles traded for Chamberlain was to have Wilt screen for them.

Boston, a well-balanced team in the championship years, had a different problem when some of the stars retired. Most of the burden in the rebuilding fell on John Havlicek. The addition of a fine shooter in Jo-Jo White eased the strain on the offense. Yet, when it counts, the Celtics prefer to rely on the special skills of White and Havlicek.

By the nature of pro basketball, there can be no such thing as a one-man team. There never should be a one-man team under any conditions; it is easier to defend against. Bill Russell was great, maybe the greatest, but he could not have done it all alone. If the other teams had only Russell to worry about, the Celtics would not have won the title so often.

Our success with the Milwaukee Bucks is a fine example. We have some outstanding individual players. But we have no super players in the class of Abdul-Jabbar and Oscar Robertson. Yet we have been able to puzzle many people over our ability to beat Milwaukee more often than it beats us because of team balance. We are a five-man team at all times and that makes it more difficult for a defense to handle.

Things to remember about team offense:

1. Basketball is a five-man game, and only one man can have the ball, so learn to move without it.

2. Keep moving. Do not stand around and watch the ball.

3. Establish a well-balanced attack. The efficient team is one that strikes a balance between the fast break and controlled offense.

4. Call plays against a defense that is set up. Get to know options so well that they can be employed instinctively when a play does not work.

LONG RANGE. There is little time for the defense to relax when a team has a mobile center like Jerry Lucas. He adds to the resourcefulness of a team offense with his ability to hit from outside.

13

In other words, be prepared to work a series, as we do on the Knicks. Some teams, such as the Celtics, like to call all their plays. We call some while others just come in the natural flow of the game because our players know each other so well.

5. If the other team is hurting you with an accelerated offense, it may be wise not to run with it. Slow things down. Work some patterns. Try to control the pace of the game.

6. Spread out against the press. Use as much of the court as possible. Avoid dribbling unless you are 1-on-1 and can get around the man without moving into a trap. Short passes have less chance of being intercepted by a team that is gambling to steal the ball. Avoid crossing and come back to help a teammate in danger. Know where your teammates are at all times in case you need an alternate receiver.

7. If you are freezing the ball, take your time. Spread out and make sure of the passes. Let the best dribbler handle the ball and meet all passes. Stay away from the middle where the defense is most likely to jam up. Do not cross and give the defense a chance to double up on the ball. Avoid being trapped in the corners. Move laterally from sideline to sideline and use screens to free teammates for the ball. Be aware of the ten-second line. Score only if a layup is sure but keep in mind that two more points is not necessary if you are leading and time is running out. If stuck, call a time-out to avoid a jump ball. We won a big game against Baltimore in the 1971–72 playoffs because Earl Monroe was trapped in a corner and was alert enough to call time before he got tied up. Take your man away from the ball once you have given it up.

8. Maintain floor balance, especially against a fast-breaking team with an outstanding rebounder. Players should rotate with the purpose of having someone always in position to protect against a sneak attack.

9. Do not hurry shots. If a play does not work, start over. Be patient. That may sound strange coming from one who is involved with the twenty-four-second clock, but it remains true in the NBA. A basket scored just before the buzzer counts just as much as one scored with fifteen seconds left on the clock. A good team is one that is not rattled by the clock and works to get a good shot.

10. Players should move with a purpose. If you are not in on a play, clear your man out or set a screen for a teammate. That is the kind of team movement we try to create on the Knicks. If Bradley gives the ball to Frazier, we know Bill is either going to run behind a screen or move to the opposite side to set one on the weak side.

11. Keep the offense simple. Forget the fancy stuff. Work the ball in as close as possible.

12. Cut down on dribbling. Use a passing attack. Move the ball around. There have been times when the Knicks have made four or five passes without the ball touching the floor and it ended with a basket.

13. Use the give-and-go against players and teams that play the ball. Also against a team that does not switch well. It is a system that develops good teamwork. We use it on the Knicks because it creates the kind of team movement we prefer. We keep giving the ball up and going to different spots on the floor while looking to create a defensive mistake. Maybe someone will turn his head. Maybe we can run someone into a pick. Maybe Frazier can give the ball to Lucas and then cut behind him for a return pass and a shot.

14. Designate someone on the floor to call the plays. There can be mass confusion otherwise. That does not mean a teammate cannot suggest a play if he detects some defensive weakness. Jerry Lucas noticed that Wilt Chamberlain would play him tightly above the foul line but differently on the side of the lane. So Lucas suggested we run one of our plays a little wider toward the sidelines to give him a shot behind a screen.

15. In the pros, where everyone is a good shooter, we believe in the guards keeping the forwards happy. The guards can shoot anytime because they have the ball so much, but we prefer they look for the forwards. That keeps everyone happy and helps create an unselfish attitude and good teamwork.

16. Never underestimate the defense. Keep it busy at all times, but never forget the other team is just as smart, sometimes smarter, than you. So work your plays crisply. Protect the ball and make sure passes. Move with or without the ball. Generally speaking, it is the passer's fault if something goes wrong—unless the ball goes right through a man's hands.

CHAPTER

8

SPECIAL PLAYS

Nothing is overlooked in the game of pro basketball. Every second must be considered. Every second must be treated with importance. There is no way of knowing just what play will determine the winner in a forty-eight-minute conflict.

That is why we prepare for any eventuality. We even carry it down to working on last-second plays. When a game comes down to the final tick of a clock, as it often does, that is no time to start improvising. A team had better be ready.

I remember a game the Knicks played against the Detroit Pistons in Madison Square Garden during the 1970–71 season. We were losing by a point when the Pistons scored with one second to go. We called time. In the NBA, a time-out in the last two minutes of the game allows a team to pass-in from midcourt when play resumes.

We huddled. We ran over our last-second play. The one we had practiced for just such an occasion. We had tried it once before in a game but it didn't work. Joe Caldwell, then with the Atlanta Hawks, pressed Walt Frazier on the sideline and deflected the pass-in.

There was another time the Boston Celtics tried it on the Knicks. It failed then, also, because Willis Reed got in front of Bill Russell near the hoop. Russell had to take the lob pass and put it in over Reed and wound up hitting the floor so hard, they had to take him to the hospital.

They kept Bill overnight but he got his clothes out of the closet and sneaked out of the hospital. It is difficult to forget that incident because it occurred near the end of the 1968–69 season and Russell did not play again until the playoffs. Then the Celtics, finishing fourth in the Eastern Division, swept to the championship by defeating the Lakers, making Russell's last hurrah an exciting one.

This time we made the play succeed against the Pistons for victory. Frazier took the ball out near midcourt. Bradley and DeBusschere moved toward the pass-in to create a flow in that direction. Reed rolled to the hoop and took a lob pass from Frazier and banked it in off the board while in the air.

Bang, bang. Just like that we had won. It seemed impossible with only one second to go and the ball over forty feet from the basket but we had done it. We have learned there is nothing impossible, so we prepare for every possibility.

So do the other teams. Baltimore used an option on our last-second play to almost beat us out of a game in the 1971–72 season. Instead of lobbing the pass at the hoop, it was thrown to Wes Unseld along the baseline at the far side of the basket. The Bullets had set a pick to free Wes for a short jumper because there were only two seconds left—enough time for a shot. Unseld missed, fortunately.

We work on situation plays. What to do when there is a jump ball. What to do in out-of-bounds situations. What to do when a game comes down to a final shot.

There are few surprises in these special plays. Every team uses them. The key is execution. Know the fundamentals and apply them. Plays are only as good as they work.

TAP PLAYS

It is a rare occasion when the Knicks have an edge with the center jump. If Willis Reed is playing, he sometimes runs into an opponent who does not tower over him too much and he has a chance to get the tap. Jerry Lucas has a more difficult problem because he is smaller—the smallest center in the league.

32
18

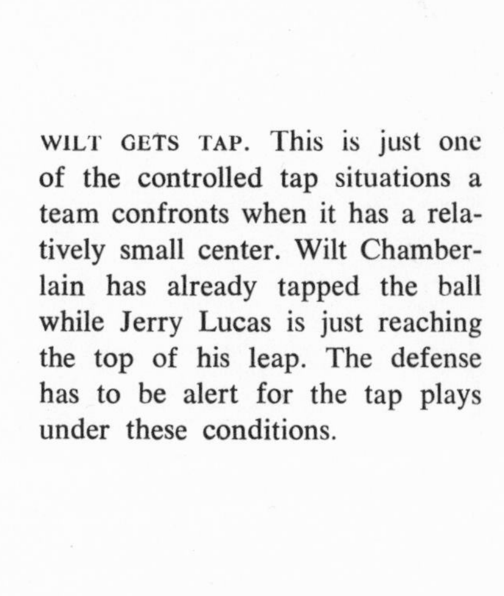

WILT GETS TAP. This is just one of the controlled tap situations a team confronts when it has a relatively small center. Wilt Chamberlain has already tapped the ball while Jerry Lucas is just reaching the top of his leap. The defense has to be alert for the tap plays under these conditions.

Diagram 8-1 Tap Play at Center Jump or Held Ball: Guard Around

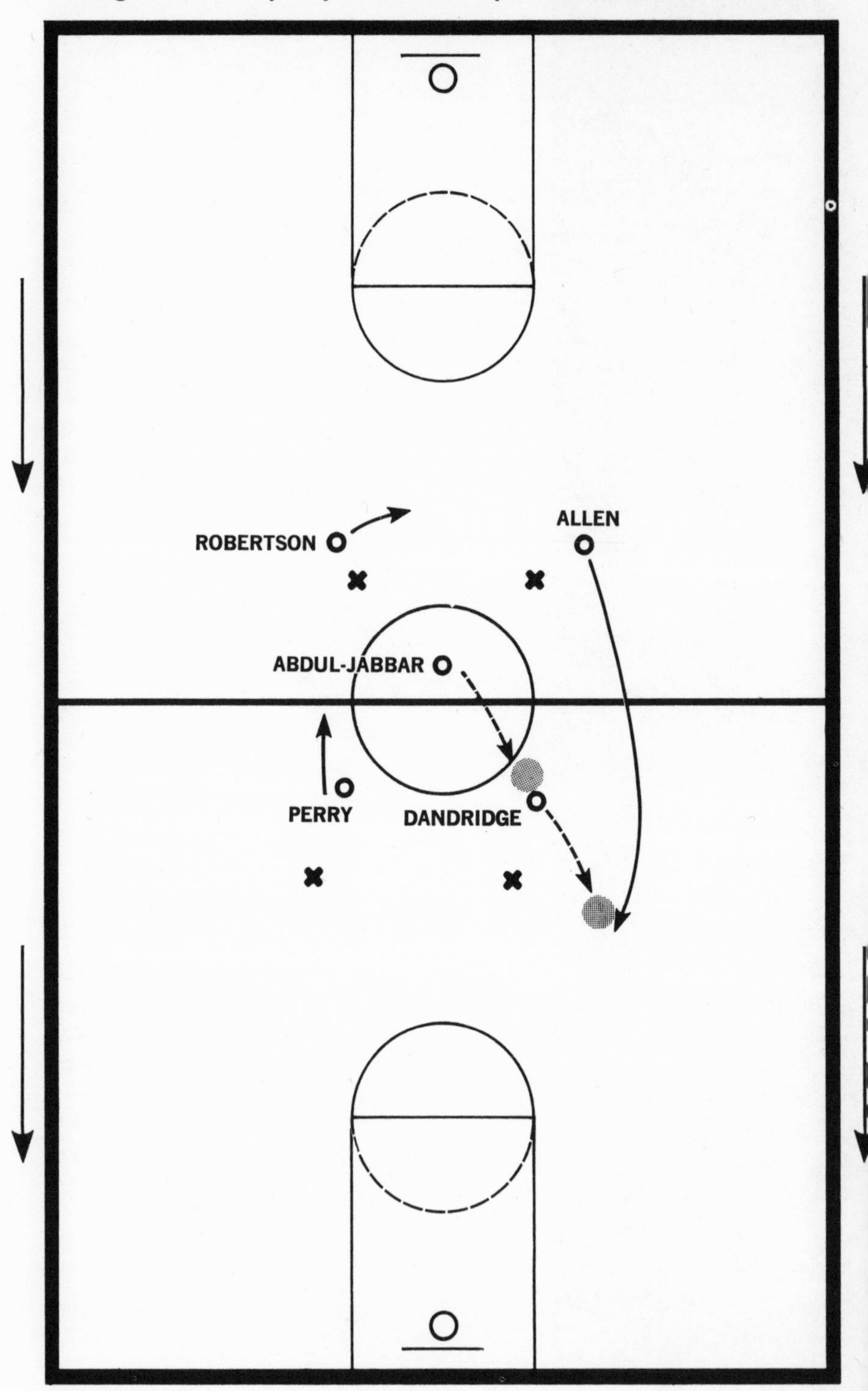

Most teams use the "box" when they think they can control the tap. Milwaukee, with Kareem Abdul-Jabbar, will put Bob Dandridge and Curtis Perry up ahead and keep Oscar Robertson and Lucius Allen back. Kareem will tap to Dandridge and Allen will cut past him to take a pass and drive for the basket. Perry and Robertson are responsible for protecting on defense in case something goes wrong (see diagram 8-1).

There is a simple option. Kareem taps to Dandridge but this time Robertson breaks past Perry, using him as a screen, to take a pass and is off to the basket. Perry and Allen protect on this one (see diagram 8-2).

Some teams use the 1-1-3 in the front court when they think they can control the tap. The Lakers, for example, when they had Elgin Baylor playing and Wilt Chamberlain at center, might like to set up Elgin in a 1-on-1 situation. Baylor would take a position below the foul line and ahead of Wilt. The other Lakers, Happy Hairston, Gail Goodrich, and Jerry West, would line up behind Wilt. That way, they kept the defense from bunching near the basket.

Wilt would tap to Baylor, who had a shot, or could pass off to West as he sliced around Chamberlain. The Lakers might even have Goodrich crisscross with West and give Baylor another target (see diagram 8-3).

In all these plays, the positions are interchangeable. For example, should Baylor be involved in the tap, Wilt would assume the front position. Should West be jumping, Baylor would move to his spot. The idea is to maintain floor balance at all times, never forgetting that the object is to get the ball no matter how serious the mismatch.

When the other team figures to win the center jump, then a steal formation may be used—maybe the 1-3-1. John Havlicek and Jo-Jo White flank Dave Cowens, with Don Nelson up ahead and Don Chaney back. Havlicek and White will try to steal the tap. No matter what happens, this formation enables a team to maintain a strong defensive position if it does not come up with a steal.

There is a box variation. Havlicek and Nelson are up front, with Chaney and White back. As soon as the referee throws up the ball, Havlicek and Nelson break toward Chaney and White. The idea is to double up on the opponent for whom the ball is intended. This is another play that may be used against a team that figures to dominate the tap (see diagram 8-4).

The 2-1-1-1 is an effective formation for which to run plays off a center jump that can be controlled. Nate Thurmond will tap the ball to Cazzie Russell and break around him. Clyde Lee screens for Jeff Mullins and then breaks down the middle if his man switches to Mullins. The Golden State

Diagram 8-2 Option: Opposite Guard Around

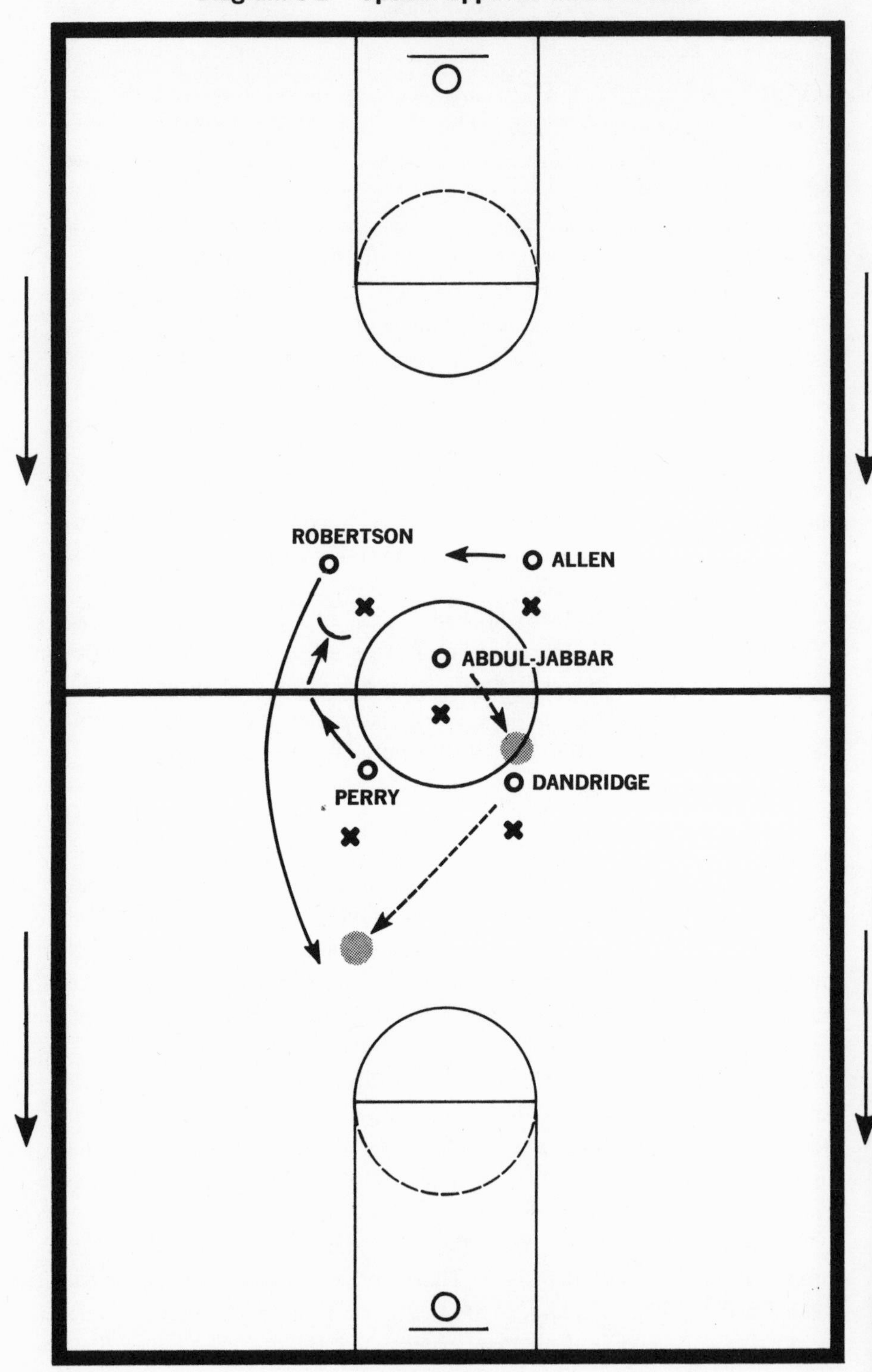

Diagram 8-3 Front-Court Play: Control of Tap-Certain—a 1-1-3 Formation

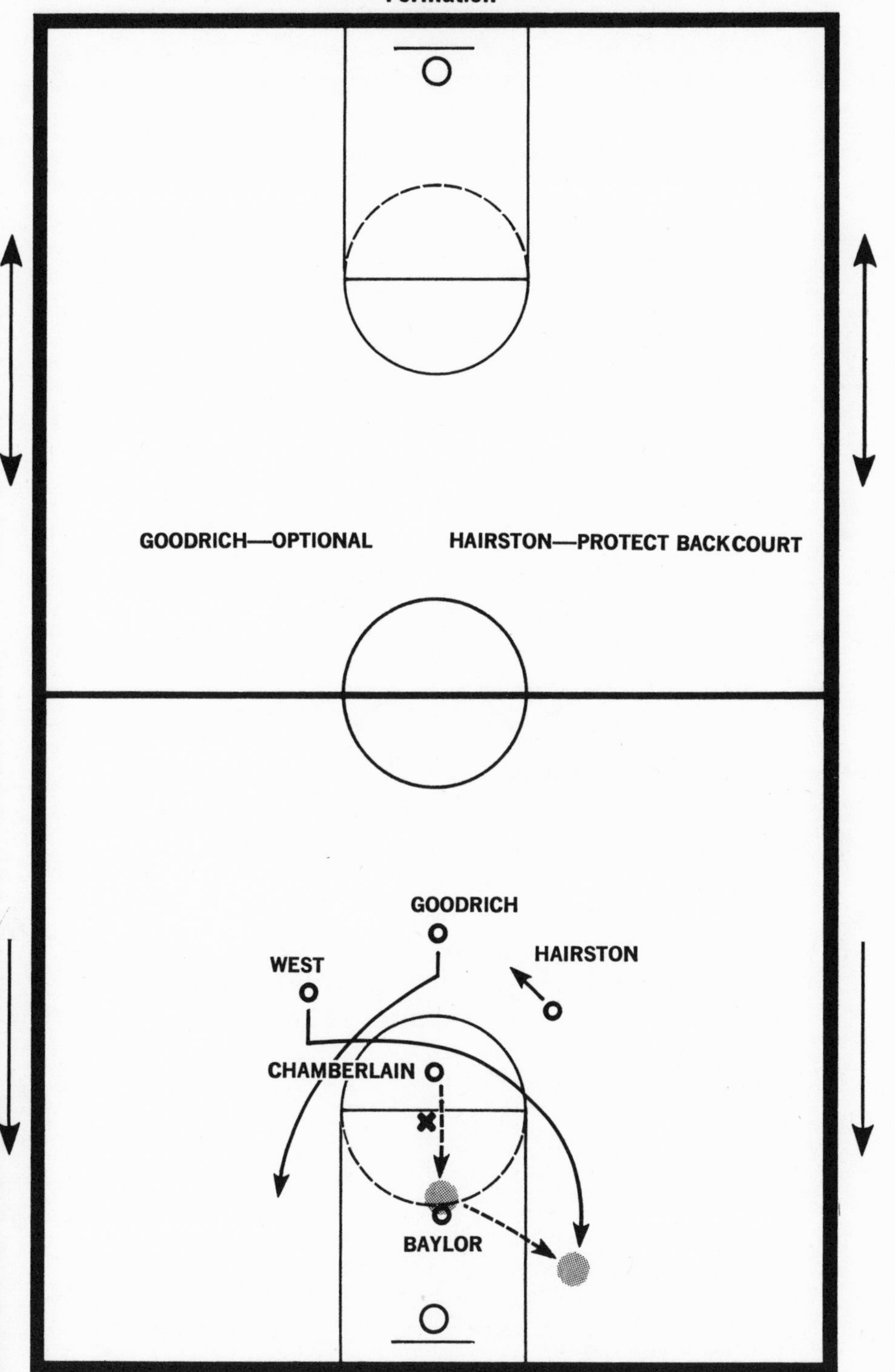

Diagram 8-4   Defense Against Opponents' Control of Tap

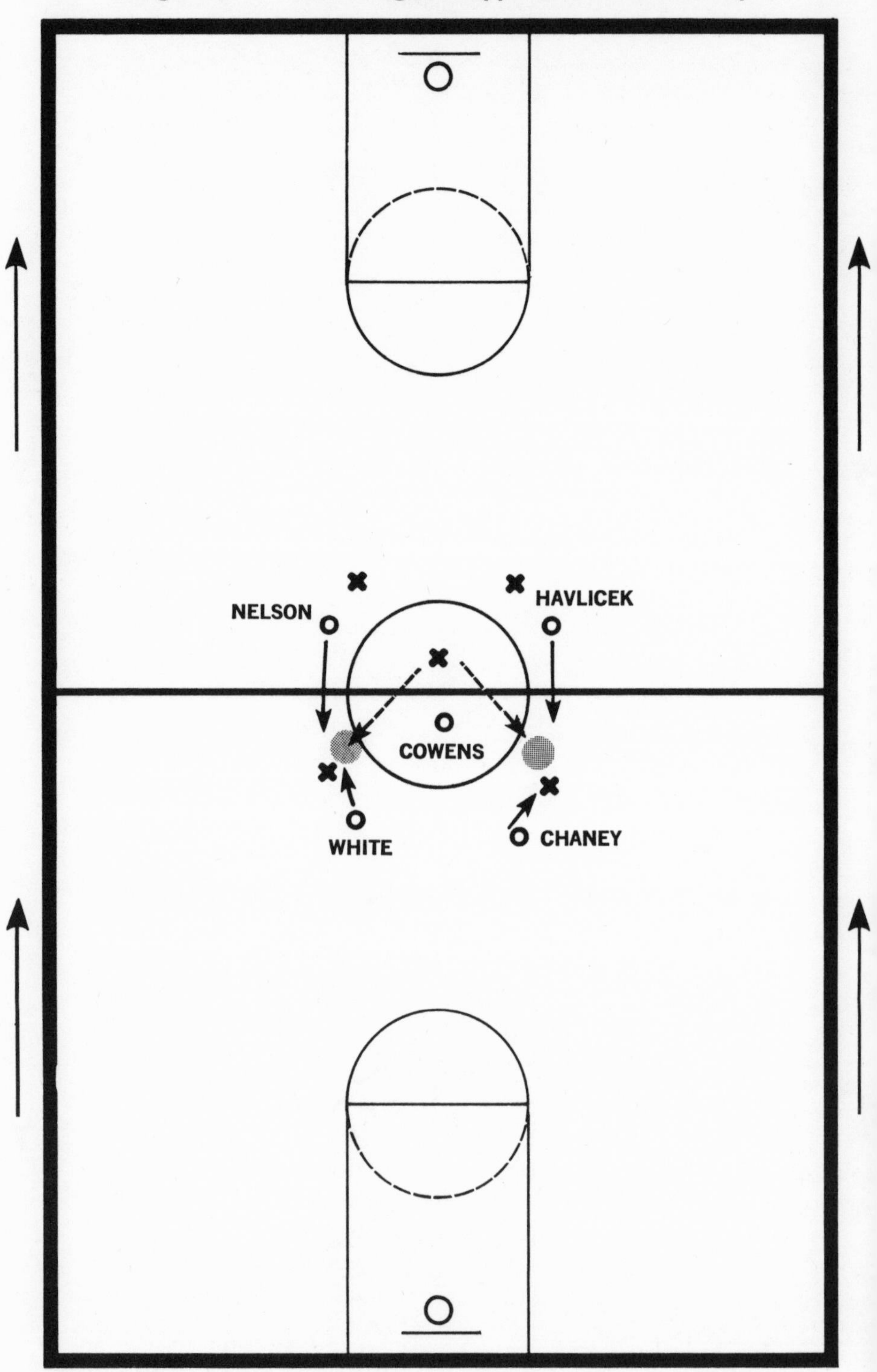

Diagram 8-5 Offense Held Ball: Play for a Mobile Big Man and Assured Tap Control

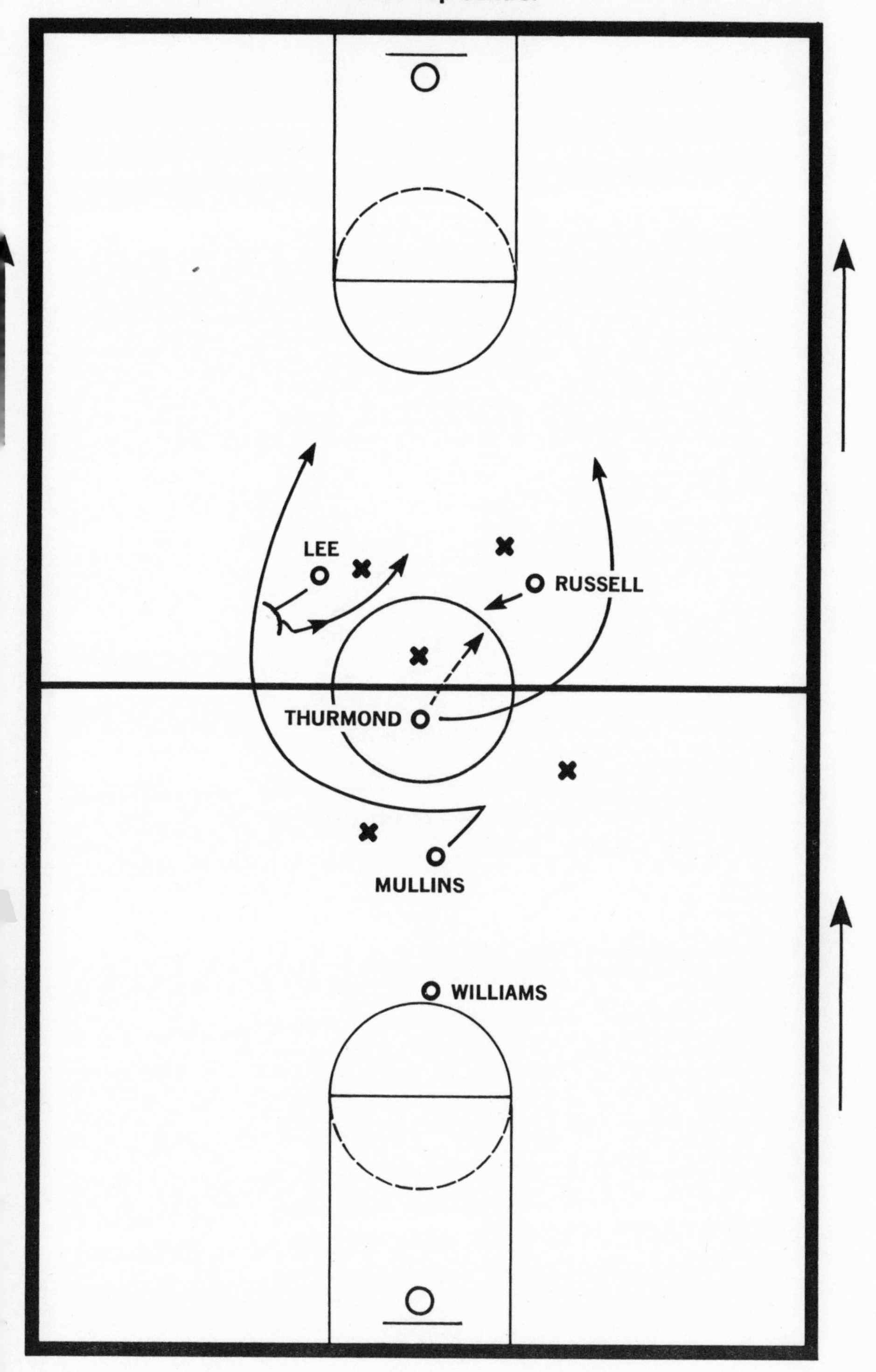

Diagram 8-6 Defense Against Opponents' Control of Tap

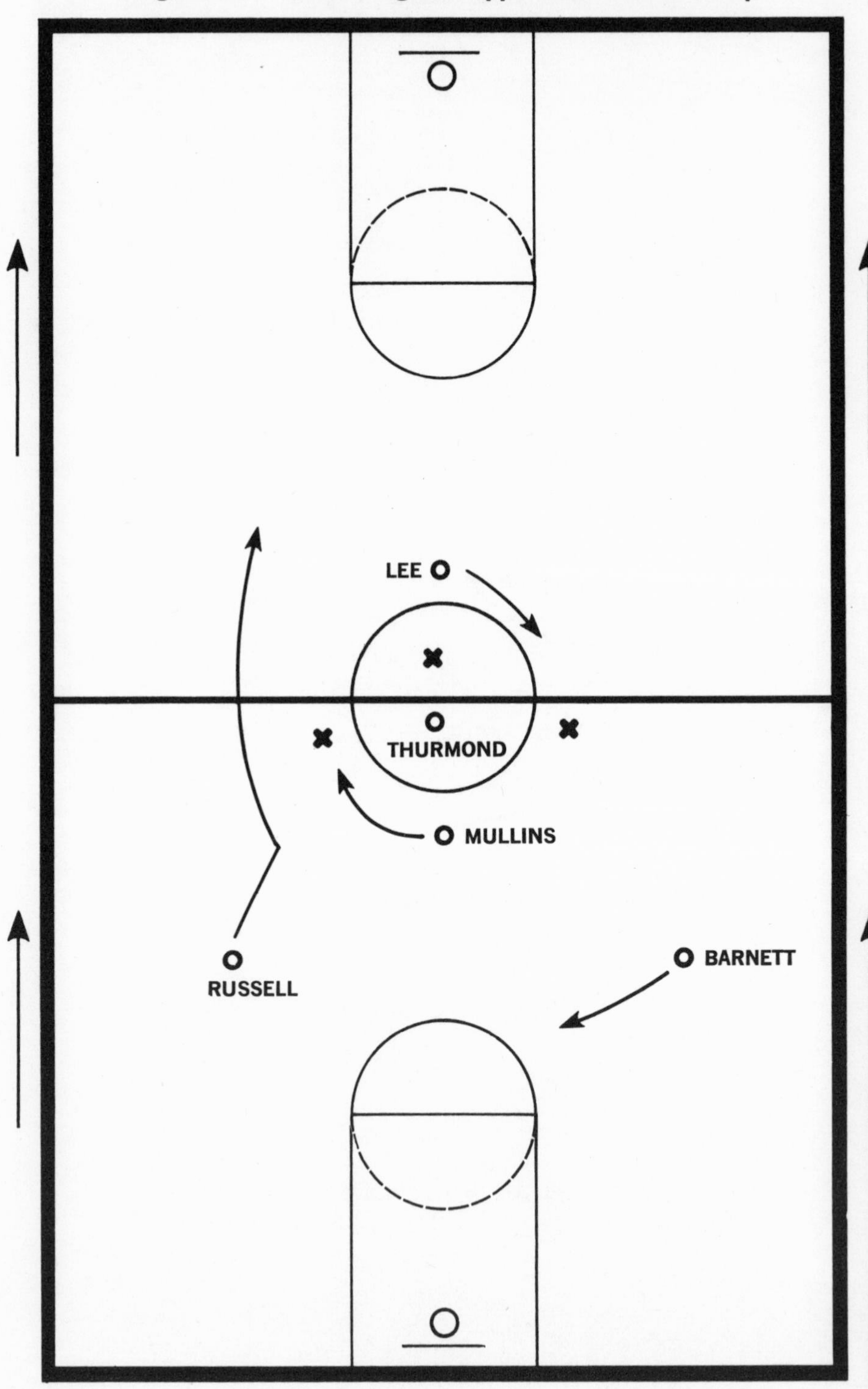

Warriors have three men heading for the hoop in Thurmond, Mullins, and Lee (see diagram 8-5).

The 1-1-1-2 offers a defensive formation that creates the opportunity to steal the ball. While the opponent may control the tap, the defensive team has enough men back to protect. In addition, Thurmond might be able to tap the ball back to Mullins and set off a play. Russell will break when Mullins gets the ball and take a pass. Mullins will swing around Russell while Thurmond breaks for the basket. If Lee or Mullins steal, Russell breaks for the basket (see diagram 8-6).

There are backcourt plays for jump ball situations, but since there are no guarantees that a team will control the ball at any time, it is safer to think defensively when you are close to the opponent's basket. The big men should set up deep and the guards play back. Connie Hawkins and Gus Johnson of Phoenix protect the inside by playing between their men and the basket. Dick Van Arsdale, the guard, "cheats" and lines up even with Neal Walk, the center, while Clem Haskins, the other guard, lays back. Van is in position to go either way: toward his own basket should Walk get the tap or to the inside should the ball go that way (see diagram 8-7).

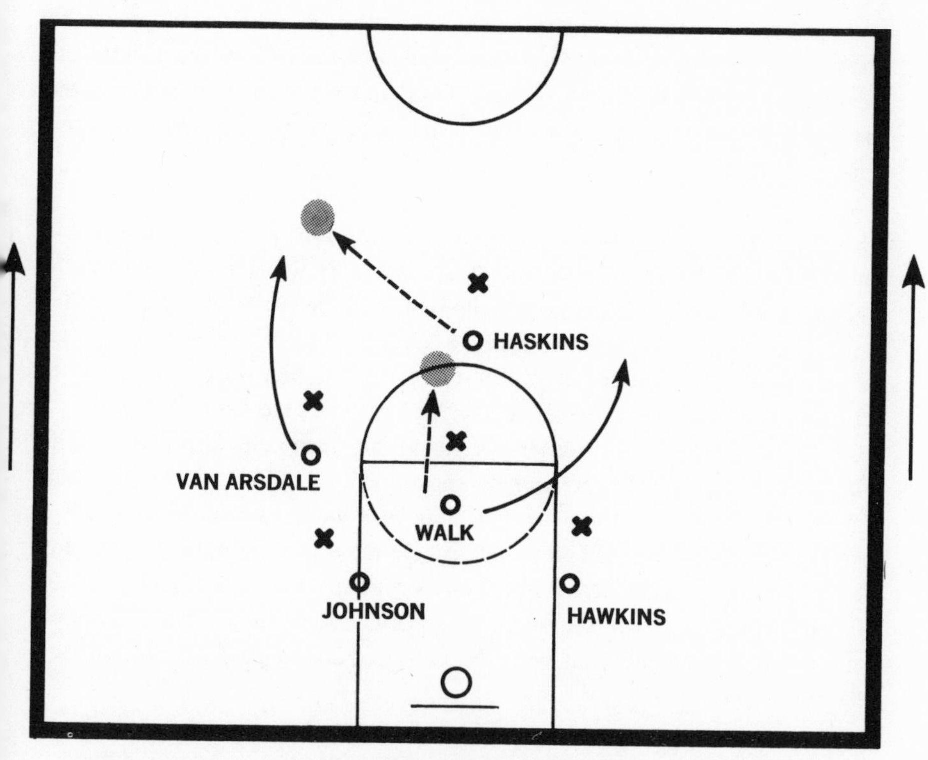

Diagram 8-7 Defensive Formation in Backcourt (Although Tap Control is Assured)

There was a fine example of what an alert defense can do on a tap play in one of the NCAA playoffs. Jacksonville had a one-point lead and was seemingly in position to control the tap after a held ball. Jacksonville used a back tap that was stolen and led to a winning layup as the buzzer sounded to end the game.

OUT-OF-BOUNDS PLAYS

These plays are generally confined to the attacking zone. They are either for use along the sidelines or under the basket. Sometimes you may see the weirdest formations: Four men lining up like the forward wall of the Minnesota Vikings. Four men lining up one behind the other like the chow line in an Army mess hall. Four men linking their arms in a human chain as the Boston Celtics do at times. Anything and everything to effect the pass-in and score if possible.

Why should a coach spend time on such special plays when a routine play might be sufficient? It has been estimated that a team gets the ball out-of-bounds in its own territory anywhere from ten to fifteen times a game, which means scoring opportunities for a potential thirty points.

That is a lot of points when you consider how many games are won by a point or two. Most of these plays are based on screens and picks to create a good shot. It is obvious that the nearer the basket, the greater the scoring opportunity. Therefore, the plays under the basket or along the baseline are designed for a quicker score than those out-of-bounds plays along the sidelines.

On plays from under the basket many teams use their big man to screen. Bob Lanier of Detroit will set up alongside the foul lane. Bill Hewitt will cut off him and take a pass from Dave Bing. If the defense switches to pick up Hewitt, then Bing can give the ball to Lanier for a shot. On another option, Lanier feints right and breaks left. Bing gives him a bounce pass and cuts around him for a return pass, leaving him with a shot or in position to hit Curtis Rowe as he slices off Hewitt (see diagram 8-8).

All pro teams have at least two good big men and effective outside shooters. That kind of personnel lends itself to a box formation. Wilt Chamberlain sets up along the foul lane and moves across to establish a screen for Jim McMillian. Now, Happy Hairston has the option of passing to McMillian, cutting across the lane, or giving the ball to Jerry West, moving behind a screen set by Gail Goodrich. If nothing works, Hairston can sweep around the man with the ball and take a pass for a shot (see diagram 8-9).

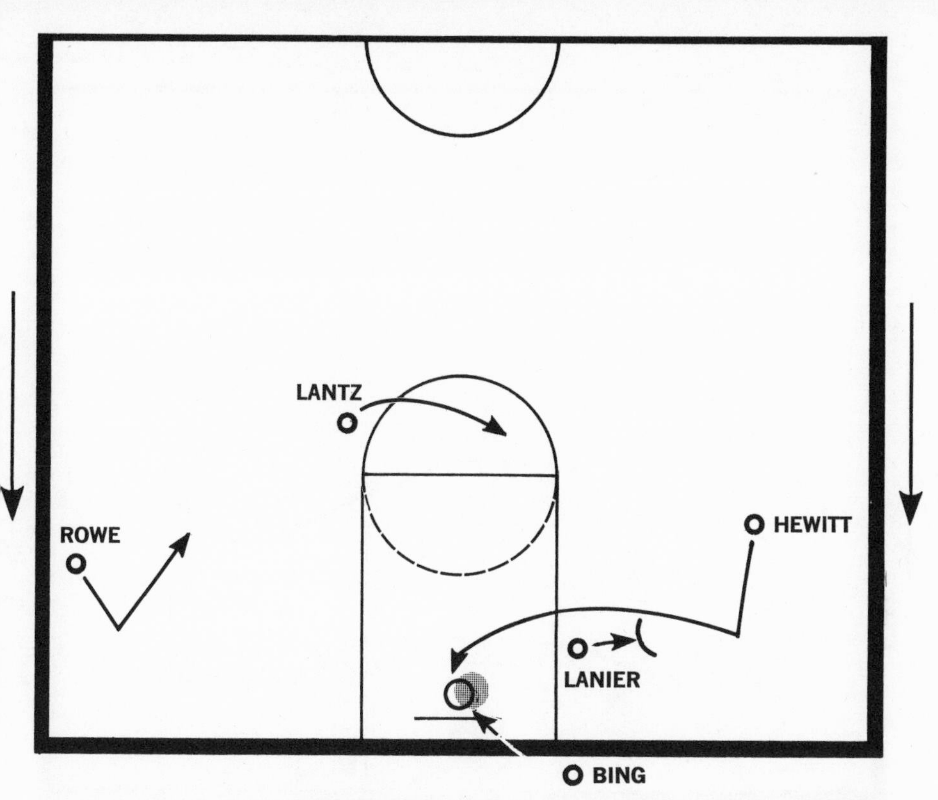

Diagram 8-8 Out-of-Bounds Underneath: Big Man Screen with Options

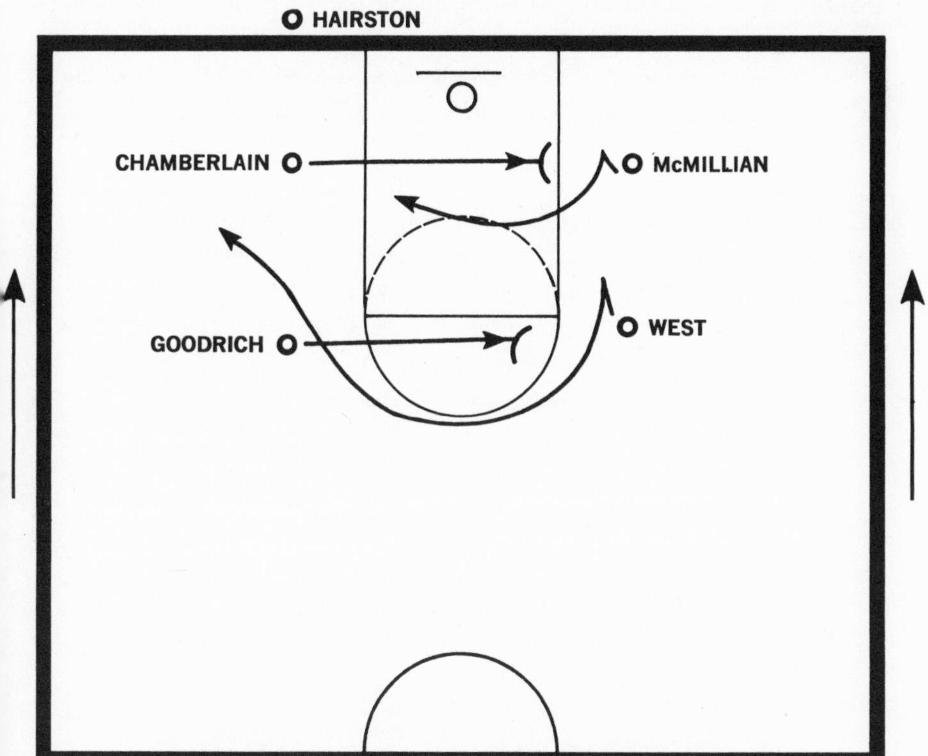

Diagram 8-9 Out-of-Bounds Underneath: Box Formation

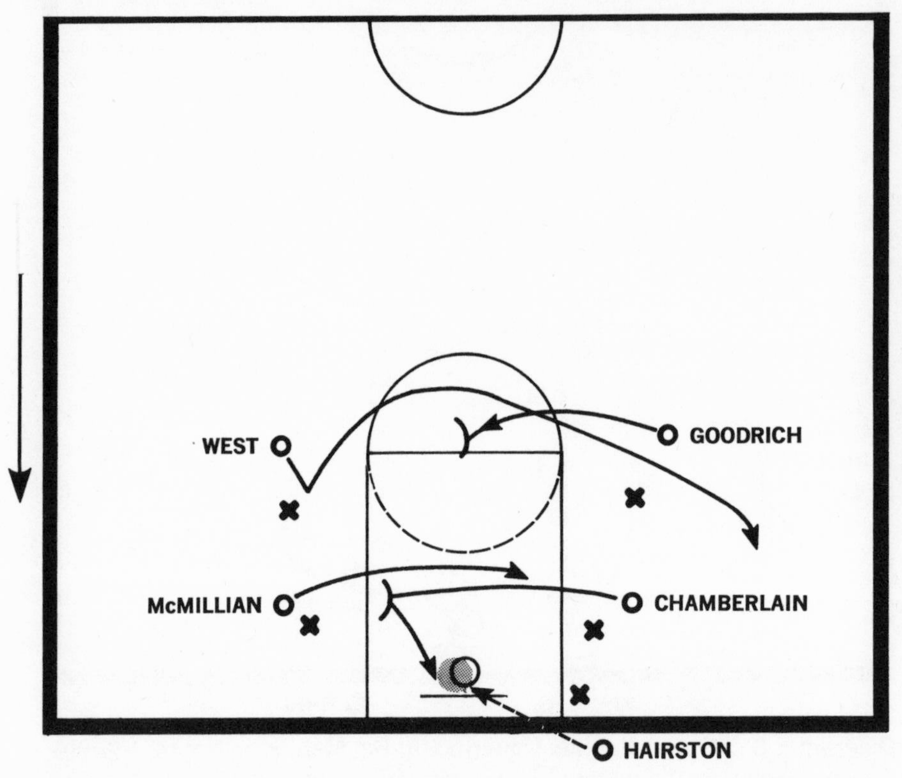

Diagram 8-10 Out-of-Bounds Underneath: Variation on Box Formation

Now, on an option, if Chamberlain's man switches to McMillian, then Wilt may be able to roll in and take a pass before the defense can react (see diagram 8-10).

Suppose the Boston Celtics want to set up John Havlicek, a fine outside shooter. Dave Cowens, Satch Sanders, and Jo-Jo White can line up along the foul line, with Havlicek behind them. If Havlicek cannot receive the in-bounds pass, Cowens can break toward Chaney for a possible pass or to set up a screen so Chaney can take a shot. Meanwhile, Sanders can set a trap on White's opponent—screening for Jo-Jo so he can take the in-bounds pass from Chaney for a possible layup (see diagram 8-11).

Another play for a good shooter such as Havlicek can involve a crisscross around the post. On this one, Sanders, the decoy, and White crisscross around Cowens. Now Havlicek fakes a cut around Cowens but stops and steps back for the out-of-bounds pass from Chaney and the shot. Sanders and White are in excellent position for the rebound.

In another situation, the shooter can be set up with a double screen at the foul line. Sanders drives his man toward the hoop, then moves to his

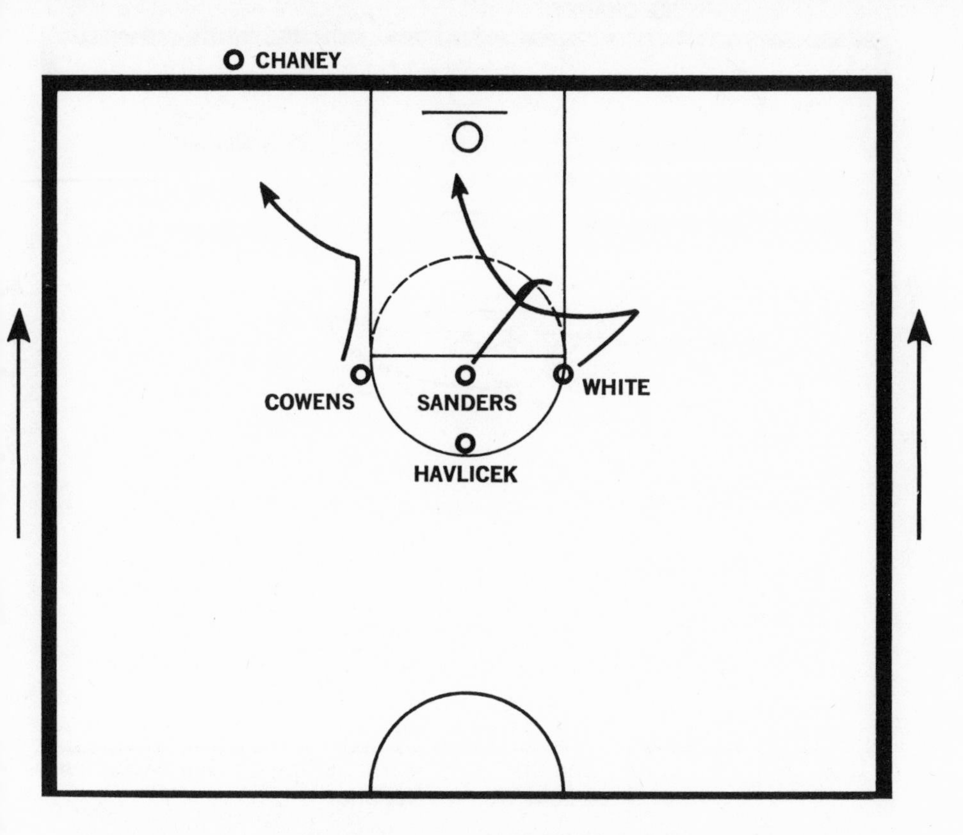

Diagram 8-11 Out-of-Bounds Underneath: Three Men on Foul Line

left to take the in-bounds pass from Chaney. In the meantime, Cowens and White move to the foul line to set up a double screen. Havlicek cuts behind them for a pass from Sanders and a shot (see diagram 8-12).

Cleveland has an outstanding shooter in Austin Carr. The Cavaliers would prefer to set him up in a sticky situation. Carr lines up behind Walt Wesley, the center. Now Butch Beard and John Johnson crisscross to draw the defense with them. Dave Sorenson flips the ball to Carr for the shot or, should Johnson or Beard break free, he can pass to either of them (see diagram 8-13).

The Philadelphia 76ers might use a slice off the high post to set up a guard going in for a weakside pass. Luke Jackson will take the ball out under the basket. Hal Greer fakes going left then cuts around Bill Bridges and heads for the basket, where he gets a bounce pass from Jackson. In the meantime, Bill Cunningham decoys by faking a cut to the basket. That enables Bridges to release and come around Cunningham for a safety pass should the defense stop Greer.

One popular formation is the lining up of four players across the foul

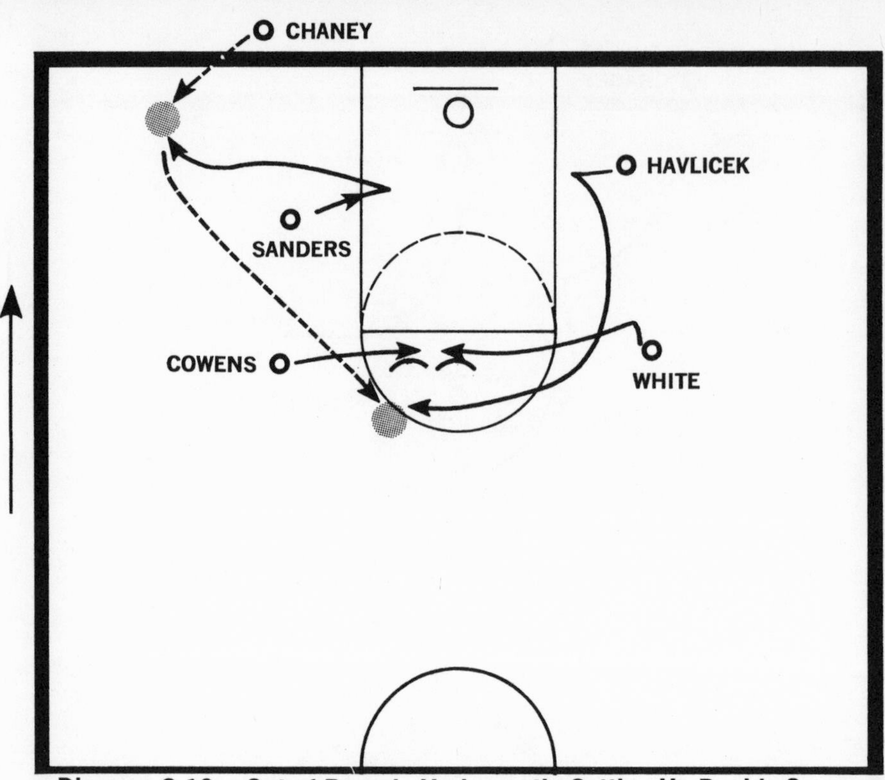

Diagram 8-12 Out-of-Bounds Underneath: Setting Up Double Screen at Foul Line for Set Shot

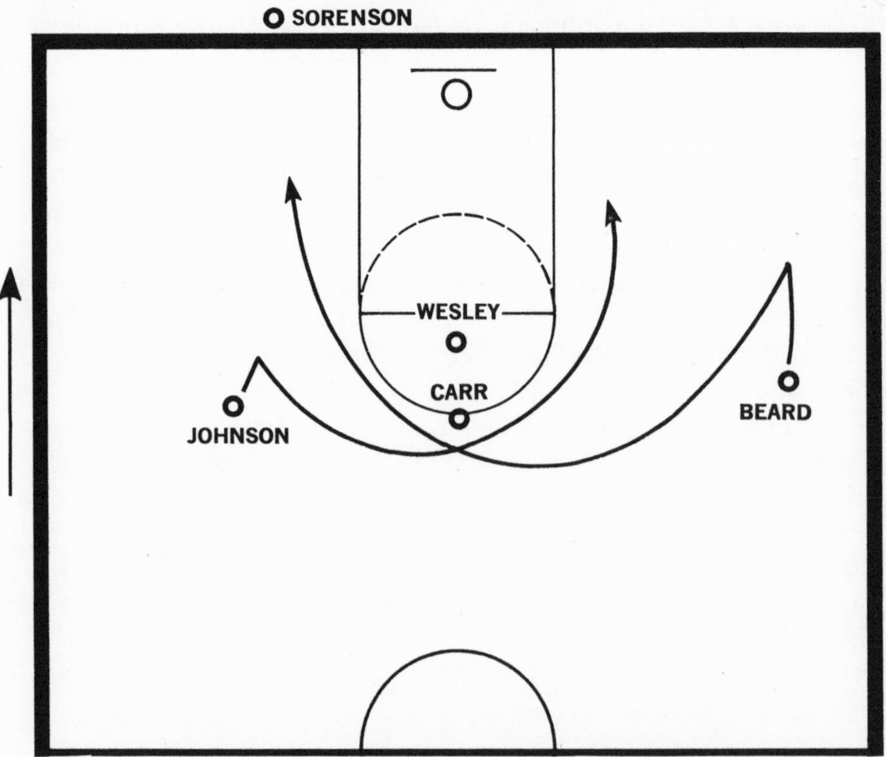

Diagram 8-13 Out-of-Bounds Underneath: Variation on Crisscross and Setting Up Screen for Shot Behind Foul Line

line. The key here is timing. Each player must break together. Jim Washington will be Atlanta's safety man on this one as he swings back for defense. Walt Bellamy, Lou Hudson, and Don Adams break for the basket on a signal from Pete Maravich. As soon as the pass-in is made, Maravich heads for the backcourt to help Washington on defense. In international basketball and Olympics competition, there can be no out-of-bounds plays underneath the basket. The ball is always put in play from the nearest sideline (see diagram 8-14).

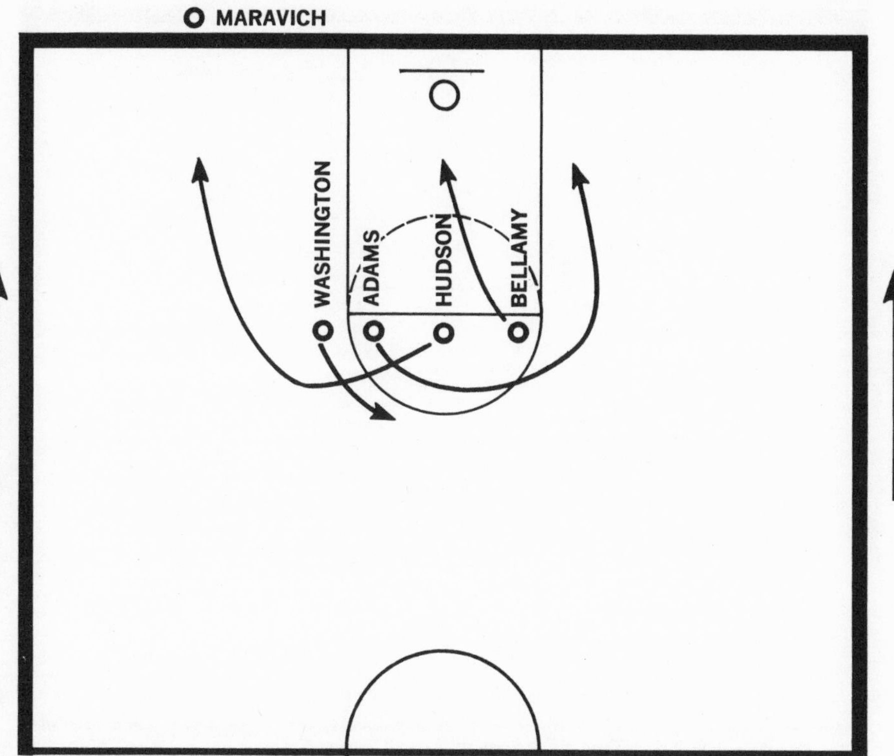

Diagram 8-14 Out-of-Bounds Underneath: Four Across on the Foul Line

The same four-man formation can be used on out-of-bounds plays from the sidelines. Hudson breaks in back of Washington to take a pass from Maravich. At the same time, Adams swings behind Hudson while Bellamy cuts to set a screen for Maravich, breaking for the basket. If the play works right, Hudson should be able to hit Maravich with a pass. If not, Hudson has a safety valve in Adams. In the NBA, the in-bounds pass at midcourt must be made into the forecourt. In college ball, the first pass may be made into the backcourt, with the offensive team having ten seconds to get across midcourt.

On another play from the same formation, Hudson fakes forward, then doubles back for the pass-in from Maravich. Now Washington swings around Bellamy and Adams, faking, going wide, and then sliding to the basket. Maravich also breaks for the hoop. Hudson can give the ball to Washington or Maravich (see diagram 8-15).

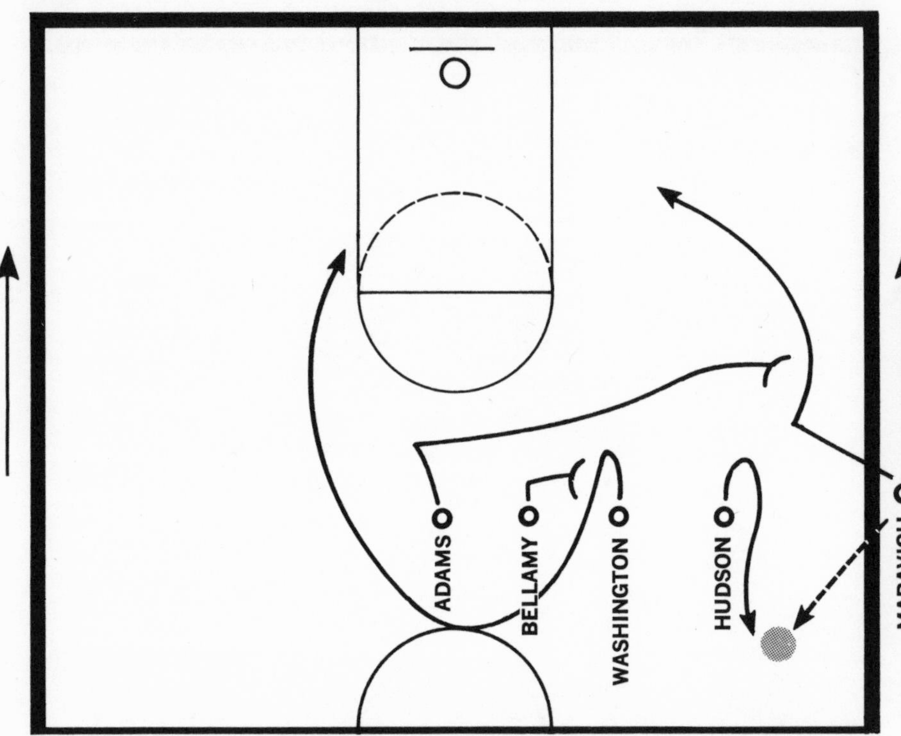

Diagram 8-15 Out-of-Bounds Side Court: Four Across Variation

These out-of-bounds plays do not necessarily require the advanced kind of personnel that you find in professional basketball. City College, where I played, used a play in the closing minutes against Bradley University to help with a national championship. It since has been adopted and used by many teams, including the pros.

In this formation, Bellamy, Washington, Adams, and Hudson line up side-by-side, facing their defensive opponents. At a signal from Maravich, out-of-bounds, Bellamy feints to the left and swings wide to the right.

Washington breaks toward the corner and then buttonhooks to be available for an escape pass. Hudson is the primary receiver, and the play is set up for him. As Adams swings back to protect the backcourt, and, also, to become a potential receiver, Hudson fakes a move to the spot vacated by Adams and changes direction. Lou swings clear of all the traffic and takes a breaking pass from Maravich (see diagram 8-16).

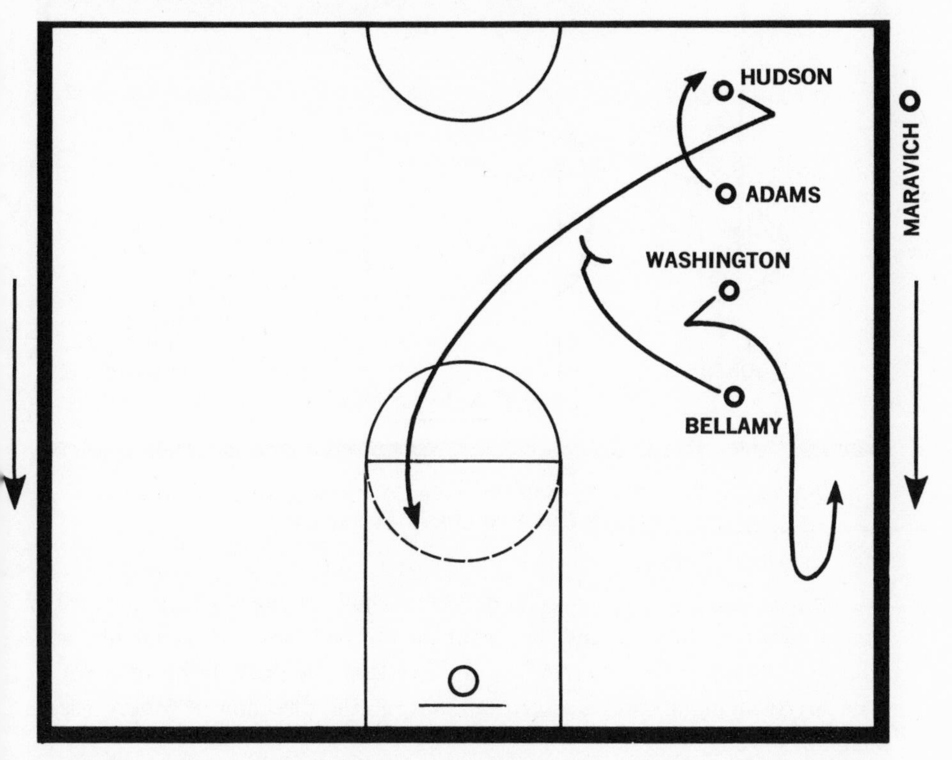

Diagram 8-16 Out-of-Bounds Side Court: Four Across Tandem Play

It is always a good idea to spread the defense to create more room for movement and passing. Everyone becomes a potential receiver. Rudy Tomjanovich of Houston, deep in one corner, takes his man toward the basket, then pivots back toward Cal Murphy, the passer. Otto Moore, the center, in the opposite corner, swings out to crisscross with Greg Smith, the forward. The other guard, Jim Walker, moves at his man, feints going right and can either reverse back for a pass from Murphy or slice off Moore should he get the ball (see diagram 8-17).

The 3-2 may be used in many ways. Murphy can pass directly to Walker who now has two routes available. He can feed Tomjanovich in the corner,

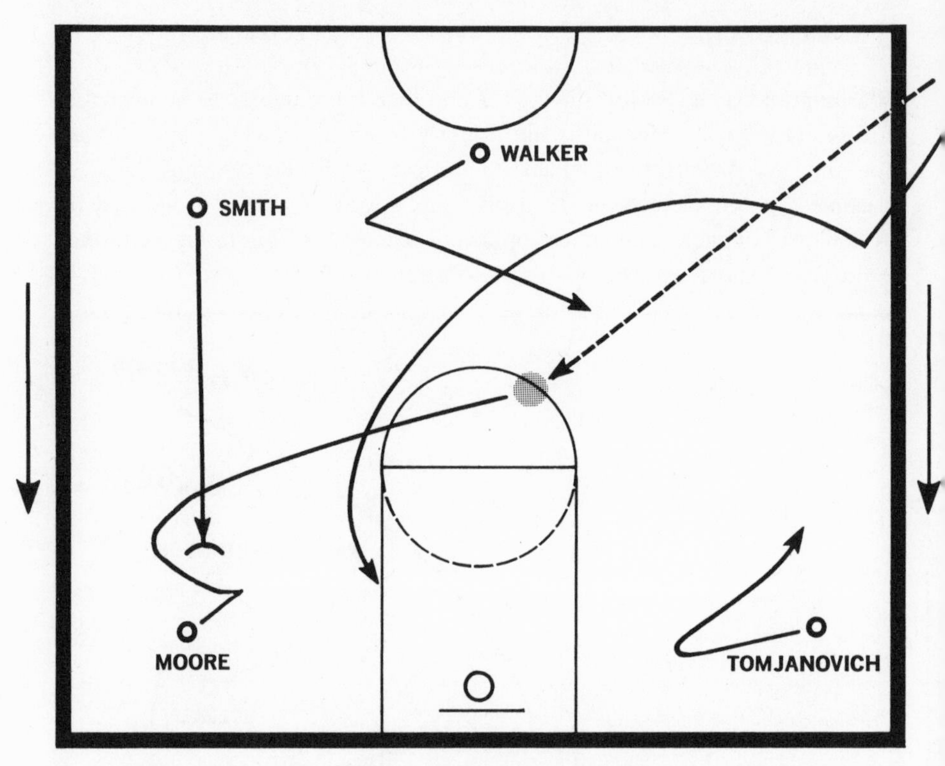

Diagram 8-17 Out-of-Bounds Side Court: Scissor on High Post (Three Out Two Under Formation)

whereupon Murphy, cutting behind Walker, can set up a screen that will enable Smith to slice around and head for the ball and a pass. Or he can fake left and run the play to his right, giving the ball to Moore, with Murphy swinging around a screen by Smith in the direction of Moore (see diagram 8-18).

Suppose the Seattle SuperSonics want to set up Dick Snyder, a good shooting guard, for a last second shot. They might use the 3-2 to create a double screen to clear him. The play starts with Snyder passing to Lennie Wilkens, who dribbles toward Don Smith and hits him with a bounce pass. John Brisker swings behind Wilkens and moves toward Spencer Haywood, setting up a double screen that releases Snyder for a pass from Smith and a short jumper (see diagram 8-19).

For additional variation, if Snyder goes baseline behind Haywood, he might draw Spencer's man on a switch. That will permit Haywood, now guarded by a smaller man, to roll around Brisker and take a pass from Smith for a jump shot from the foul line.

Many teams use a 2-3 variation on which they set up a pivot screen for the weakside forward. Snyder will pass to Wilkens, get the ball back, and

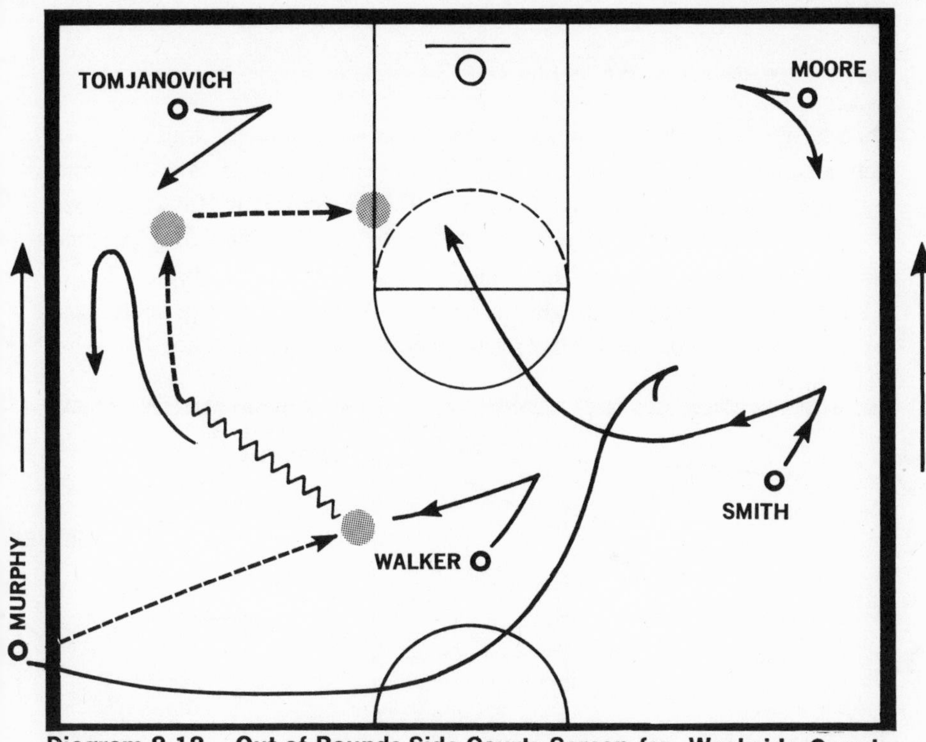

Diagram 8-18 Out-of-Bounds Side Court: Screen for Weakside Guard (Three Out Two Under Formation)

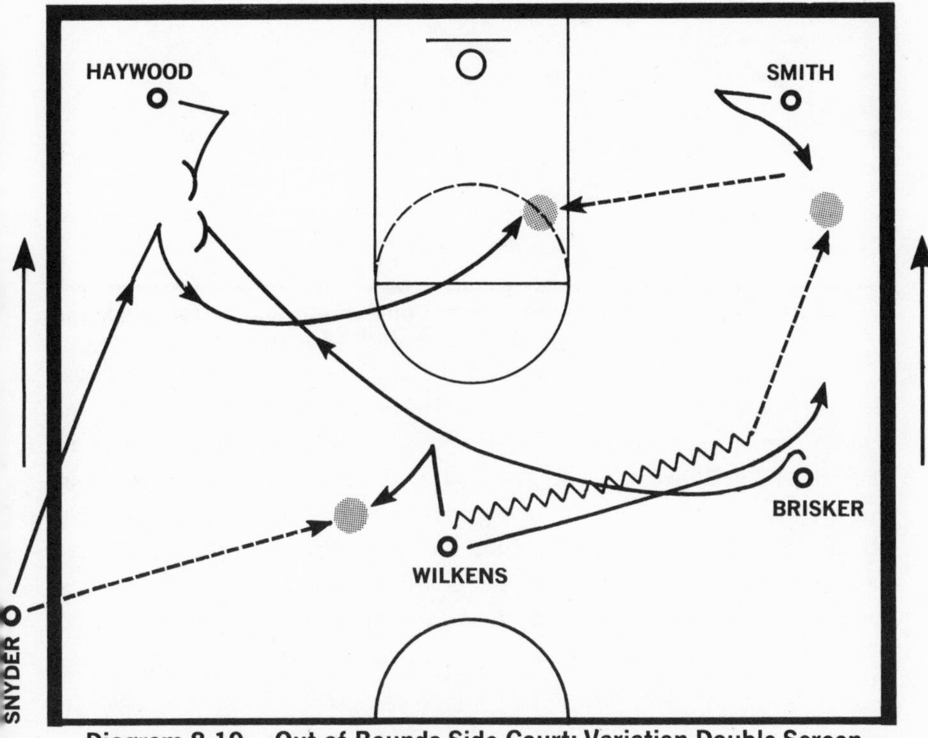

Diagram 8-19 Out-of-Bounds Side Court: Variation Double Screen

then hit Brisker with a bounce pass. Smith moves across the foul lane and sets a screen for Haywood, the weakside forward. Spencer fakes left and cuts right to take a pass from Brisker. After the screen, if Haywood goes to the foul line, Smith rolls underneath for rebound position or a possible pass if the defense is caught in a mismatch on a switch. If Haywood cuts back to the baseline, Smith will move to the foul line for a possible pass or to set up a screen for Brisker, who may dribble and drive for the hoop (see diagram 8-20).

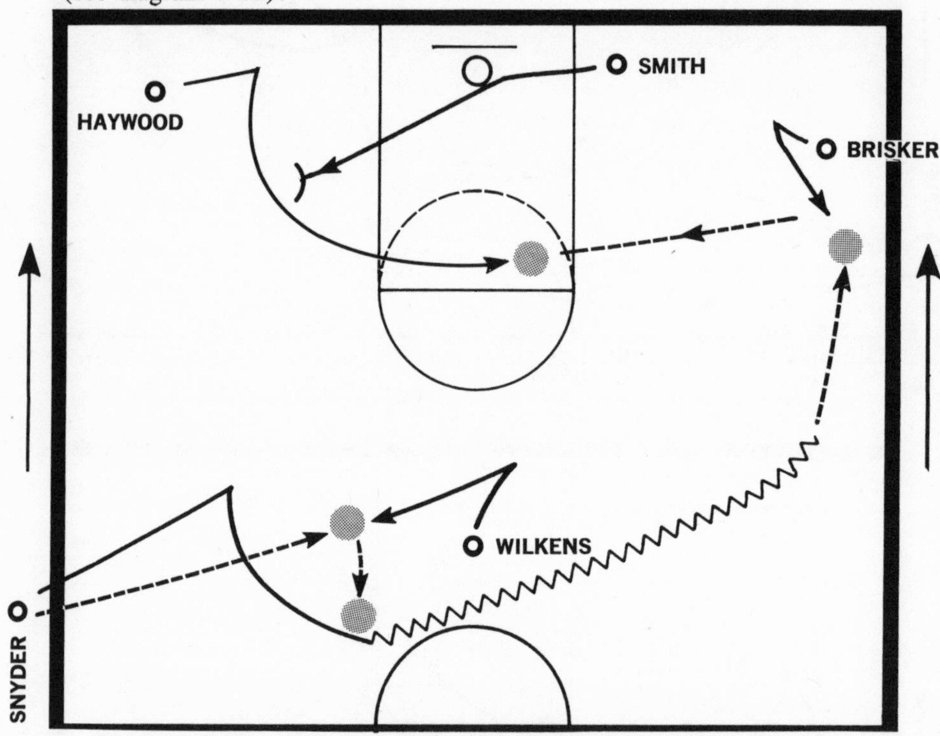

Diagram 8-20 Out-of-Bounds Side Court: Pivot Screen for Weakside Forward (Two Out Three Under Formation)

A double screen can be worked off the same formation. We used it for Bob Pettit when I coached the St. Louis Hawks. It can be run for any good outside shooter, such as Jack Marin, now with Houston. Walker passes to Murphy and gets the ball back. Marin, deep in the left corner, swings along the baseline as Moore moves alongside Tomjanovich to set the double screen. Walker hits Marin behind the screen for the jump shot. This play can be worked in deep, close to the baseline, with Tomjanovich moving toward Moore and Marin going into the opposite corner (see diagram 8-21).

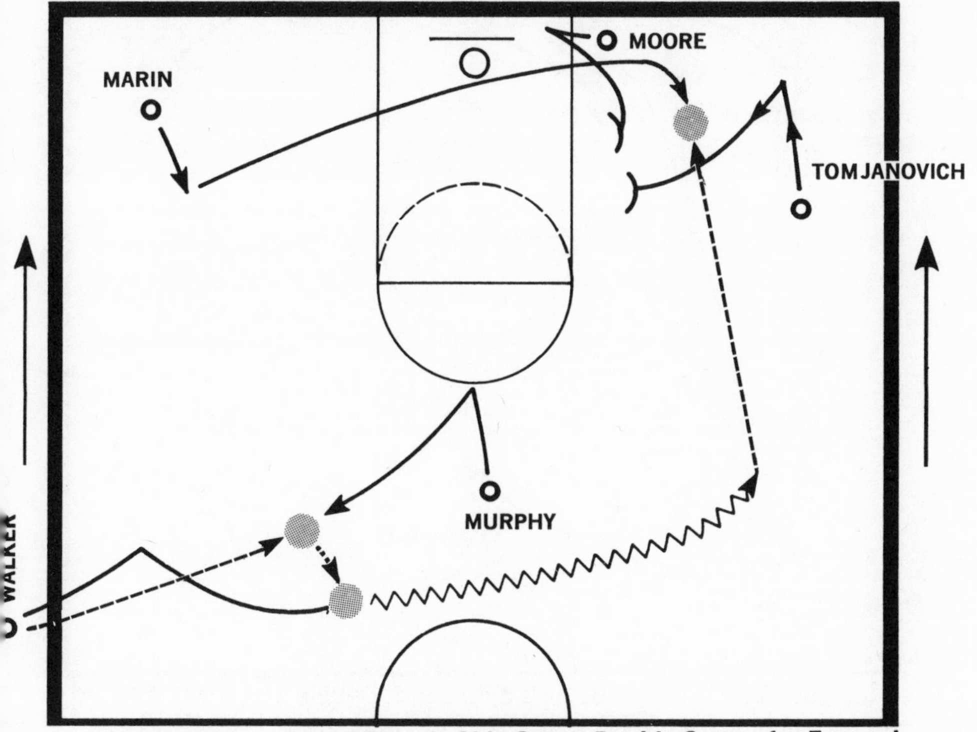

Diagram 8-21 Out-of-Bounds Side Court: Double Screen for Forward (Two Out Three Under Formation)

It is possible to break a man in close with some direct, quick moves though the pass-in may be at midcourt. Marin and Murphy decoy by moving around each other. Tomjanovich breaks from the corner and takes a pass from Walker. Now Tomjanovich stops and turns as Walker uses him as a screen that will permit Moore to come out for a pass and shot.

Then there is a two-out, three-under formation, setting up a double screen for the weakside forward. Walker passes to Murphy and then drives past Moore in deep and toward the baseline. Moore releases and moves slowly through the lane to screen for Marin, coming baseline from the opposite corner. Marin swings past the screens set by Moore and Walker and goes to the corner for a pass from Murphy and a shot (see diagram 8-22).

Using out-of-bounds plays reduces the risk of the ball being stolen. Players cannot stand around; they must move; they must meet the ball.

It is difficult to determine what situation will take place at what stage of a game. The only guide a coach has is the knowledge that the defense does certain things at certain times. Given the chance to get set, the defense can create pressures that can disrupt an offense. The idea is for the

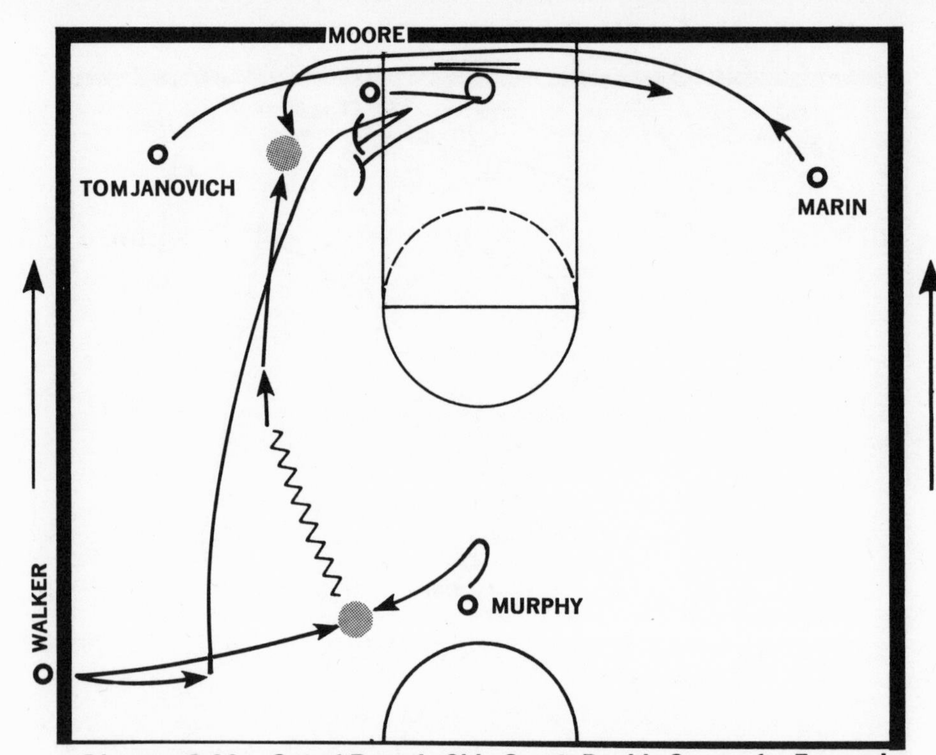

Diagram 8-22 Out-of-Bounds Side Court: Double Screen for Forward Coming from Weak Side (Two Out Three Under Formation)

offense to cut down on the risks and, at the same time, exploit the defense any way possible.

These special plays are designed for just such a development, and they can be used in the routine flow of a game. They can be used to meet a crisis. They provide an element of surprise when a team is trying to get the ball into play against a pressure defense or is faced with winning a game on a last shot when time is running out.

It is important to avoid complicated plays; keep them simple and easy to perform. A team has only five seconds to make the pass-in and the defense generally jams up the passing areas. If the maneuvering is too fancy, the passer may have trouble getting the ball into play in time.

Rotate the players when practicing the plays. That way, each players gets familiar with every assignment, a useful thing in an emergency. In pro basketball, the referee makes the man nearest the ball take it out under the basket. Therefore, some plays require a switch in assignments.

One player calls the play and the one handling the pass-in should be the best ballhandler. Some teams have the man making the pass-in slap the ball as a signal for the play to start. It is wise to arrange some system of signaling so the players react together. There is fine timing to these plays, and they must be run off with precision.

CHAPTER

9

THE PLAYERS' VIEWPOINT

Dean Meminger was drafted by the Knicks as a No. 1 pick. The 1971–72 season was his first in the NBA, yet, for such a young player, he displays a remarkable insight into the game of basketball. He had certain theories that were good for him and, quite frankly, might be good for every player.

Meminger learned his basketball in the schoolyards of New York. "Everybody has his tricks," he says in explaining how he steals the ball. "I try to catch the ball when they bring it up. I put my hand on the pit of their stomach. When they bring the ball up to shoot, it has to hit my hand."

Dean is only six-foot-one, a small man in a land of giants. Yet, he is an astonishing rebounder for his size—especially off the offensive board. "That's where the ball is," is his reason as to why he invariably winds up fighting bigger players for missed shots. "It's an asset being small. They're not looking for me."

He might have mentioned hustle and instinct. "I pick my spots," he adds. "I look for the side shot, because sixty percent of the time it's not going to bounce off where the big guy expects it to. I got three or four baskets on Wilt [Chamberlain] that way in one game."

Walt Frazier makes the All-Defensive team every year. He is one of the few players in the league who does not play with his hands on an opponent. "Then he knows where I am," he says. "My man never knows where I am. That way, I can surprise him and steal the ball."

He likes to fool an opponent by giving the impression he is relaxing on defense, then striking. Before that happens, he studies his man. "You watch a guy from the start," he explains. "You watch his reactions. Study the way he passes. Look to see if he prefers to drive the same way all the time."

That gives him a reading and helps his anticipation. He knows what to expect and waits for the proper opportunity to use the knowledge. "I wait for my man to get careless, then I make my move," he points out. "After I've played a man long enough, I can pick up the rhythm or cadence of his dribble. Stealing is a calculated risk and you need help from your teammates when you do it. Never lunge. It leaves you out of position."

Mike Riordan, a former Knick and now with Baltimore, also stresses the importance of knowing an opponent and anticipation. "Try to figure out what your man is doing and prevent him from doing it," he says. "Force him away from his strength and to his weakness. If he's a good jump shooter, play him close and try to take the jump shot away. If he can drive, play loosely and give him the outside shot. If he likes to drive right, overplay that way and force him left."

Dave DeBusschere is one of the finest rebounders in the league. "You must go after every ball and try to keep yourself between your man and the basket," he explains. "You must be ready to go to the boards as soon as the ball goes up. You have to know when to leave your man. Speed and mobility are much more important than height. I'd much rather go against a bigger man than a smaller, quicker one."

Willis Reed was Most Valuable Player the season the Knicks won the championship and his merit as an all-around player is recognized by his making the All-Star game every year. "I try not to be stationary in the pivot," he points out. "I keep moving so my man can't get set. I try to keep myself and the ball in motion. I look for my shot but I also look for the open man to pass to. I try to mix things up so the other team cannot figure out whether I'll shoot or pass."

Dick Barnett, knowledgeable in every phase of the game, has always been considered an artist when it comes to shooting. He is the master of the unorthodox—a recoil jumper on which he falls away from the basket. This puzzles the fundamentalists but he makes his shots.

"All good shooters do basically the same thing," says Barnett. "No

SHOOTING STYLIST. Dick Barnett says all good shooters do basically the same thing. See if you can pick out what he means from this picture.

matter how unorthodox, their elbow to their wrist is straight and the ball rests in the hand, controlled by the fingertips. How you hold the ball is an individual thing."

He points out there are certain basic things that every good shooter considers. "Find the range where you can make the shot," he says, "get some height on the ball, have some rhythm on the shot, and follow through." As easy as that, if you know how.

These are individual approaches. They represent the experience and knowledge that the players gained on their way to earning their status as professionals at the top of the rung. The fundamentals of the game that have been refined to the point of high quality.

Yet they have their problems: The competition is so great and they are human. They perform in an accelerated game where the team defenses are motivated by the application of constant pressure to create mistakes. So they experience turnovers and anxieties and shooting slumps.

Even a great shooter such as Jerry West loses his touch once in a while. It was impossible to believe how he shot against the Knicks in the first three games of the 1971–72 championship series. He missed layups and, sometimes, he missed the basket completely with outside shots he ordinarily could hit blindfolded.

"They don't have to put anyone on me the way I'm shooting," he said, 3-for-15 in the first game, 6-for-21 in the second, and a slightly better 10-for-28 in the third. "My shot's gone now. It's on vacation." West kept shooting, which is the way to climb out of a slump. The worst thing to do is go into a shell and shoot with fear.

John Havlicek remembered a slump. "It was in college," said Havlicek, a forward on a great Ohio State team. "I was missing. I found I was following the flight of the ball. By taking my eyes and putting them on the ball, I was losing concentration on the rim."

He discovered what he was doing wrong in a strange way. He would shoot an hour a day in the gym, but nothing happened. He still could not make his shots. "One time I was working at night outside," he recalled. "There was a light above the hoop. I discovered if I didn't keep my eye on the rim, I lost the ball in the blackness of the sky."

He also discovered, or rediscovered, that if he kept his eye on the rim, his shots went in. "A lot of great shooters," he said, "can follow the flight of the ball. I have to keep my eye on the target—the rim."

Havlicek came to the Boston Celtics for the 1962–63 season. He found his position in the front court crowded. Tommy Heinsohn, Tom Sanders,

EYE ON RIM. John Havlicek drives through traffic and zooms in on target. *Nothing* will break his concentration.

23
HUDSON
CELTICS
17

and Jim Loscutoff were getting the playing time. Red Auerbach suggested John learn the intricacies of playing guard, though Bob Cousy, K. C. Jones, Sam Jones, and super-sub Frank Ramsey, the swing man in the backcourt and at forward, were available for most of the duty.

ABOUT PLAYING GUARD

"When I first started playing guard with the Celtics," recalls Havlicek, who played on six of the eleven NBA championship teams, "I had to go through a whole process of changes. One of the biggest problems was ball-handling. A guard has to move the ball up the floor."

Havlicek considers himself lucky because Cousy was on the team. Bob, one of the gifted ballhandlers and dribblers, made the rookie from Ohio State a personal project. "He taught me to use either hand when I dribbled," says Havlicek. "I would go up the floor with one hand and back down the floor with the other hand."

Hondo, as he is called by his teammates, learned to change hands and, also, that there were various types of dribbles. "The spin and straight-forward dribble," he cites as an example, "where the ball bounces higher. The change of pace dribble. The crossover dribble, where you have to bring it back to you and switch hands—you can't leave it out in front or they'll steal it."

There are others, almost too numerous to mention, but part of the instinctive repertoire of good dribblers. "The between the legs dribble to set yourself up for a real good shot," Havlicek points out as another weapon. "Jimmy Walker was the first to use it very effectively. He comes right at you and you can see it cross over and go between his legs but it is too quick for you to adjust."

Then there is the behind-the-back dribble used by Cousy, Frazier, and Monroe quite efficiently. "I don't use it—maybe once a year," points out Havlicek. "I do use the control dribble, where you keep your body between the man and the ball. I've learned the reverse dribble. Monroe is great at it. He has a better sense of balance than anyone as he comes at you and then reverses."

He discovered that the shorter the bounce on the dribble, the easier to control. "The margin of error is greater as the bounce gets higher," he explains. "I found out the best way of all. I would always give the ball to our other guard. I'd tell Cousy and K. C. Jones: 'Here, you take it up.' "

CONTROL THE DRIBBLE. John Havlicek learned the lower the dribble, the easier it is to control the ball. Here Dean Meminger keeps the ball close to the floor as he jockeys for position with Gail Goodrich of the Lakers.

NEW YORK
7

PROTECT THE BALL. Dick Barnett is doing everything he can to press John Havlicek and get the ball. The Boston star is using his body and outstretched arms to avoid serious trouble.

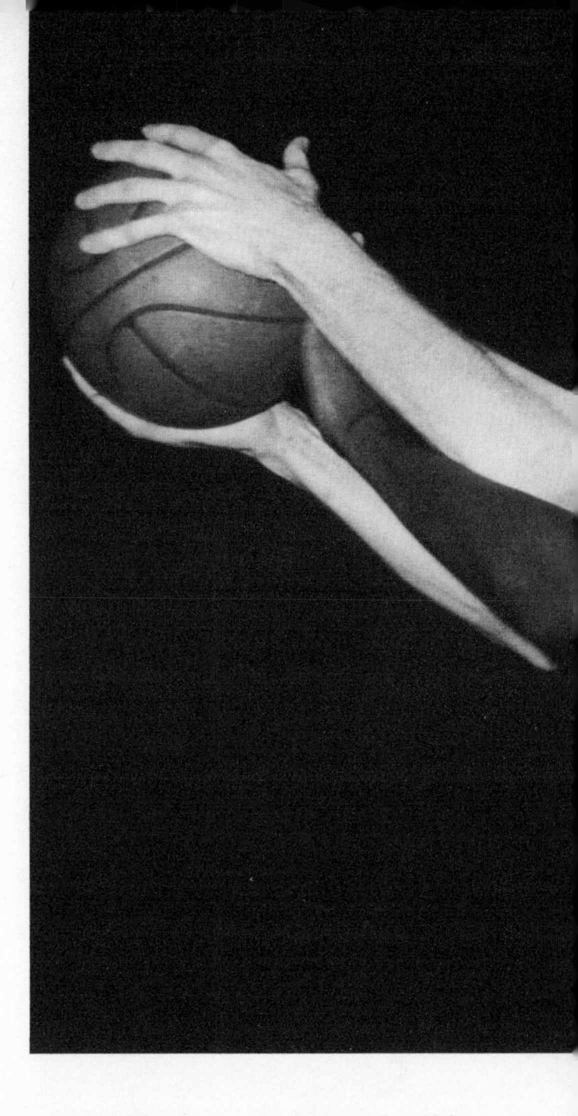

He learned the different types of dribbles then he had to learn how to use them without looking at the ball. That is the biggest problem for unnatural ballhandlers: they must look at the ball. "It was my biggest fault at the beginning," he confesses. "I was being overprotective. I couldn't see anyone cutting."

Once Havlicek gained confidence, he managed a style of his own. "I like to take the dribble right at someone," he says. "I want to make him commit himself so I don't have to jockey with the ball. I do this because of my speed. I can take the ball from the weak side to the strong side and get out of pressure situations."

He is not a penetrating dribbler. He does not have the control type of dribbling that is needed to maneuver the defense. "Lennie Wilkens does it

best," he says. "His successor will be another small guy, probably Nate Archibald."

Havlicek considers Wilkens and Archibald two of the best at penetration. "They put pressure on a defense," he explains. "Someone has to help out and that leaves an open man. They're quick and have complete control of the ball. A lot of times it is great for a penetrator to keep 'em honest, to even take a charging foul to let the defense know he has incorporated that [penetration] into his game."

In other words, if the defense is aware Havlicek might go all the way on a penetration, it must play accordingly. "You get the defensive man backing up on his heels," says John. "Now you can move him back and stop for your jump shot."

Havlicek is an expert on shooting. Nobody on the Celtics had to teach him that. "I'm a scorer, not a shooter," he says, modestly. He means he knows how to work for his shots and what to do when he gets them. "You must know where you are going to shoot," he points out. "Know your range on the floor. The distance and the proximity of the lines. There are times when you are not looking at the basket. You get into a scoring area and have no time to look for the basket. Sometimes you see a guy dribbling and he's up and shooting without even looking and you wonder how he does it."

The pros are adept at it because they have done their homework. They are familiar with certain spots on the floor. They know from where and when they can shoot. "Let's say you dribble across the key from left to right," says Havlicek. "If you're five feet away from the key, you know it's going to be a difficult shot. If you're only a foot away, it's not going to be that difficult."

There is no reason to worry about picking up the basket. "Enough time for that," explains John. "You take a jump shot and hang just a little longer and pick it up while you're going up." His approach to passing is hit the man in the chest with the ball and try to hit the waist when you use the bounce pass.

He never had to concern himself about working without the ball at guard because he learned how to do it at forward, his natural position. "It's the same for both positions," he points out. "You try to apply the principles that you don't like to happen to you."

That's familiar. I feel the same way about many things in basketball. If a team works something well against the Knicks, I put it into our practices. We work on it and use it against someone else.

"I keep moving," says Havlicek. "You can't stand around and look at the ball. If you do, your man will stop you from getting the ball entirely. It was like a night off playing a guy in college who didn't know how to move without the ball. Who didn't know how to use screens."

Some people watch a game and see Havlicek running and think there is no rhyme or reason to his movement. He runs around Dave Cowens or Satch Sanders and it is assumed he is just running for running's sake. No way. He is using the screens set by his teammates for a purpose.

"I like to see a screen facing me," he explains, indicating how much thought he gives it. "I don't like them to turn the back and use the rear end. They're not using the entire body and it is easier for a defensive man

A FAMILIAR SPOT. Dave DeBusschere knows from experience that he is within his shooting range. He is familiar with every spot on the floor and can shoot without hesitation when he desires.

22
21

to roll around. There's a bigger area for blocking if a teammate faces you on a screen."

Good players emphasize details. They always think of getting the maximum out of every situation and every second in a game. "You should rub shoulders with your teammate as he's setting a pick," says Havlicek. "That way, the defensive man can't get through. It's not up to the man setting the pick as to how it should be set. It's up to the man utilizing it."

Whenever he makes a move, he precedes it with a fake. He wants to get his defensive man moving in some direction so he can have an edge moving the other way. When he cuts, he moves sharply and directly. "No banana cuts," is the way he describes a wasteful, looping maneuver.

He moves toward the ball if he wants it, otherwise he clears out to remove defensive pressure. "We weave a lot on the Celtics," he explains. "It gives movement. It lends itself to reverses, cuts, and changes."

He listens to what the defense is saying. He sometimes picks up a clue and uses it to exploit the defensive move that is in the process of being made. "It's the guard's job to try and help out," he explains. "You should move into an area where you're immediately effective. You should always be in position to make a shot or move."

"Jerry West likes to get his man involved in picks and screens and move away without the ball," says Havlicek. "He likes to work outside. I like to go inside a lot because I'm generally bigger than my man and I don't think guards rebound that well."

There are exceptions. Walt Frazier and Jerry Sloan, for example. "Sloan is an excellent rebounder for a guard," says Havlicek, "so I try and drive on him and get him involved in a lot of picks. You like to keep him away from the boards."

He does not forget that he cannot only think of what he would like to do. He might like to drive on Sloan, but there are other considerations: his teammates and floor balance. Somebody has to be back if one of the guards decides he is going inside.

"Chaney likes to go to the board a lot on our team," explains Havlicek. "So I don't go that much. There may be times I could go but there's no one back. That comes first, so I just stay back. The Knicks have great floor balance. You can't break on them that much. They're always rotating. They always have someone in position to protect."

Havlicek learned that part of the game at Ohio State. "We were aware of it there," he claims. "We always had someone back. We had a smart team. Make a mistake and you're like a dummy. You don't want to make it again."

You have to be smart to play guard in the NBA because you run into such talented players as Frazier. That is one of Havlicek's many assignments when he is in the backcourt. "Frazier tries to force you toward defensive help," says John. "I'll just take off and move a lot against a fellow like that. Take him away from the ball. Once he plays the ball, you have to take advantage and move where it hurts the defense."

Offense means motion. The idea is to spread out and create enough motion so the defense will get careless or impatient and make a mistake somewhere. No matter what style of attack a team employs, that is the basic philosophy. The best and most logical way to get the job done.

On defense, Havlicek has certain principles that really are no different from those of other ballplayers who work in the backcourt. He studies his man's shooting range so he can tighten up when they are in that area. "There are so many shooters," he suggests, "not many are true playmakers."

There are enough, however. Havlicek and the other guards know them. Familiar names such as Wilkens, Archibald, Frazier, Archie Clark, and Oscar Robertson, of course. No one can relax against them. They all make the play and can get points.

"I have certain principles," says Havlicek, speaking about his approach to defense as a guard. "Against a scorer, you have to prevent him from getting the ball; he's not going to score if he doesn't have it. You have to beat him to spots."

He considers defensive guard the hardest part of the game. The guards are quicker, mobile, and generally good shooters. They have the ball most of the time and know what to do with it. "You have to play the passing angles against them," observes Havlicek. "You must keep your hand in the passing lane. If I throw a hand out there, I might deflect a pass. At the very least, it makes the offensive players change their passes. They cannot throw them directly through the lane where I have my hand extended."

He talks about the use of peripheral vision. How he works himself into a defensive position so he can watch the man and the ball without losing sight of either. That is not easy when you play against someone like Clark. He comes right at you and then changes direction faster than you can blink an eye, let alone shift one. He dribbles straight at his man, feints once or twice, puts the ball low on the floor, and sweeps in the other direction faster than anyone in the NBA.

The players in the NBA are so far advanced and tricky, the defense has to create some guidelines to stay with them. Havlicek has his own rules of thumb. "I look at a guy's number or the letters on his chest," he says.

"They have to go wherever he goes. I also try and play a man to his strong side. Make him go away from his strength."

That is on straightaway defense or against a ballhandler or opponent moving laterally. Penetrators create a different set of rules. In other words, if Havlicek is playing Archibald or Wilkens, he must be concerned about them driving past him through the middle. "I watch the crotch or the ball," is the way John handles those cases.

There is more. "A lot of guys get into trouble by always slapping at the ball," he points out. "They go up on their toes and get themselves off balance. The weight is forward and that makes it easier for a man to drive around them. What I do is keep my palms up. That gives me better balance."

He always makes his man try to beat him to the outside. Wilkens is a fine example. Lennie likes to drive the middle and pressure the defense. He will go all the way to the basket if they let him. If someone switches to help inside, he will lay the ball off to the open man.

"You try to make him shoot from outside," explains Havlicek. "He is left-handed, so you make him move right or force him into a corner if you can. You don't play him tight. He'll go right around you." Don Chaney normally gets the Wilkens assignment on the Celtics and Havlicek spends a lot of time helping his younger teammate adjust to the intricacies of playing the tricky Seattle backcourt star.

Archibald provides the same set of problems except he is faster, though not as knowledgeable or mature as Wilkens. The little backcourt performer for the Kansas City-Omaha Kings also is left-handed. "You make him shoot outside and force him to his right," says Havlicek. "He's so left. I think it is wise to overlook his fake and let him drive right."
fast, though, he keeps you off balance. He starts you right, then comes back

Clark, a different type, is a dangerous shooter if you let him penetrate to the fifteen-foot range he desires. He sets everything up with his crossover or change of direction dribble. "He's great on the crossover," observes Havlicek. "If you want to take that away from him, you must play low on his dribble, maybe with your hands at your knees. He has great speed and gets you moving backwards. You're still retreating when he stops and goes up for his jumper."

Havlicek remembers a similar move by a player of a different era. He mentions Gene Shue, coach of the Baltimore Bullets and a New York Knickerbocker on the 1954–55, 1955–56, and 1962–63 teams. Havlicek, of course, played against Shue in 1962–63, which was John's rookie season.

TURNABOUT. John Havlicek gets his opportunity to play defense and pressure his man at times. Here he is closing in on Walt Frazier and reducing the area of maneuverability.

NEW YO
ROIT

BE CAREFUL. Dave Bing seems to be concentrating on Walt Frazier's left shoulder, figuring wherever the shoulder goes, Frazier must go. The Detroit guard is making sure he has the middle blocked off.

"Shue had a reverse dribble that was amazing," recalls Havlicek. "He'd come right at you, whirl and pivot. He'd be so open for a shot, it was wild." It must have been if Hondo cannot forget after so many years and so many exciting basketball developments in his life.

When I was playing ball with the Rochester Royals, our Bobby Davies could do all those things with a basketball. He was the first I ever saw use the behind-the-back dribble as an offensive weapon and I am talking about when he was an All-America at Seton Hall around thirty years ago.

Not everybody resorts to fancy dribbling; Oscar Robertson, for example. He is the perfect example of what a guard should be capable of doing on offense. "You can stay with him," says Havlicek, "but he's going to wind up with what he wants. He is real strong and nobody controls the ball better or knows what to do with it. At lot of guys try to steal the ball from him but it is next to impossible because of his big body. You just have to play him honest all the time and not give him an inch."

ABOUT PLAYING FORWARD

When Havlicek first entered the NBA he was considered an in-between. He was a little big for a guard at six-foot-five but a little small for a forward. That, no doubt, had something to do with Auerbach's decision to have John learn to play the backcourt, a second position.

Two seasons later, Frank Ramsey retired and Havlicek stepped right into his role as super sixth man for the Celts. They each had that rare ability to come in cold off the bench and help a team immediately, at two positions. Ramsey was only six-foot-three but he did a lot of damage at forward when asked.

"I'm a small forward," concedes Havlicek, thinking of seven-foot Mel Counts, six-foot-nine John Block, six-foot-eight Spencer Haywood and Connie Hawkins, and others who tower over him. "I'm not a big man, so I have to move a lot without the ball when I'm at forward."

He thinks of Gus Johnson—the Gus Johnson before he had operations on both knees prior to the 1971–72 season and went through another operation when traded by Baltimore to Phoenix for the 1972–73 season. "Gus, he puts a hand on you and it's like carrying around another person," says Havlicek. "He's physical. You have to be on the move or it will kill your whole game."

Bill Bradley is something else. "A guy like Bradley has very good de-

CAUGHT IN SWITCH. John Havlicek finds himself with Jerry Lucas, a bigger man, on a switch with Dave Cowens (18). Havlicek protects the middle and pressures Luke so he cannot get inside for an easy shot over a shorter man.

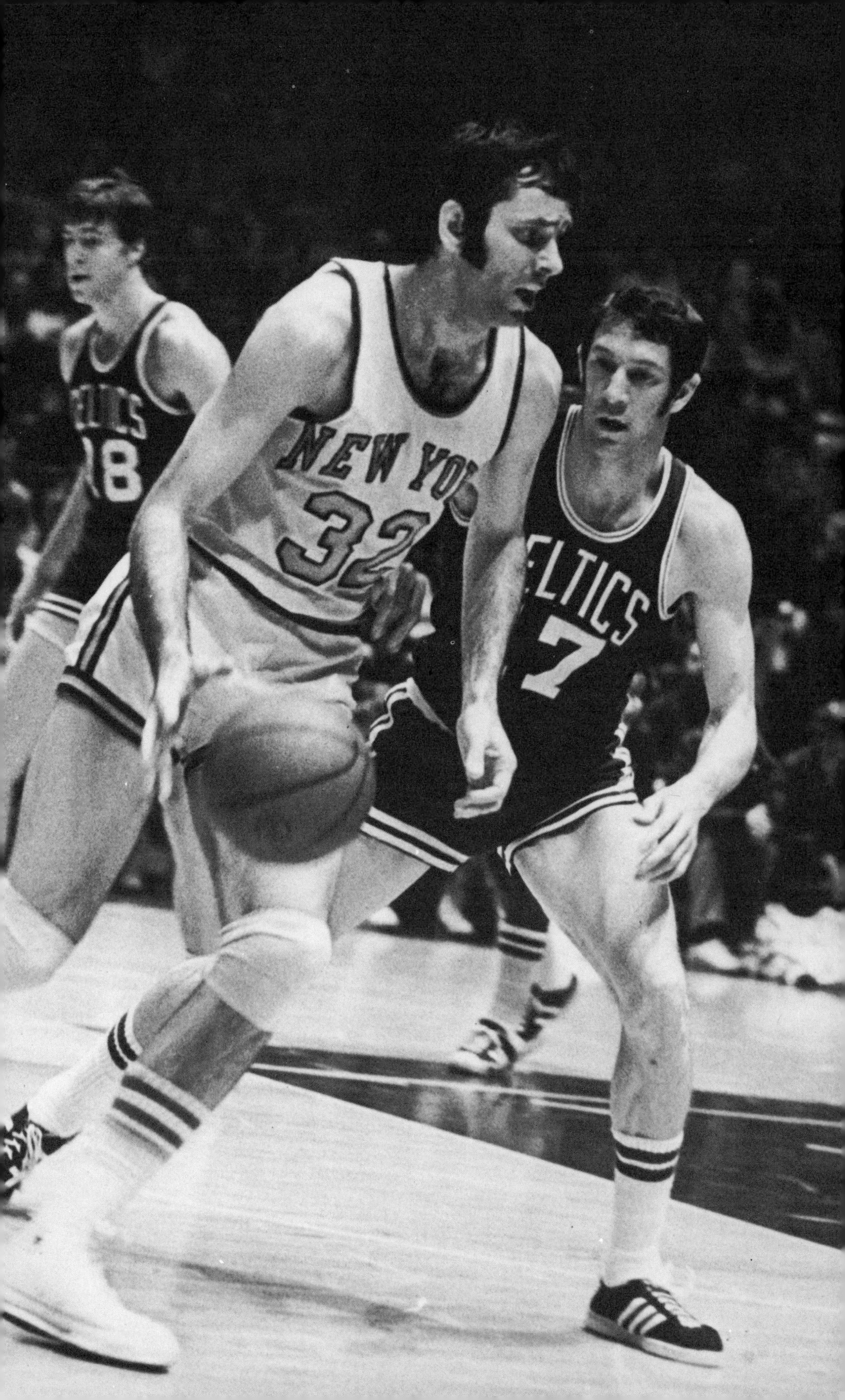
NEW YO
32
ELTICS
7

fensive ability," explains John. "He is as quick as I am. He is as tall as I am. You got to keep moving. You got to keep using your screens. If you don't, he'll keep you from getting the ball entirely."

There was a game the Celtics played against the Lakers. It was tough. Tommy Heinsohn, the Boston coach, was moved to try something new. The Los Angeles forwards, Jim McMillian and Happy Hairston, were getting the better of it. Jerry West and Gail Goodrich in the backcourt were disrupting the Celtic game.

"They kept trying to make me go left along the baseline toward Wilt," recalls Havlicek. "Heinsohn decided to switch positions. He put me and [Don] Nelson in the backcourt and [Jo-Jo] White and Chaney up front. Now the Laker forwards had to play defense where the guards usually play. I like to bring the ball up real fast. I was running all over the place. It was one of the most tiring games—but we won."

As a forward, Havlicek feels it is important to get the ball inside—from the foul line to the baseline. "Extend the foul line to the sidelines and that is the area," he says. "When you get the ball, you should be a triple threat. Unless someone cuts, you should be looking for the shot. If there is a cutter, you should be able to pass to him. Or you should be able to drive on an individual move."

He thinks many players do not fully understand. They will wander to a spot on the floor where they cannot be productive. They become a total waste. "A lot of forwards get the ball with their back to the basket," he says. "The first thing they have to do now is turn around. By then, the defense comes up on them."

When he gets the ball, he wants to be in position to do something about scoring right away. Once again, he moves with a purpose—into an area with a purpose. He thinks that should be fundamental with all forwards.

"Another thing that's so fundamental, yet unbelievable, is the way starters play a lot but have great difficulty getting the ball to the pivot man," he says. "Pivotmen like the ball up around the chest and shoulders. It's just a matter of faking your defensive man and then making the pass. Your hands are much quicker than his when you know what you are doing."

Havlicek, in his microscopic examination of the game, brings the art of playing forward right down to running. "Did you ever try to run forward and look backward?" he asks, knowing how difficult that is. "You got to see the ball all the time, so you cannot run straight back."

You either back-pedal or run in a way that you can see what is going on behind you. "I know some players who just take off down the middle

PERPETUAL MOTION. Here are Bill Bradley and John Havlicek working against each other. Bill has come around a screen set by Dave DeBusschere, and John is trying to maintain position and force Bradley away from the basket.

of the floor," says Havlicek, "and go right to the corner without looking. They should know where the ball is and go to the hoop."

The reason? Havlicek, seeing a teammate break, no doubt will throw a lead pass toward the basket. That is the right play when a teammate breaks into the open behind the defense. Now if the teammate, running without looking, suddenly breaks to the corner, the ball will be thrown away.

"I never turn my back on the ball," says Havlicek. "When I play a cornerman, I take the passing angle away. I open up and if he tries to get behind me, I feel for him. I may turn my back on him, but not the ball."

Havlicek is a strong rebounder for a player his size because he is an intelligent rebounder. "Blocking out is the most important thing in rebounding," he says. "You must shut off your man. I have a two-second rule. When the shot goes up, I count one-thousand-one, one-thousand-two, before I move for the rebound."

He has studied the situation and is prepared to guarantee the ball will hit the floor two seconds after a shot. He estimates that the majority of rebounds come off at a forty-five-degree angle, so he concentrates on taking away the bouncing areas. "The idea is to cut your man off before going for the rebound," he advises. "If I don't get the rebound, he's not going to get it."

Havlicek goes the way of most small forwards in the NBA—he is taken inside. "I wind up with guys who take me low," is the way he puts it. "I front them if I can. If I have to go behind, I avoid contact so they don't know where I am."

He likes to give them room to confuse them. "They're always leaning back and feeling," he says. "If they don't know where you are, they will look around. When they do that, I sneak around in front."

He doesn't always play in front. That can be dangerous at times. He likes to mix things up and keep the bigger man guessing. "If I cheat and play him on the side," he says, "I prefer to play him on the baseline side. I want to force him to the middle or make him pitch the ball out."

Havlicek learned his lessons well. He says he prospered through playing with a smart team at Ohio State and, thereby, establishing a sound foundation for his years with the Boston Celtics. "It was a very smart team," he insists. "Audibles were never called. Everything was automatic."

No plays were called. The players went into them automatically. "Everything was keyed off Lucas," says Havlicek, who had Jerry at center and

Larry Siegfried, a future teammate in Boston, at guard. "We were drilled in it. It was uncanny. It just depended on where Luke was."

ABOUT PLAYING CENTER

Lucas came to the Knicks after an eight-year professional career playing forward in Cincinnati and San Francisco. We dealt for him to double at forward and play behind Willis Reed at center. Then Reed played only eleven games because of tendonitis in his knee, so Lucas went to center and was a revelation to many. No one who knew Jerry's background should have been that surprised. He says center is his natural position and who could question that after the season he had in 1971–72.

"A center is involved in almost all the plays," he says, supporting what Havlicek had to say about the days at Ohio State. "He is on two-on-twos, three-on-threes but not the five-man weaves. He has to learn how to pass."

He mentioned a number of different passes. The first was the release pass after a rebound at which Lucas is adept. "Get a friend to help with a release drill," he suggests. "Put him under the basket and try to throw the ball through him after taking the rebound. Move from right to left and throw before you hit the ground."

He thinks the thing to remember on all passes is that a teammate is moving. "The pass has got to be soft, so it can be handled," he says. "If it's a shovel pass, protect the ball, get a good grip on it and make the pass waist-high. Use the hook pass to throw long downcourt. If it's a bounce pass, use one or two hands. The bounce pass is the easiest one to handle by a man cutting off a post."

A center must know where he is and where his defensive man is. "This may sound ridiculous," he says, "but when he has his back to the basket, he must know the angle and the distance to the basket. He doesn't waste time looking for the hoop. He becomes familiar with the markings on the floor, when to use the board, if he's too low and can't drive."

Basketball is a science to Lucas and all intelligent players. "Feel your man on pressure and know where he's shading," he suggests. "Glance at his feet. Know where he is so you can move against his weakness."

The first thing he recommends in the pivot is a simple drop step. "Most players who overplay to the right use the left foot to pivot," he points out. "Step back with the left foot and hook your man's left leg and then pivot straight to the hoop. That way you will protect the ball."

11
CE
EW YO
32

A center should develop a hook shot. "Too many people make the mistake of starting the shot wrong," he says. "The ball should start low around the thigh so you can control it longer. When you release the ball, the hand faces the basket."

Do not start with the arm bent and then twist the hand in movement. "It's a one-motion shot," says Lucas. "Get into release position before you start and then hook in one motion. The quicker you pick up the hoop, the better you are. It is an all-arm shot. There is no breaking of the wrist. It just rolls off the hand."

The pivot foot remains on the ground during the release. "That's very important," he says. "It can come off after the release. You should wind up facing the opposite direction."

Jerry thinks it is a waste of time to work on a left hook when the time can be spent perfecting one way. Some of the time might better be invested in the turnaround jump. "There are two kinds," he explains. "The in-close jump and turn, while at the same time, shooting. And the jump away and turn like Elvin Hayes. He turns and shoots while going away in one motion."

It is better to use the board if the shot is taken from an angle. It is wise for a center to maneuver his man on defense. "Make an aggressive move," suggests Lucas. "Take a step so he will react and move backward. Most centers do it; they do not move laterally. When you have him moving away, pull up and take the shot."

Centers should move back and forth and create daylight between their opponents. "On a turn," he says, "the first thing to look at is his feet. Once you see which way his foot is heading, you know his weight is heading the same way."

Developing fakes is essential. "When you play biggers guys," says Lucas, who does only that for the Knicks, "the thing to do is show them the ball. A fake with the head and shoulders is effective. Let him see the ball. In close, you want him up and down. Show it to him up and down so he's on a pogo stick."

You can't show the ball without protecting it. "Know where your man is," suggests Lucas, "so you can hold the ball away from him. Away from where he shades. Control the ball with two hands. Stay away from one-hand fancy stuff. Be aware of what's going on. Don't expose the ball so he can steal it. Bend over if he's giving you heat. That gets him further from the ball if he is playing straightaway."

OPEN UP. Jerry Lucas takes a deep breath and harnesses all the power in his body for this tap play. He is conceding nothing, no matter how tall the other center, and is ready to launch himself as high as possible to win the tap.

HARD TO HANDLE. Jerry Lucas has stepped away from Nate Thurmond of the Golden State Warriors and is sweeping a hook at the basket. His arm is fully extended in a one-motion move and he is facing the hoop on the follow through.

32
23

Picking is next. "Lots of centers don't know how to set a pick," Lucas claims. "There are two ways: facing or with the rear end. The closer to the basket, you use the rear. Fewer mistakes can be made that way. On the pick-and-roll, get your rear to the guy. Get as close as the rules allow."

The angle is important. Where does the man with the ball want to go? "Set up at least at a ninety-degree—or more, but not less—angle in relation to the direction your teammate is going," suggests Lucas. "Reduce the angle of escape for the man who is playing your teammate. Once you set the pick, you can turn. That limits the space and the man can come off you as close as he can."

A center always turns in the direction of the ball. "If you face it, and know where it is, you can turn away; but always know where the ball is," Jerry points out. "Once the offensive player is near you, move to the hoop. The object is to get a two-on-one advantage. Every time you can, pick with your rear end. You don't lose any teeth that way. You also can take him out and release sooner."

Never lose sight of the primary objective. "Do the first job first," reminds Lucas. "Pick the man. Worry about the layup later. Be a headhunter—get your man. Don't do it by the numbers. Don't turn the body halfway. While this is for a center, because he does more picking, it's really for everyone."

He mentions Reed as the perfect example. "Willis is strong as an ox," says Lucas. "He gets you. You know it when he sets a pick. He jars a guy to his teeth."

Lucas has a lot of respect for Wayne Embry as a center. They were teammates in Cincinnati for many years before Wayne moved on to Boston and ended his career there. Embry is now general manager of the Milwaukee Bucks.

"A center has to have basketball awareness and Embry had it," says Lucas. "He has to be unselfish. He has to handle the ball a lot. He knows when the weakside player is open, and hits him."

Lucas might have said the same things about himself. He is the prototype of the ideal team player. So is Havlicek. They make the game easier for coaches. They not only know the things that should be done, they do them.

In a sense, Jerry, as a small center, has one of the most difficult jobs in pro basketball. You can say the same thing for Cowens, the young man with the responsibility of protecting the middle against the likes of Chamberlain, Abdul-Jabbar, Unseld, Bellamy, Thurmond, Lanier, Hayes, and the other old and new physical specimens of the league.

Lucas, as the center with the smallest physique, has to compensate for this disadvantage.

There was one stretch during the regular 1971–72 season that was almost inhuman. Lucas had to play Chamberlain, Lanier and Abdul-Jabbar in successive games—Los Angeles in New York on Tuesday night, the Pistons in Detroit on Wednesday, and the Bucks in Milwaukee on Friday.

I would have to say as a partial, or impartial observer, that Luke opened a lot of eyes with the way he conducted his business in those three games. For the first time, people began to take him seriously as a center who, within the context of a team effort, was capable of contributing against overwhelming size.

We lost the first one to the Lakers, 107–102, when Jerry West triggered a 15–2 streak that put them ahead, 91–82, in the final period, but Luke had done his job well. "We never got our fast break going," said Bill Sharman after the game. "Everyone says the Knicks haven't got Reed, but the way Lucas is playing, he's a superstar."

Sharman was referring to the way Luke shot when Chamberlain did not come out. Sharman was referring to the way Luke drove or hit his teammates with bounce passes when Wilt did come out. "With Wilt away from the basket," explains Lucas, who hit twenty-eight points, "it shuts off their fast break. They haven't gotten a lot off us."

The next night, we beat the Pistons, 126–102, and Luke was slightly sensational with his outside shooting. At one time he was 11-for-12 and had the Detroit defense bewildered. Lanier, of course, presented a different problem on offense than had Chamberlain. "Fortunately," says Lucas, "Wilt does not think of scoring. You play him to harass the ball and position yourself between him and the basket."

Lanier is big, strong, and mobile. He has a good hook as well as a turnaround jumper. Luke moved more on defense against Bob and tried to keep him from getting position on the floor. When Lanier got the ball, Lucas tried to press him away from the basket.

Abdul-Jabbar and Milwaukee were next—two nights later—and we won, 113–107. Kareem got his thirty-seven points and was outstanding, as usual, but we survived because of what Lucas gave us in the way of shooting, rebounding, ballhandling, and general team intelligence.

Lucas even surprised everyone by actually blocking a stuff attempt by Abdul-Jabbar while directly under the basket. "I have to hit my shots from outside against this team and Los Angeles, like tonight," Luke ex-

LUCAS
32

FROM ANYWHERE. Jerry Lucas exhibits his shooting versatility. He is off on the side and about to fire a long jumper. Wilt Chamberlain has faked at him and is about to drop back and protect the board if there is a rebound.

plained after he scored twenty-nine points. "I can't relax at all against him [Kareem]."

On defense, Luke knows Abdul-Jabbar will handle the ball a lot and shoot it often. Lucas must pressure the ball from one side of Kareem and be alert and quick enough to get back into position behind him once he gets it. Luke must stand his ground and not let Kareem back him up and get closer to the basket. He must pressure him and force him to roll away and hook going away from the hoop—a percentage risk because Kareem hits those shots fairly well.

It is fortunate for the Knicks that Lucas is the kind of player who can get points back, though he has considerable team value the way he rebounds, handles the ball, and plays the game. "I have to move and run when I play the bigger guys," he explains. He has to move them away from the middle and basket, a job he does as well as any center I know.

Chamberlain, physically, gave Lucas a rough time when he decided to look for his points in the second game of our 1971–72 championship series with the Lakers. In the first few minutes, Wilt had not only begun to score, but he also drew two quick fouls on Luke. It was 17–11 in favor of Los Angeles, with Wilt having accounted for seven points. He had eleven and the Lakers were leading, 44–42, when Dave DeBusschere suffered the hip injury that was to affect him and the Knicks for the rest of the series.

The Lakers won that game, 106–90, and behind Chamberlain, playing a magnificent series, they went on to capture their first NBA title for the city of Los Angeles. "I have to do something about Wilt," said Lucas, nevertheless, "I just can't let him roll in on me. I'm not going to get out of his way. I'm going to get more physical. I'm going to lean on him and stay in his way. I'm even going to get knocked down if I have to, but it's the only thing I can do."

That is the way Lucas thinks and acts when he plays center. A good player must be able to adjust to any situation. A good team must be conditioned to play, know the fundamentals, and play together. That is about all there is to basketball.

CHAPTER

10

THE TRAINER'S VIEWPOINT

"An athlete's best friend is his icebag," says Danny Whelan, the trainer for the Knicks. That may sound funny and even strange, but to know Danny Whelan is to be impressed by his wisdom and humor and what a good trainer can mean to a team.

Whelan has the pedigree. He has been associated with world champions in two different sports—the 1960 Pittsburgh Pirates and the 1969–70 New York Knickerbockers. He started as a trainer back in 1946 with the Rochester Red Wings, then part of the St. Louis Cardinals' farm system.

That means he has had over twenty-five years of experience with the complaints, ailments, and personal problems of players. He is the first in training camp and the last to leave. He goes to our site at Monmouth (N.J.) College to set things up about a week before everyone reports.

He greets everyone with a smile and a locker full of equipment so they can get started without any delay. When a player walks into a Knick camp he is prepared to run and scrimmage immediately. He finds two pairs of pants, two reversible "T" shirts with blue on one side and red on the other, a half dozen sweat socks, a half dozen jocks, and three pairs of basketball shoes.

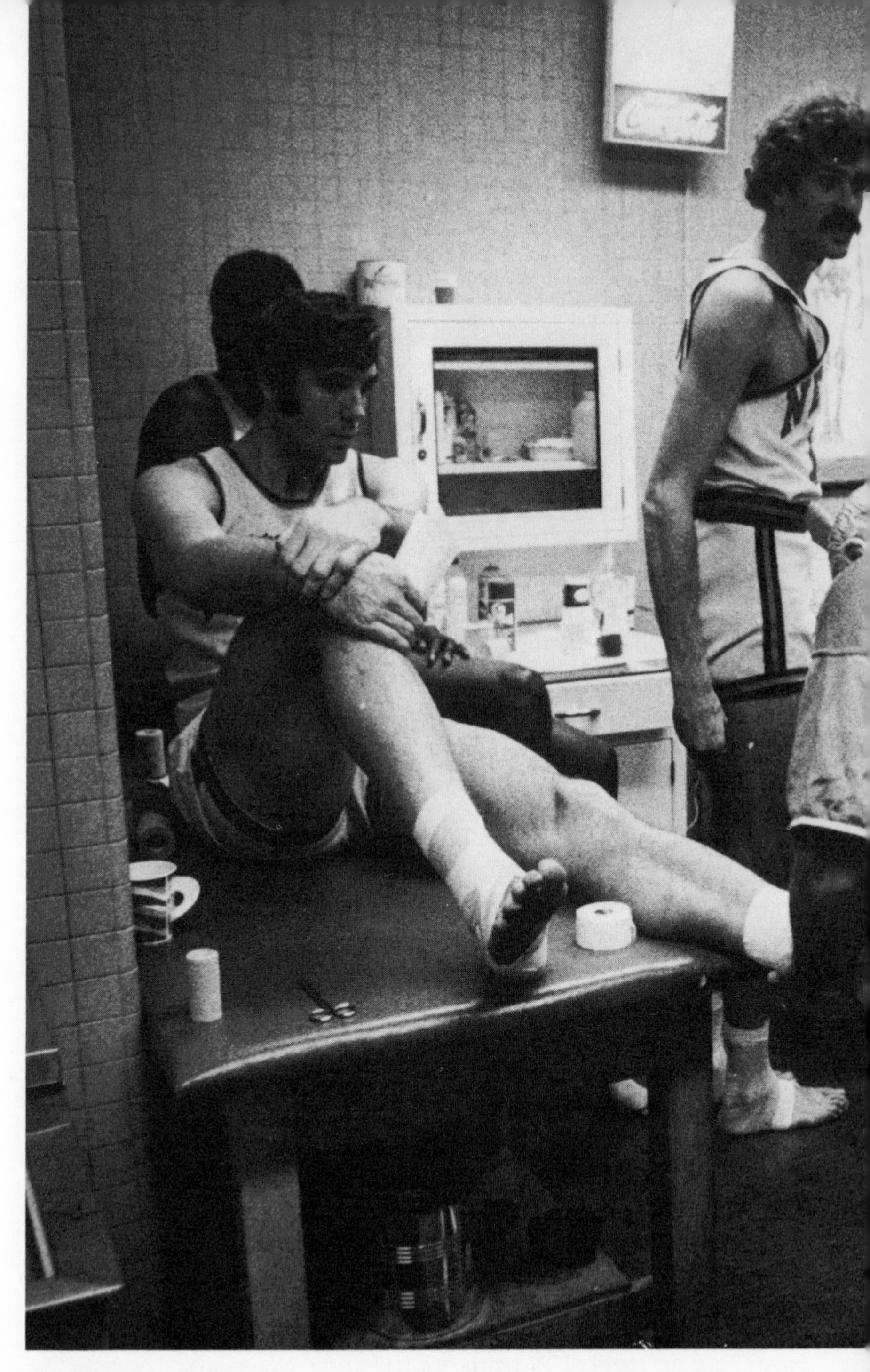

TRAINING ROOM. Danny Whelan tapes Dave DeBusschere's ankles. That's Phil Jackson with the mustache and Eddie Miles taping himself on the other table. Willis Reed, out with an injury, is the visitor.

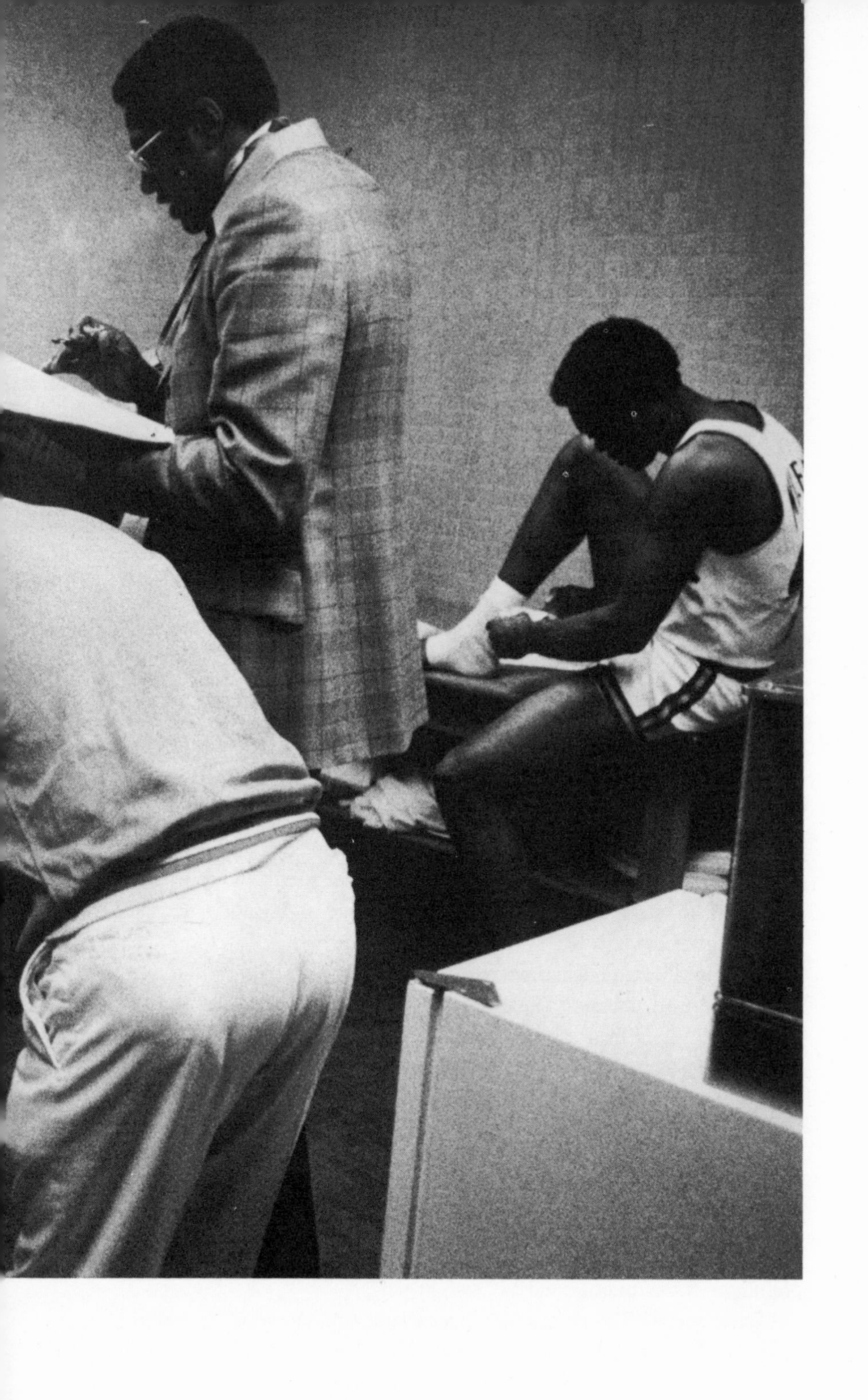

"You got to know who's who," explains Danny. Different players wear different shoes. Whelan has to know which is which. Fortunately, he has a good memory book. He remembers from season to season, unless a player crosses him and changes his endorsement without telling him.

Otherwise, he knows which brand of basketball shoes to put in which lockers. "Bradley wears Converse," he says. "Barnett wears Adidas. Frazier wears Puma, different colors. Reed has his own brand made by Uniroyal." Whelan passes the test every time.

He is right there to handle the sore muscles that always occur. They are inevitable even though I write to every player two months before camp opens to explain what is expected of them. We expect everyone to be in top physical condition before he arrives. We do not want to waste any time with exercises. I believe it is an athlete's responsibility to a team and, mainly, to himself to stay in shape and report in shape.

If an athlete has pride in himself and wants it badly enough, then he will take care of himself. That goes for high school and college players also, but even more so for professional athletes, who get paid for what they do. That is why I alert everyone that he is expected to be ready to participate in running drills and scrimmages from the moment he reports to camp.

Whelan agrees. He has been around athletes all his life. He was an infielder at St. Mary's (California) and knows what it means to stay in shape. "There is no reason why an athlete should be told to take care of himself," he says. "If he needs exercise, then he should do it without being forced. If he needs to limber up before practice or a game, then he should do it without being told."

I can recall only one time when we had to make a serious suggestion to one of our players. Dave DeBusschere, the season he came to the Knicks, played a little heavier than we thought was good for him and the team. He had a good excuse. He had fractured a bone in his foot during a charity game in the off-season and reported to the Pistons overweight and never had a chance to take it off.

We traded Walt Bellamy and Butch Komives for DeBusschere after the 1968–69 season had started. When it was over, we suggested Dave go on a diet. He was under a doctor's care in Detroit, his home, and the doctor reported his weight to us every week. He took off about fifteen or twenty pounds and has maintained his weight since.

"Every person knows if he's overweight and in good condition," says Whelan, the house expert on such things. "You don't go to a doctor and say: 'I think I'm fifty pounds overweight.' You know you are before you go. There is no excuse for any athlete in any sport not to have a sense of responsibility about getting himself in shape."

Whelan is prepared to suggest special exercises should a player express an interest or need them. We prefer to deal with rehabilitation exercises, unfortunately. I say unfortunately because rehabilitation exercises mean injuries—the rebuilding of weakened areas—and no one wants players involved with those problems.

"Bill Mazeroski always had hamstring problems when I was with Pittsburgh," recalls Whelan. "Mazeroski was big from the waist down, and there was too much pressure on the muscles in his legs. The hamstring."

There is a preventive exercise for athletes such as Mazeroski. "Stretching exercises," says Whelan. "To avoid these problems, try to touch the toes with your hands. Then try placing the palms of the hands on the ground. Then extend the hands further out. That should help strengthen the hamstring area."

Barnett presented a different problem when he ripped an Achilles tendon near the end of the 1966–67 season, when he was thirty-one. "We had him running in the sand at the seashore," recalls Whelan. "Jog fifty yards through the sand, then go to the water and walk back. Run fifty yards through the sand, then walk back in the water. He ran as much as he could take."

Near the end of the 1971–72 season, Barnett came up with a bad back. He missed some games before the playoffs and never fully recovered. He called Whelan one day after the season and wanted to do something to strengthen his back. Barnett suggested lifting weights. Danny ruled it out. He does not like weight lifting. "Makes an athlete muscle-bound," he says. "I wouldn't recommend anything over twenty pounds. That wouldn't hurt and, at the same time, might build strength and not make anyone muscle-bound. That's why so many linemen are muscle-bound—they lift weights. It is not good for an athlete."

He suggested isometrics to Barnett. "He had a real simple back problem," Whelan remembers. "It was muscular. I told him to lay on his back and put his legs under a table and try to lift it. I told him to come over to the Garden and I would help him."

The isometrics he had in mind for Barnett worked like this: Dick laid on his stomach and Whelan applied pressure to his right leg. Barnett tried to lift it. "I'm trying to keep it down while he's trying to raise it," Danny explains. "The pressure I apply is what does it. We do it one leg at a time—once a day, nine seconds each leg. If he wants to work alone, he can hook a foot under the couch and try to lift it."

TIME OUT. Group sessions are an integral part of any workout. It is a good idea to stop practice to discuss problems of technique and strategy whenever they develop.

These are not the kind of ailments that show up the first day in training camp. "The players just get sore," says Whelan. "Rarely do the veterans complain. They get sore muscles but they won't tell you. But the rookies out of college are not used to the one-and-a-half-hour drills that start right away. They're running right from the beginning. They had a picnic in college, where the coaches take a lot of time teaching fundamentals."

Our first day in camp is no easier or tougher than our last. Every day is the same. We run and we play basketball. I feel basketball is the best conditioner so we do not waste any time with exercises, though I see no harm in calisthenics if anyone wants to do them. We have two sessions a day. The first from eleven to twelve-thirty and the second from five-thirty to seven.

The players usually start drifting in about a half hour before practice starts. They can tape or limber up. I don't care what they do as long as they are all on hand and ready to start when I want them—which is at eleven o'clock in the morning.

We start with a warm-up drill. The players line up along the baseline and start running. To the foul line and back. To halfcourt and back. To the other baseline and back. We do that for five minutes.

Now we go into our playing drills. We work 1-on-1, 2-on-2, 3-on-3, 2-on-3, and 3-on-2 for forty-five minutes. We work on offense and defense. We spend the rest of the morning playing team defense. I prefer to keep it halfcourt at the start because I can consolidate things better that way.

We break for lunch. The players have five hours to nap and relax. They are back at five-thirty for another hour-and-a-half. We start with ten minutes of warm-up drills; maybe some five-man breaks. Then we play 2-on-2 for ten minutes and 3-on-3 for ten minutes.

We'll separate the centers and play 2-on-2 for individual defense. The guards will work with the guards and the forwards with the forwards to learn reactions. We will spend fifteen minutes on that.

Now I'll work them half-court defense for twenty-five minutes, concentrating on pressure defenses and who does it best. Then it will be twenty minutes with half-court offense, getting everyone acquainted with the team patterns we use on the Knicks.

We do our foul shooting at the end of each workout when everyone is tired. That is about the closest to game conditions as you can get. The players break for dinner or to go to see Whelan about their sore muscles.

"They come to me and the back is either bothering them or the legs are bothering them or they have blisters," says Danny. "It's natural soreness. I tell them to take it a little easier. Their muscles are tired. Slow it down. Be aware that they do have soreness. Tell the coach about it. Indulge but not heavily."

I rely on Whelan in these matters. We will not push a player if Danny tells me he has a sore muscle or blisters. "When the workout is over," says Whelan, "Bradley and DeBusschere and some of the other veterans like to take whirlpool. It's a massage. It stimulates circulation. Some won't do it because they don't want to let you know they are sore but they will go back to the motel and take a warm bath."

Whelan feels no player should ignore soreness though it may be routine. He should treat it to avoid complications. He advises whirlpool or a warm tub. "It's a great relaxer," he says. "Put about five pounds of Epsom Salts in the water, that's why the ocean is so great—the salt. They walk racehorses in the ocean to take soreness out of their legs. They even have whirlpool pools for sore horses."

We do not restrict the players to any diet but rely on their good judgment. The players are on their own for breakfast and lunch but we arrange dinner for them at the college. We would probably eat all our meals together if we had the proper setup. Unfortunately, the college is in session while we are in training, so that creates a complication about having every meal on campus.

"The players should eat proteins," advises Whelan. "They should stay away from fried and fattening foods. They are tough to digest and not the best kind of food when you are in training." He suggests a healthy breakfast of juice, cereal, eggs, and milk.

Lunch is not that important in the Knicks' camp. "They usually eat a sandwich, have a cup of soup, and drink milk or soda," says Whelan. "Something light and then they hit the sack for a few hours. Or, if you are Phil Jackson, go and play some tennis—if you can find Eddie Mast."

Danny has seen a lot of strange eating habits in his many years around athletes. "In baseball, the hot dog was the greatest meal in the world," he says. "I've seen them eat them in the clubhouse before the game. I've also seen them heave it up at second base after they hit a double."

He recommends that athletes eat no later than three hours before a game. "Like Reed eats," he suggests. "He will have roast beef, or some broiled meat, baked potato, salad, and tea or soda around four-thirty when we play at seven-thirty. No milk later than two hours before a game because the body gets heated and milk will churn and curdle."

Whelan thinks tea, coke, or an orange drink is the safest. "That's what the Knicks use," he says. "Cazzie [Russell], when he was with us, carried around his own teapot and made his own tea before every game. He would put honey in it and drink it. He also drank carrot juice. He was on the health food kick."

So are many other Knicks. Players such as Barnett, Lucas, and Frazier are deep into wheat germ and vitamins. "Lucas carries twenty-eight different kinds of vitamins with him," says Whelan. "After they [the other Knicks] saw what Lucas did, he made a believer out of them. All vitamins are not that good. There are a lot on the market and a doctor should prescribe them. Nobody should take vitamins without seeing his doctor first."

The Knicks have cleared their vitamins with their doctor or doctors. Otherwise, pills on our team are taboo. "I wouldn't think of carrying pills,"

COOLING OFF. Jerry Lucas indulges in a Knicks clubhouse ritual.

NEW YORK
32

says Whelan, who believes in certain vitamin pills and that's all. "A lot of players take Vitamin B_{12} and Vitamin E for energy. The doctor will prescribe that for people who do not eat regularly and require some body balance."

Danny has seen more than his share of bruises and injuries in his career. We have had more than our share on the Knicks in recent years. Every season, it seems, we have a serious problem with someone in the playoffs. Barnett missed them in 1966–67 because of his Achilles tendon. Frazier missed the last two games against Philadelphia in 1967–68 and was hampered by a groin injury while playing the final two games against Boston in 1968–69.

Reed hurt his hip in the fifth game of the NBA championship series with the Lakers in 1969–70 and played only eleven games of the 1971–72 season because of tendonitis above the knee. DeBusschere, of course, was hardly the same after injuring his hip in the second game of the 1971–72 championship series with the Lakers.

There were other assortments of back, ankle, leg, and hand injuries that had to be handled by Whelan and our team doctor, Dr. Andrew Patterson. The bone spur on Earl Monroe's left foot, after the Knicks obtained him in a trade with Baltimore. The spinal fusion that kept Phil Jackson out of the 1969–70 season and limited him to only forty-seven games the season before.

So Whelan has had his hands full—fortunately, he has good hands. They know how to handle the serious and routine physical problems that are a part of an athlete's life. "All injuries, when they occur, should be treated with ice immediately," says Danny. "On the Knicks, the first thing is ice—always ice. Then an X-ray to make sure there is no break."

Whelan estimates that the Knicks go through about three dozen icebags a year. "I feel more like an iceman than a trainer," he says. "If we are going to a workout on the road, I borrow a basket from my room and bring it to the arena. I figure there's not going to be any ice and I've got to go and get it myself."

It has been an interesting and educating experience in a way. "I found out how much ice costs," says Danny, whimsically. "Ice in New Jersey, where we train, costs a dollar for twenty-five pounds in an ice machine. I never really stopped to think how much ice has gone up. I used to get a hundred pounds for thirty-five cents in the last ten years."

Whelan is responsible for providing an adequate supply. "You never can tell what's going to happen," he explains. "Frazier is always coming up with bumps and bruises. So is Jackson. With Reed it's always been his hand, shoulder, knee, hip, or shins. Lucas needs ice for the two icebags he uses on his knee after every practice and game. You go with ice first when something happens to prevent swelling and help the circulation."

Suppose there is a twisted ankle? "Pack it in ice right away," advises Whelan. "Bradley had one. We put ice on it. Then when he went back to the hotel, he wrapped an icebag on it. He kept using ice for seventy-two hours. After that, after the swelling is controlled, you go to heat. The ice is for soreness and swelling."

Whelan remembers a day when Freddie Crawford, in the days when he played for the Knicks, hurt an ankle in practice at the old Garden. There was no ice available. "I went out on Eighth Avenue to a bar," recalls Danny. "I asked the bartender to fill up my icebag. He put two ice cubes in, that's all. He said he had no more."

It was understandable in a sense. "It was eleven in the morning," says Whelan. "But whoever heard of a bar without ice? I went to another bar and gave the bartender a dollar to fill up the bag. He filled it up. I found out why they don't give any ice away in the winter in New York—it's expensive."

He discovered another thing. No athlete should be without an icebag. "It should be standard equipment," he suggests. "It's as important as basketball shoes. It makes no difference if it's the Little League or a sandlot game. The icebag is more important than the ball. You need it if someone hurts a finger or a hand or an ankle. You can always get ice. The Knicks always have ice. We use fifty pounds a workout and a game. We couldn't survive without it. The coaches in our league don't realize that the easiest way to beat the Knicks is to steal our ice."

Heat treatments consist of whirlpool and ultra sound. "If the injury is very bad, get off it and rest," says Whelan. "On the Knicks, we have the meals brought to the room if a player is hurt badly enough for us to make him rest."

Whelan thinks many young athletes, especially high school players, are vulnerable to poor advice as to how to treat an injury. "The average kid will sprain an ankle," says Danny, "and his mother soaks it in hot water right away. Now he really gets swelling. He should put on the ice immediately. He should sleep with an icebag on the ankle and, if he wakes up, fill the icebag up if it has melted. Wrap it with an ace bandage to apply pressure on the injured area."

When the soreness subsides and the swelling is controlled, then it is time

DEE-FENSE! It is safe to assume Red Holzman is working on defensive strategy with his players in this 1-on-1 session. Why? Because the Knicks spend 80 percent of their time on defense.

to switch to heat. "Use a hot water bottle," Whelan suggests. "Wrap a towel around it and you can sit and watch TV. A heating pad is okay but moist heat is the best all the time." Of course, Danny recommends that doctors should be consulted as soon as possible.

Whelan points out that most accidents are simple and occur in the home. The treatment is the same whether or not you are an athlete. "The icebag and hot water bottle are the most important things for first aid," he says. "People buy heating pads and apply infra-red lamps to the injured areas and burn themselves."

That reminded him of the good old days. When there was no such thing.

"They had pot-bellied stoves in the clubhouses in those days," recalls Whelan, going back a long ways. "The trainer, if they had a trainer, would put the pitcher near the stove to warm up his arm before a game. They didn't know any better."

Now every team has a trainer. Every team has a doctor. "Things are much better today," acknowledges Whelan. "In the old days of baseball, a trainer had a roll of tape and a bottle of iodine, the cure-all for everything. Now it's the difference between a horse and buggy and a cadillac. Now the trainers are educated and fully equipped. In the old days they were just valets who made sandwiches and ran errands."

A trainer has to be reliable and professional because he is entrusted with valuable merchandise. "He is handling players making one hundred thousand dollars or more a year," Whelan points out. "He gets better treatment. People think the modern athlete is pampered. What they don't realize is that in the old days, no one knew any better, so the players played with injuries that were not treated properly."

Whelan was reminded of the way they used to handle hamstring pulls. "Honestly, they used to use a rolling pin on them," he insists. "Every clubhouse had a rolling pin. A guy would get up on the table and roll that pin over the sore spot. Guys used to jump off the table and never come back."

He compares that treatment with the way some athletes think they can run out a hamstring pull. "It's just like the rolling pin," says Whelan. "They're doing more damage. The first thing is ice. Then heat treatment and rest. You cannot work out a hamstring pull. It has to heal before you can be active again."

Many of the Knicks like to be massaged before a game. Some of it is necessary, such as when Barnett wants his back rubbed or Reed asks to have a sore shoulder or the muscles over his tender knee massaged. "A lot of massaging is just mental," says Whelan. "But if it relaxes an athlete, then it's worth it. A pitcher needs a rubdown. His arm gets all knotted up. Baseball players like to be massaged. Basketball players seem to prefer the whirlpool."

Reed's hip injury during the 1969–70 championship series epitomizes the kind of treatment Whelan suggests for athletes, or anyone for that matter. Willis hit the floor hard and had to be helped to the dressing room. "We applied ice right away," recalls Whelan. "He was in a lot of pain. We feared a cracked hip."

The doctor examined Reed. He felt for a break. He found none. "We kept the ice on for better than an hour," Whelan's story continues. "I went out for the second half but Willis sat in the dressing room and listened to the game. He then went to the hospital for X-rays. There was no crack."

Reed went home and applied ice all night. "The next day," Whelan recalls, "we left for Los Angeles. We had an offday and figured we'd treat him out there. The doctor went along with us. We went right to the Century Health Club when we arrived."

Willis was put into an ice cold tank. "It was like a small pool," says Whelan. "He stayed in there for about five minutes but it must have seemed like five hours to him because it was so cold."

Next a walk-in whirlpool. "With fifteen jets," Whelan remembers. "It was one hundred and ten degrees. We wanted to get more circulation. He was not responding. We went hot to cold to hot to cold. It was not a routine injury. It was almost like a fractured hip."

The swelling had been contained, which is why heat was being used along with cold. "It was ten minutes in the heated whirlpool," says Whelan, "then back to the cold pool for five minutes. Another ten minutes in the whirlpool and back to ice for five minutes. Then we let him take a sauna bath for fifteen minutes. Finally, a medium shower that ended with cold water." When Willis got back to the hotel he applied ice, again.

The next day, the day of the sixth game, Reed used more ice in the morning and went to the Forum around eleven in the morning. "We gave him ultra sound treatment," says Whelan, "then he went back to the hotel and kept ice on it. When he arrived in Los Angeles, he couldn't raise his foot. After a full day's treatment, he could walk up stairs without pain."

There was only one hitch. He could not play. "It was decided it would be better to give him two more days," says Whelan. "We had a day off before we were to play the seventh game in New York. He sat on the bench and watched us lose. Then the three of us left the team to go back to New York on a midnight plane."

Reed, Whelan, and Dr. James Parkes, Dr. Patterson's assistant, arrived at the Garden around seven in the morning. "We gave him whirlpool and ultra sound and told him to go home, apply ice, and get some sleep," says Whelan. "Willis woke up around seven that evening and said he felt better."

On the day of the seventh game, Reed met with Whelan in the trainer's room at the Garden. "It was around three o'clock," recalls Danny. "I gave him some hot packs. We used ultra sound. We went to dinner around four o'clock and had steak, salad, and tea and then back to the dressing room for more hot packs until six-thirty."

That's when Willis went on the floor to test his hip. "When he went out to shoot," says Whelan, "Wilt was there. Willis knew he was watching. It hurt while he was shooting but he didn't want to let Wilt know it."

Reed played. He gave the Knicks just enough time to help us win. So did the doctor and Whelan. The next season and the next it was the tendonitis over Reed's knee.

A weight-lifting program was recommended to strengthen the muscles around the knee. They gave Willis a special metal shoe that fit over his regular one. He tied it on as though it was a roller skate and then slid the iron weights onto an iron bar that ran along the front of the shoe.

Willis started with five pounds in a program that was designed for him to reach an ultimate thirty-five pounds. It was the type of weight program that Whelan endorses. Anything to strengthen and rehabilitate a weakened area. Not for muscle building alone. "Kids in the YMCA go into a weight room," says Danny, "and it's uncanny to see the weights they pick up. Those kinds of muscles look beautiful on the beach at Santa Monica, but he will have problems combing his hair."

Whelan believes in letting nature take its course for athletes. "Kids think they're too skinny but don't realize they are not matured yet," he says. "He will fill out in time but he wants to be fifteen and look like Bronco Nagurski."

He thinks that is nonsense—especially if a young man wants to be an athlete. He may be ruining everything with an injudicious use of weights. "Look at the pictures of [Walt] Frazier when he first came to the Knicks," says Whelan in support of his theory, "and look at him now. What a difference. And he did nothing but rest properly, eat good food, and let nature take its course."

Whelan thinks basketball players are the best conditioned athletes in the world. "They play for six months," he says, "and most of them work out in the off season. A lot of them play summer basketball. They lay off between seasons in the other sports."

He thinks athletes should adhere to certain standards. "Good pros get plenty of rest," he says. "As soon as they arrive in a city when they are traveling, they go to bed. Some sleep around the clock. They even eat their meals in the room. It's a rarity to see a player sightseeing. He's resting most of the time."

He believes a player is foolish to abuse himself or his body. "I don't believe in bedchecks," he says, nevertheless. "That's a lot of hooey when you have to take men and put them to bed. If they punish themselves, it will show in their performance and they will not play. They have everything to lose but nothing to gain."

Some teams use weight charts to check on the players. "We use the chart in the training camp," says Whelan. "Once a month during the season we get serious about it. Let's face it, the fellows who gain weight that affects their performance don't play."

He recommends lots of running to build up wind and no smoking to preserve it. "Eat proper foods," he says. "Don't drink a lot of liquids when playing. Water is always the best. Do certain exercises to condition the body and make the muscles supple. Watch the weight. Don't neglect injuries. Stay in condition."

Can you imagine anyone ever thinking that a trainer is not important?

TRAINER AT WORK. Danny Whelan gives Dave DeBusschere courtside treatment for an injured eye. The proper treatment and care for all athletes cannot be overly emphasized.